Engaging Thomas Merton

Engaging Thomas Merton

Spirituality, Justice, and Racism

Daniel P. Horan, OFM

ORBIS BOOKS

Maryknoll, New York 10545

Founded in 1970, Orbis Books endeavors to publish works that enlighten the mind, nourish the spirit, and challenge the conscience. The publishing arm of the Maryknoll Fathers and Brothers, Orbis seeks to explore the global dimensions of the Christian faith and mission, to invite dialogue with diverse cultures and religious traditions, and to serve the cause of reconciliation and peace. The books published reflect the views of their authors and do not represent the official position of the Maryknoll Society. To learn more about Maryknoll and Orbis Books, please visit our website at www.orbisbooks.com

Published by Orbis Books, Box 302, Maryknoll, NY 10545-0302.

Manufactured in the United States of America.
Manuscript editing and typesetting by Joan Weber Laflamme.

Library of Congress Cataloging-in-Publication Data

Names: Horan, Daniel P., author.
Title: Engaging Thomas Merton : spirituality, justice, and racism / Daniel P. Horan, OFM.
Description: Maryknoll, NY : Orbis Books, [2023] | Includes bibliographical references and index. | Summary: "Essays on the Trappist monk, his enduring significance, and his contributions to spirituality and social issues"— Provided by publisher.
Identifiers: LCCN 2023017740 (print) | LCCN 2023017741 (ebook) | ISBN 9781626985445 (print) | ISBN 9798888660034 (ebook)
Subjects: LCSH: Merton, Thomas, 1915-1968 | Monks—United States. | Christianity and justice. | Christianity and culture.
Classification: LCC BX4705.M542 H669 2023 (print) | LCC BX4705.M542 (ebook) | DDC 271/.12502—dc23/eng/20230810
LC record available at https://lccn.loc.gov/2023017740
LC ebook record available at https://lccn.loc.gov/2023017741

To my colleagues and friends in the
International Thomas Merton Society and
The Thomas Merton Society of Great Britain and Ireland

Contents

IV

The Spirituality of Racial Justice

V

Social Justice and Ethics

Introduction

Thomas Merton has fascinated me for nearly my entire adult life. When asked how I became a Merton scholar, a question that inevitably surfaces when I lecture or teach a course or lead a retreat on Merton, I almost always say that, for me, "Merton is a hobby that grew out of control!" I didn't set out to become an expert in the life and writings, thought and legacy of the American Trappist monk and author. It was not planned, and it still surprises me to this day that I have and continue to spend so much time and energy studying and sharing the wisdom of Merton. Like so many readers who become interested in Merton, I started reading his work for my own spiritual nourishment. As a young man, just out of college—St. Bonaventure University, the same college at which Merton taught English literature for three semesters before entering the Abbey of Gethsemani—I was taken with Merton's own conversion story and spiritual journey as he relayed it in *The Seven Storey Mountain* and *The Sign of Jonas*. From there I found myself reading his early books on prayer, contemplation, and the spiritual life. Books like *New Seeds of Contemplation* and *Thoughts in Solitude* became regular companions.

Over time, I came to read more and more of his extensive written corpus, not just the books on prayer but also his journals, letters, poetry, and writings on social issues. It was this last category that became especially captivating for me. Merton, who died in 1968, writes across the decades as if he were alive today, addressing many of the same issues that continue to plague our world in the twenty-first century. With a prophetic sense of accuracy and insight, Merton was able to see the world as it actually is and the world that God is calling us to become with clarity that is only possible from the vantage point of a monk on the margins, a man of faith and prayer at the periphery not only of his contemporary society but also at the periphery of his own monastic life. The more he sought solitude in his hermitage, paradoxically, the keener his sense of social criticism and the more accurate his religious response became.

While I have and continue to remain interested in and inspired by Merton's explicitly spiritual writings, especially those texts from the first two decades of his monastic journey, I have also become increasingly convicted by Merton's writings on social issues and the ongoing relevance and timeliness of his insights. I have written dozens of articles and delivered even more lectures on these themes, especially on Merton's writings on racism, violence, and contemporary Christian living. This book is a collection of some of those essays. In my previous book on Thomas Merton—*The Franciscan Heart of Thomas Merton: A New Look at the Spiritual Inspiration of His Life, Thought, and Writing*—I laid out a singular, constructive argument, studying the manifold ways the Franciscan spiritual and intellectual tradition informed the Trappist monk's theological vision. The format of this present book is decidedly different, offering instead a collection of both previously published essays and new contributions gathered into one volume. The inspiration for this style comes from Merton's later work itself. Although he was capable of writing monographs and books on a singular theme, Merton was also an accomplished essayist whose most important writings on racial justice, war and violence, and other social issues most often appeared as discrete essays that were ultimately collected into volumes like *Seeds of Destruction* (1964), *Raids on the Unspeakable* (1966), and *Faith and Violence: Christian Teaching and Christian Practice* (1968). It seems fitting to me that my own engagement with many of Merton's contributions in the areas of social justice take a similar form.

Many of the chapters included in this volume have been previously published in an earlier form. These essays have been revised and expanded, some substantively so. Others are appearing in print for the first time in this book. These were first presented as lectures. But all these essays take as their starting point the continued relevance and insight of Merton for our times. While I have made a concerted effort to rework individual essays so that repetition could be minimized across the chapters, certain themes and details of Merton's life and work inevitably recur, although in such cases it is my hope that a new angle or perspective is added.

The chapters in this book are organized into five sections. The first section focuses on Merton's life and continued relevance, appeal, and significance. It opens with a chapter that originated as a sermon delivered on the fiftieth anniversary of his death preached at Corpus Christi Church in Manhattan, the same church where Merton was baptized in

1938. The second chapter, which first appeared as an article around the same anniversary, considers some of the ways in which Merton continues to remain relevant even fifty years after his death. Chapter 3 takes up this same theme but looks to young adults and explores why Merton offers wisdom and insight for a new generation. The section closes with a short reflection on the role Merton continues to play in bringing people together through his writings and inspiration.

The second section examines some of the ways that Merton's thought and writing provides insight into contemporary Christian life. Chapter 5 focuses on an admittedly counterintuitive theme when one considers the author's social context as a Roman Catholic monk and priest: the spirituality of marriage. The next chapter looks at young adults, specifically members of the Millennial Generation and Generation Z, and presents wisdom from Merton for navigating the spiritual journey in a digital age. Chapter 7, the last in this section, examines the insights Merton offers to those ordained ministry in the church.

The third section, "Insights about Key Christian Virtues," examines four central themes to the Christian tradition: revelation, holiness, poverty, and love. Chapter 8 offers a study of Merton's theology of revelation with attention focused on the importance of mercy in his reflections. Chapter 9 engages the writings of Pope Francis and Merton on the subject of Christian holiness and the universal call to holiness shared by all the baptized. Chapter 10 likewise engages the writings of Pope Francis and Merton, but this time on the subject of evangelical poverty. The last chapter in this section explores a theme that is ever-present in Merton's writings, but that has not been substantively studied in Merton scholarly circles—love, and what I call "true and false love."

The fourth section turns to Merton's prophetic and prescient writings on racism and racial justice. Chapter 12 looks at how Merton's social analysis anticipated what scholars of racism would later term "interest convergence theory" and at how the Trappist monk recognized the intersection of spirituality and racial justice as essential for Christian responses to injustice. Chapter 13 considers Merton's repeated view that "racism is a white problem." While a growing amount of Merton scholarship has engaged his writings on civil rights and racial justice, very few scholars so far have explored what role Merton's whiteness played in his own perception, insight, and critique. The last chapter in this section considers the at-times-complicated relationship Merton had to two civil rights giants, Martin Luther King, Jr. and Malcolm X, and how his perspective of the latter developed in the 1960s from dismissal to admiration and respect.

The last section of this book contains essays that engage Merton's writing as a resource for thinking through contemporary questions on social justice and ethics. Chapter 15 returns to the contemporary teaching of Pope Francis on care for creation and examines the ways Merton's model of "ecological conversion"—to borrow a phrase from *Laudato Si'*—might offer us insight in our age of climate catastrophe. Chapter 16 explores four ways that Merton models for us what it means to be a person of dialogue. Finally, the last chapter of this book engages Merton's thought with the contemporary philosophical and ethical thinking of John Caputo and Stanley Hauerwas to consider how these three thinkers provide us with ways to think about Christian nonviolence in our time.

I

The Continued Appeal and Significance of Thomas Merton

1

Seeds of Inspiration

Remembering the Life and Legacy of Thomas Merton

It was eighty years and twenty-four days ago that Thomas Merton was baptized in this church of Corpus Christi. Nine years later—while a monk in the Abbey of Gethsemani, but not yet the publicly recognized Thomas Merton of *The Seven Storey Mountain*—he composed the poem "On the Anniversary of My Baptism" (1947), which concludes with the following lines:

> The day You made the waters,
> And dragged them down from the dividing islands
> And made them spring with fish,
> You planned to bless the brine out of the seas
> That were to be my death.
>
> And this is the ninth November since my world's end
>   and my Genesis,
> When, with the sting of salt in my dry mouth,
> Cross-crowned with water by the priest,
> Stunned at the execution of my old companion,
>   death,
> And with the murder of my savage history,
> You drowned me in the shallow font.

[A version of this essay was originally delivered as the homily on the fiftieth anniversary of Thomas Merton's Death at a liturgy celebrated on December 10, 2018, at Corpus Christi Church in New York City and later published in *The Merton Annual* 31 (2018): 49–55. Used with permission.]

My eyes, swimming in unexpected infancy,
Were far too frail for such a favor:
They still close-kept the stone shell of their empty
    sepulcher:
But, though they saw none, guessed the new-come
    Trinity
That charged my sinews with His secret life.[1]

It is extremely fitting for us to be commemorating the earthly death of
Thomas Merton—Fr. Louis to his Trappist brothers—in the space where
he was not only received into the church but also, and more important,
was received into *new life through baptism.*

It is fitting because what we commemorate taking place fifty years ago
today *began* in this place. Baptism and earthly death are in many ways the
bookends of Christian life. They have liturgical and theological similari-
ties that are often overlooked but which have tremendous significance.

Take, for example, the following: Both the rite of baptism and the
funeral liturgy begin at the entrance of the door; both begin without the
Sign of the Cross or the usual introductory rites; at both we are dressed in
the white garment—an outfit or cloth at baptism, a funeral pall draped
over the coffin at the funeral liturgy; at both we are placed beside the
light of Christ symbolized in by the Paschal Candle; at baptism we are
immersed in the water of the font, at the funeral that water is sprinkled
on our deceased bodies; at baptism the presider blesses the water by praying: "May the power of the Holy Spirit, O Lord, we pray, come down
through your Son into the fullness of this font, so that all who have been
buried with Christ by baptism into death may rise again to life with
him"; and at the funeral the presider sprinkles the font with water and
prays: "In the waters of baptism the deceased died with Christ and rose
with him to new life. May he or she now share with him eternal glory."

---

[1] Thomas Merton, "On the Anniversary of My Baptism," in *Figures for an
Apocalypse* (New York: New Directions, 1947), 39; *The Collected Poems of Thomas
Merton* (New York: New Directions, 1977), 157; and *In the Dark before the Dawn:
New Selected Poems of Thomas Merton*, ed. Lynn R. Szabo (New York: New Direc-
tions, 2005), 59–60. It was first published in *Commonweal* 43 (April 12, 1946),
640, but it was presumably composed at the time of the anniversary the previous
November. I wish to thank Patrick O'Connell for his assistance in tracking down
the publication history of this poem.

Life and death are intimately tied together, one impossible without the other. Baptism to new life cannot take place without a share in the life, death, and resurrection of Christ. And this is what is articulated in words found in the Letter to the Ephesians, which was the Second Reading proclaimed at the liturgy this evening. These bookends of life and death are seen as one through the eyes of God in Christ Jesus. It was God's plan from the beginning that no one and nothing should be lost or forgotten. God has freed us through unimaginably generous forgiveness and love.

While at times it may be difficult for us to see in the present, particularly in our extremely hectic and distracting modern lives, what seems to us to be ultimate in terms of earthly death is merely a moment, a part, a *transitus* as St. Francis of Assisi would say. Death is a passing from here to there, which is not a separation or an absolute end but a continuation of life, albeit in a new form or register.[2] But what is proclaimed in the rite of baptism and affirmed at the funeral liturgy is the assurance given to the early Christian community in Ephesus: That it is, in fact, God's plan from the fullness of time to sum all things up in Christ Jesus, to bring all of creation back to God's self. This is what we call salvation.

In an Easter homily written in 1967, Merton reflects on this dynamic of life and death in Christianity. He writes: "The risen life is not easy; it is also a dying life. The presence of the resurrection in our lives means the presence of the Cross, for we do not rise with Christ unless we also first die with him. It is by the Cross that we enter the dynamism of creative transformation, the dynamism of resurrection and renewal, the dynamism of love."[3] On a personal level Merton seemed to understand well what he described here as "the dynamism of creative transformation, resurrection and renewal, and love." His life was marked not by a singular instance of conversion, as if with baptism here or an encounter at 4th and Walnut streets in Louisville comes a static shift in his life. Instead,

---

[2] This is a loose allusion to the title of the book on the spirituality of death written by the great Merton scholar William H. Shannon, *Here on the Way to There: A Catholic Perspective on Dying and What Follows* (Cincinnati: St. Anthony Messenger Press, 2005).

[3] Thomas Merton, "He Is Risen," *The Merton Annual* 9 (1996): 2.

his journey was a lifelong series of conversions. Merton came to experience that the death one encounters in baptism, the death occasioned by the waters of new birth, inaugurate something new, ongoing, dynamic.

I was recently asked to reflect on why anyone should care about Thomas Merton fifty years later at a time so different than that of Merton's.[4] While at first it sounds like a disrespectful question, it is in fact an opportunity for us to pause and consider what motivates our gathering here this evening, our participation in regional chapters devoted to studying his writings and life, our continuing to purchase books written more than half-a-century ago.

There are many ways that Merton's world is different from our own. Despite the increased technocratic paradigm of his time, marked as it was by global violence and conflict—from two world wars early in his life through the Vietnam War that set the context of the end of his life—the fast-paced world in which we find ourselves today would seem unimaginable to a person who died in 1968. With the rapid decline in women and men entering religious life and the increasing disaffiliation of young people from institutional religions, the very context of monastic life would likely appear foreign to most people today. To ask about what is still relevant about the thinking, writing, or life of a monk who has been dead for five decades is in fact neither insulting nor absurd, because at first glance there is hardly a clear or compelling answer. In fact, it would seem that there is nothing that a white, male, American, Catholic priest and monk can say to those searching for meaning in our ever-shifting cultural, social, and ecclesial context.

But I don't believe that is actually true. I don't believe we are here at this church merely to recall some nice guy and an historically significant author, even if he was both. I don't believe that Merton has nothing to offer contemporary people, especially those seeking meaning today.

I believe that it was precisely Merton's recognition of what he called in that Easter homily the simultaneity of the "risen life and dying life," which is a life of ongoing conversion, that is at the core of the many reasons we should care about Thomas Merton today. While I am personally inspired and challenged by his many writings, I don't think that is the most significant legacy Merton leaves to us (although I certainly recommend them to all). It is something more fundamental

---

[4] See the next chapter in this volume.

that continues to draw me—and I suspect many others—to him all these many decades later.

What I mean is that the most significant reason why we should and do continue to care about Merton today is his unabashed humanity. This may very well be his greatest gift to us. What we see in the example of a life captured in writings and recordings, photographs and drawings—this is what grounded his life, his writings, his prophetic stance in the world. They are not simply historical artifacts or well-written texts. Merton's work serves as a vehicle to convey an honest sense of humanity not often witnessed among religious figures, especially in the Catholic Church. Merton's prolific nature interrupts the tendency we have as a faith community to remember only the "inspirational" or "holy" aspects of a revered Christian's life. Hagiography is the expectant format for telling the story of great Christian witnesses, but Merton's own self-narrative—especially in his extensive correspondence and personal journals—pulls the rug out from beneath any attempt to gloss over his complex personality and, at times, complicated life.

Merton struggled with how best to use his gifts for the church and the monastery. But he always found a way to express both encouraging words of inspiration, especially when it came to supporting the prayer lives of all women and men, and prophetic words of admonition, especially in the face of social injustices. Both modalities of proclaiming the gospel message arose from his fully human experience.

We can take his challenging exhortations to respond in true Christian fashion to the structural injustices in our society and church—violence, racism, religious intolerance, poverty, and so on—because he is not preaching to us from some place of perfection or distance. Merton's voice is so powerful because it is, in a counterintuitive way, also our voice. It is a voice of conscience, perhaps, but it is also a voice of uncertainty and questioning and struggle and faith. Merton never had all the answers, nor did he ever pretend to. In an age of "fake news" and "alternative facts," where younger generations have no patience for being lied to or "spun," Merton's humanity on full display offers a refreshing model of Christian living that is honest. In this way Merton is relatable, even for those who may have every reason to resist institutional religion.

✧✧✧

Returning to the reason we are gathered to celebrate this Eucharist today, the commemoration of the end of Merton's earthly journey, I want us to return to the Gospel proclaimed this evening. The primary setting of this short discourse Jesus offers in John's account anticipates the impending death and resurrection of the Lord. Declaring to his followers that the time is coming, he draws on a metaphoric image very familiar to readers of Thomas Merton's work: the seed. Jesus says: "Unless a grain [a seed] of wheat falls to the ground and dies, it remains just a grain of wheat; but if it dies, it produces much fruit" (Jn 12:24).

It is fitting that we remember the death of Merton with these words. While Merton wrote a lot about seeds—seeds of contemplation and seeds of destruction—with the perspective of five decades behind us, we might look back and recognize that Merton's entire life was a "seed of inspiration."

During the fifty-three years Merton lived and worked on this earth, he created a potent kernel of inspiration, which after his death would continue to grow and blossom into a robust source of insight, wisdom, affirmation, solace, and challenge. During his earthly life Merton reflected on his practice of wide-ranging correspondence as an "apostolate of friendship." But that didn't end with his sudden, tragic death. He continues to bring together friends who tend the living and dynamic plant that has grown from the seed of his life and work.[5] And we are just a few of these friends. Fifty years on, the responsibility is now ours to care for, nurture, and share this plant, which continues to bear incredible fruit.

In *Conjectures of a Guilty Bystander*, Merton writes: "The things we really need come to us only as gifts, and in order to receive them as gifts we have to be open. In order to be open we have to renounce ourselves, in a sense we have to *die* to our image of ourselves, our autonomy, our fixation upon our self-willed identity. We have to be able to relax the psychic and spiritual cramp which knots us in the painful, vulnerable, helpless 'I' that is all we know as ourselves."[6]

Merton came to us as one such gift, a gift that we have opened ourselves up to receiving. Today, as we commemorate Merton's death, may we also celebrate the life and the legacy he has left us as a gift—a gift to

---

[5] See Chapter 4 in this volume.

[6] Thomas Merton, *Conjectures of a Guilty Bystander* (New York: Doubleday, 1966), 204.

be shared with others as we continue his ministry of friendship; a gift that continues to blossom and produce great fruit; a gift that the world and church desperately need in our time.

> *Eternal rest grant unto him, O Lord. . . .*
> *May Thomas Merton and all the departed, through the*
>   *Mercy of God, Rest in Peace. . . .*
> *Thomas Merton, Pray for us!*

2

Why Should Anyone Care
About Merton Today?

Merton, the famous Trappist monk and best-selling author, has now been dead for almost as long as he had lived. When he died unexpectedly on December 10, 1968, at the age of fifty-three while in Asia on a speaking tour about the renewal of monastic life, he left behind dozens of books, thousands of journal entries, and tens of thousands of letters from correspondence with people from around the world. He also left behind a legacy that included a model for modern Christian living that encouraged everyone—religious and lay alike—to pursue a life of prayer, holiness, and social justice.

But as we consider the rapid pace of change in our contemporary context, the ever-increasing role technology plays in all aspects of our lives, and the differences too numerous to count between the life and times of a mid-twentieth-century monk and our own experience, it would seem at first glance that Merton's ideas, writings, vision, and example might be set aside, like pieces in a museum. They might be treated as valuable in their own right, inspiring perhaps from a distance, but not particularly relevant for us in the twenty-first century. Merton should be considered just another dead white male author, like Dickens or Chaucer or Erasmus, to be put on a library shelf and perhaps forgotten. He can be remembered as a once important historical figure, but one not taken seriously today.

And yet I believe, upon closer examination, that Merton provides us with at least three compelling reasons for continuing to learn about

[A version of this essay was originally published in *National Catholic Reporter,* December 10, 2018. Used with permission.]

him and read his work as much today as when he was living more than half a century ago.

First, there is the obvious area of continued relevance. Merton was one of the first Roman Catholic religious leaders before the Second Vatican Council to emphasize the importance of prayer and contemplation for all people and not just the religious "professionals" (that is, nuns and priests). He articulated in his popular spiritual writing, such as *New Seeds of Contemplation*,[1] what Vatican II would more than a decade later describe as the "universal call to holiness." All of us, by virtue of our baptism, have received a vocation and to discover what that is requires prayer and discernment. Each of us also has what Merton called our "True Self," who we are in our fullness as known only to God. This means that to discover our truest identity requires seeking and discovering God in prayer. These insights are as timeless as the human quest for authenticity.

Second, there is the less obvious area of the continued timeliness of his later writings. Most readers of Merton's work are familiar with his overtly spiritual texts, but far fewer are familiar with his social criticism and urgent writings on justice. In books with titles like *Seeds of Destruction* and *Faith and Violence*, Merton's prophetic reflections on systemic racism in the United States and the relationship between fear and violence speak as challenging a message today as they did five decades ago.[2]

Take, for example, his 1965 essay titled "The Time of the End Is the Time of No Room." Here Merton's description of the scene of Jesus's birth in Bethlehem eerily resonates with what is happening at the southern border of the United States today.

> Into this world, this demented inn, in which there is absolutely no room for Him at all, Christ has come uninvited. But because He cannot be at home in it, because He is out of place in it, and yet He must be in it, His place is with those others for whom there is no room. His place is with those who do not belong, who are rejected by power because they are regarded as weak, those who are discredited, who are denied the status of persons, tortured,

---

[1] Thomas Merton, *New Seeds of Contemplation* (New York: New Directions, 1961).

[2] Thomas Merton, *Seeds of Destruction* (New York: Farrar, Straus, and Giroux, 1964); idem, *Faith and Violence* (Notre Dame, IN: University of Notre Dame Press, 1968).

exterminated. With those for whom there is no room, Christ is present in this world.[3]

This essay, which makes for a powerful Advent and Christmas reflection, challenges Christians to link the too-often-domesticated gospel with the signs of our time. When we look around our world, nation, and local communities today, it is disturbing to recognize the systemic injustices that steadfastly persist all these decades later. It is clear that few listened to Merton then; perhaps, just maybe, some might listen now. And that is one of many good reasons to keep reading Merton today.

Third, there is what I believe is the most significant reason why people should care about Merton today: his unabashed humanity. Like his friend and contemporary Dorothy Day, Merton is one of the few Christian exemplars we have that are not encumbered by hagiography and selective memory. A truly modern person, Merton's story is one with many turns, surprises, challenges, and moments of grace. He had a life before the monastery, and he had a life in the monastery: each period lasted about twenty-seven years. Both halves of his life reveal a complex man whose sanctity and sinfulness, pride and humility, ambition and regret are on wide display thanks to his prolific writing practices and his willingness not to sugarcoat his joys and hopes, his griefs and anxieties.

Even though most young adults today probably have not heard of Merton, his way of serving the church and world as a monk, priest, and writer has tremendous potential to speak to the hunger for a more authentic, honest, and transparent church as repeatedly expressed by representative young adults in the pre-synodal meeting document in March 2018.[4] At the invitation of Pope Francis, hundreds of young adults from around the world gathered in Rome to share their experiences, observations, hopes, and challenges in advance of the 2018 synod of bishops on young adults. They were bold yet respectful, direct and clear-eyed in expressing some hard truths to church leaders. Demographers and sociologists tell us that Millennials and members of Generation Z are incredulous when

---

[3] Thomas Merton, *Raids on the Unspeakable* (New York: New Directions, 1966), 72–73.

[4] See "Final Document of the Pre-Synodal Meeting of Young People" (Rome, 2018), http://secretariat.synod.va/content/synod2018/en/news/final-document-from-the-pre-synodal-meeting.html.

it comes to words without action, arguments from authority alone, and prioritization of making a good impression over honestly admitting mistakes, errors, and wrongdoing. They want leaders and mentors who can ask for forgiveness when needed and offer forgiveness when asked.

Young people—and not-so-young people—want "real" Christian models who inspire us not by their perfection in life and faith, but by their committed struggle in life to keep the faith. Dorothy Day's experience of ongoing conversion and struggles for peace and justice on behalf of the poor, and Mother Teresa's long trial of experiencing God's absence while nevertheless persisting in caring for society's "untouchables"—these are Christians that speak to women and men today. It is their humanity on display that makes them both holy and relevant.

Merton is another such model.

His wrestling with religious censors who sought to mitigate or silence his publishing about the important themes of violence, racism, and the Christian responsibility to put faith into action speaks to experiences of those whose consciences call for more than banal Christian platitudes and take the risk to work for justice in the church and world.

His ongoing struggle with ego and ambition while also sincerely desiring a simpler, prayerful, and eremitical life speaks to the conflicted motivations we all face in decision-making.

His falling in love with a nurse at the age of fifty, the genuine affection they had for one another, and the turmoil recorded in his journals and poetry about his discernment and his ultimate decision to remain a monk speak to the universal human condition of love and loss that monks and nuns and laity all experience, if in different ways and at different times.[5]

We should care about Thomas Merton today because in many ways he reveals something to us about who we are: modern men and women, religious and laity, striving to connect the faith of Christianity with the particularity of our lives. Fifty years after his death Merton not only intercedes for us from within that great cloud of witnesses that has gone before, but he has left us the story of his life and the text of his many writings to guide us on our own journey.

---

[5] See Thomas Merton, *Learning to Love: Exploring Solitude and Freedom*—The Journal of Thomas Merton, vol. 6, ed. Christine M. Bochen (San Francisco: HarperCollins, 1997).

3

Why Merton (Still) Matters

Wisdom for Young Adults

January 31, 2015, would have marked the one-hundredth birthday of the American Trappist monk and best-selling author Thomas Merton. But having died suddenly in Thailand on December 10, 1968, while overseas to speak at conferences for Catholic monastic communities in Asia, Merton never lived to see a birthday beyond his fifty-third. Yet, his insights, writing, and model of Christian engagement with the world continue to live on today.

Though his life was short, his output in terms of writing, poetry, and correspondence was extraordinarily productive. The diversity of his work makes his relevance in a number of areas related to Christian living, creative expression, and social action abundantly clear. His continued popularity among readers and enthusiasts is confirmed by the perennial status he holds as a best-selling author, a rare accomplishment illustrated by the fact that many of his books have never gone out of print. His depth of thought and spiritual genius is confirmed by the ever-increasing bibliography of new articles and books written about Merton by scholars in diverse fields from theology and spirituality to American history, literature, and peace studies.

While a general consensus appears to have formed with time affirming the enduring status and legacy of Merton's life and work, there are detractors who claim Merton is outdated and his appeal overstated. Among the most recognizable critics of Merton's legacy and relevance is the former

[A version of this essay was originally published in *America Magazine* 211, no. 20 (January 19–26, 2015): 20–23. Used with permission.]

archbishop of Washington, DC, Cardinal Donald Wuerl. In 2005, when Wuerl was bishop of Pittsburgh, he chaired a committee that oversaw the production of a new American Catholic catechism aimed particularly at young adults. Each chapter of this catechism was to include a profile of an American Catholic whose life and work served as a model for Christian living. As author and peace activist Jim Forest recalls in an afterward to his biography of Merton, *Living with Wisdom*, Wuerl decided that the profile of Merton originally included in the catechism should be taken out of the draft text. Among the reasons Wuerl gave for this decision was that "the generation we were speaking to had no idea who he was."[1]

As both a member of the Millennial Generation, having been born in the early 1980s, and a professional scholar of Merton's work, I have taken Wuerl's remark very seriously during the decade since he expressed his opinion. In a sense, he is right. Not many of my peers—let alone those younger than me—know Merton in the same way that previous generations have, many of whom read Merton's spiritual autobiography *The Seven Storey Mountain* and recognized Thomas Merton as a household name. But in another sense, Wuerl's view discounted the power of Merton's true legacy, overlooked the way Merton's words do resonate with the young adults who are introduced to his work, and eschewed the responsibility the American church has to remedy precisely what Wuerl was diagnosing—the need to pass on to the next generation the wisdom and example of Merton so the youth and young adults of the American church could know him.

Because of Wuerl's remarks a decade earlier, it was especially exciting to hear Pope Francis deliver his address to the special joint session of the United States Congress in September 2015. The pope talked about four exemplary Americans: Abraham Lincoln, Martin Luther King, Jr., Dorothy Day, and, you guessed it, Thomas Merton. What made this event so monumental, beyond the pope unequivocally lifting up Merton as a significant American model of Christian discipleship, was that Cardinal Wuerl was sitting in the front row of the United States Capitol, just a few feet away from Pope Francis as he addressed the nation and world. I wonder what was going through Wuerl's thoughts at that moment. I imagine it is possible that he was rethinking his exclusionary decision

---

[1] Quoted in Jim Forest, *Living with Wisdom: A Life of Thomas Merton* (Maryknoll, NY: Orbis Books, 2008), 242.

and dismissive remarks about Merton ten years earlier. Either way, the pope vindicated so many of us who had always known Wuerl and his likeminded fellows to be misguided at best when it came to their assessment of Merton and his legacy.

In celebrating the centenary of Merton's birth, it seems fitting for us to take a closer look at some of the ways Merton's relevance remains strong today and may continue into the future. Among the myriad ways Merton continues to be relevant stand several that are especially timely, particularly for young adults.

From "Slacktivism" to Solidarity

In a sense, one might assert that conversion is the theme most central to Merton's life and legacy. Those who came to know Merton first through his 1948 spiritual memoir *The Seven Storey Mountain* might recognize this theme as the thread that drives the narrative. Born to creative but largely unreligious parents—both of whom died before Merton turned sixteen—Merton's childhood and young adult life was mostly devoid of religious practice or reflection. From the time of his memoir's publication onward Merton was hailed as a contemporary "St. Augustine" whose "modern-day *Confessions*" highlighted how God's grace breaks through an all-but-atheistic young man's self-centeredness to inspire conversion to Christianity and eventually religious life. This is how Merton presented his story, which concludes with his entrance into the Trappist Order at the Abbey of Gethsemani in Kentucky.

But Merton's conversion didn't end there. Real conversion never does.

In fact, like Augustine's *Confessions*, Merton's spiritual memoir bears the marks of what literary critics call the "unreliable narrator." We are presented with a compelling narrative, undoubtedly grounded in truth, but one that nevertheless emphasizes some elements and overlooks others. With time on our side, as well as the resources of his journals, correspondence, and impressive official biography by Michael Mott, we know that Merton's young adult life was probably much more like the experience of the average college student today.[2] He questioned his beliefs, experimented with political associations, including communism,

---

[2] See Michael Mott, *The Seven Mountains of Thomas Merton* (New York: Harcourt, 1984).

developed his creative and artistic side, made lifelong friends, got into trouble, and was shaped by his undergraduate mentors. If anything, it was a closed worldview from which Merton suffered most acutely, something characterized by his lack of awareness of the needs of others, especially those outside his immediate circle.

This introspective worldview followed the young man into the monastery and can be seen in the style and themes of Merton's early writings. It is not that Merton was misanthropic or dismissed those who suffered elsewhere. It was just that his preoccupation was with his own spiritual journey. The 1940s and early 1950s witnessed books and essays by an enthusiastic young monk who wanted to share his faith with others, but the themes verged on the solipsistic: solitude, contemplation, asceticism, the monastic vocation, each of these often viewed as ends in themselves. If we take Merton at his narrative word in *The Seven Storey Mountain*, then the conversion we are left with is one from the self-centeredness of "secular life" to the navel-gazing of "religious life."

However, as Lawrence Cunningham, emeritus professor of theology at the University of Notre Dame, has written, "The period of the 1950s was a time of deep change in Merton's thinking, a change radical enough to be called a 'conversion' (or, perhaps better, a series of conversions)."[3] Merton's experience of graced conversion did not end with profession of religious vows and the donning of a Trappist habit. Rather, the shifts in Merton's outlook on the world and God's presence in it powerfully influenced the monk's writing style and subject matter. It was as if a veil was lifted or his eyes opened to the realities of violence, injustice, and suffering around the world. He began to correspond with civil rights activists, world leaders, and artists. He established what he would later describe in a letter to Pope John XXIII as "an apostolate of friendship" that allowed him to reach out to so many through his writing and correspondence.

Merton's turning toward the world and the prophetic shift in his priorities seem to offer a timely lesson for today's young adults. The neologism *slacktivism* has gained currency over the last decade to describe the minimal efforts people engage in, often by means of social media, to "support" an issue or cause, but efforts that have in fact very minimal or

---

[3] Lawrence Cunningham, *Thomas Merton and the Monastic Vision* (Grand Rapids, MI: Eerdmans, 1999), 51–52.

no practical effects. The primary result of such measures is some sense of satisfaction with oneself that arises from having "done something good."

In an age of hyper connectivity and rapid communication, young women and men are instantly aware of what is happening around the globe. The result is something like a preliminary conversion, a move toward awareness of something beyond oneself. However, the slacktivism of today is not unlike the religious interiority of Merton's early conversion. Over time Merton came to realize that he was (to be anachronistic) a slacktivist, someone who thought he was doing something good for others, but without taking the risk or putting himself in relationship with those he sought to help. Young adults can look to Merton as a model of someone who remained open to continual conversion, open to the challenge of God's spirit, open to doing something more and risking much for the sake of another. He used his social location within the monastery as one on the margins of society to critique those injustices of his time—racism, nuclear armament, poverty—and then reach out to support, comfort, guide, and help organize change.

Reading across Merton's corpus, beyond *The Seven Storey Mountain* into his social criticism of the 1960s, can offer young people today a model for moving from slacktivism toward solidarity, from tweeting about an issue toward doing something real about it.

Interreligious Dialogue

Near the end of his life, in October 1968, Merton spoke to a group of monks in Calcutta and ended his talk with these now-famous lines: "My dear brothers, we are already one. But we imagine that we are not. And what we have to recover is our original unity. What we have to be is what we are."[4]

Merton's ongoing conversion opened him up to a variety of encounters and relationships that traversed the boundaries of the early-twentieth-century insular world of American Catholicism to dialogue with people of different faiths and those with no religious affiliation at all. As early as the 1950s Merton anticipated one of the monumental shifts that would emerge from Vatican II. Even to this day Merton is criticized by

---

[4] Thomas Merton, *The Asian Journal* (New York: New Directions, 1971), xx.

some who hold to a naive reading of the patristic saying *Extra ecclesiam nulla salus* ("outside the church there is no salvation"), and believe that Merton overstepped his bounds as a Catholic priest in dialoguing with Muslims, Jews, Buddhists, and Christians of other denominations. Some have even gone so far as to spuriously claim that Merton had "abandoned his faith" for some syncretic religious view. This could not be further from the truth.

There is absolutely nothing in Merton's published works, or in his private journals and correspondence, that would indicate an interest in leaving the Catholic Church. In his 1966 book, *Conjectures of a Guilty Bystander*, Merton writes:

> The more I am able to affirm others, to say "yes" to them in myself, by discovering them in myself and myself in them, the more real I am. . . . I will be a better Catholic, not if I can refute every shade of Protestantism [or other faiths], but if I can affirm the truth in it and still go further.[5]

What rooted Merton's engagement with people different from himself was the sense of "original unity," which he recognized bound all people together as children of God. He understood that he could not have an authentic conversation about faith with others if he didn't have a firm commitment and deep love for his own tradition. Before Vatican II promulgated *Nostra Aetate*, Merton already understood that "the Catholic Church rejects nothing that is true and holy in these [other] religions" (*NA*, no. 2).

There is so much that can be said about the still-timely insights Merton presents to us about engaging other religious traditions.[6] Perhaps the most pertinent is the need to live honestly in the tension between maintaining one's own faith commitments and humbly learning from the experiences of others, all the while holding onto the belief that we are indeed, somehow, "already one."

His Holiness the Dalai Lama, in a 2010 *New York Times* op-ed piece, writes, "While preserving faith toward one's own tradition, one can

---

[5] Thomas Merton, *Conjectures of a Guilty Bystander* (New York: Doubleday, 1966), 140.

[6] For example, see William Apel, *Signs of Peace: The Interfaith Letters of Thomas Merton* (Maryknoll, NY: Orbis Books, 2006).

respect, admire and appreciate other traditions." He went on to explain that it was none other than Thomas Merton, with whom he met personally in 1968, who offered him this insight. "Merton told me he could be perfectly faithful to Christianity, yet learn in depth from other religions like Buddhism. The same is true for me as an ardent Buddhist learning from the world's other great religions."[7] For Merton then, as for the Dalai Lama later, compassion for and personal encounter with people of other faiths do not diminish one's own religious convictions; if anything they strengthen them. Merton shows us as much by living out what he came to realize was his "vocation of unity," to borrow a phrase from Merton scholar Christine Bochen.[8]

The Potential Appeal

Merton continues to speak a prophetic word to us today, but who is listening?

Returning to Wuerl's contention that young people don't know Merton, the cardinal may be correct about that when Millennials and Generation Z are compared with earlier generations, but it is not for the lack of Merton's appeal to young adults. In addition to courses on Merton's life and work being taught at colleges and universities around the United States today, the International Thomas Merton Society (ITMS) established the Robert E. Daggy Scholarship program to fully fund youth and young adult participation at the biennial ITMS conference. Since the Daggy Scholarship's establishment in 1996 by the late Fr. William Shannon, the renowned Merton scholar and first president of the ITMS, there have been hundreds of young people who have had the opportunity to delve more deeply into the popular and scholarly discussions about Merton's life and work. My own travels speaking around the United States and abroad offer anecdotal confirmation that when young adults are exposed to Merton's writings and thought, they are captivated and often can relate to his experience of conversion, his witness of imperfect humanity, his openness to the diversity of others, and his radical commitment to social justice and peace.

---

[7] Tenzin Gyatso, "Many Faiths, One Truth," *New York Times,* May 25, 2010.
[8] See Christine M. Bochen, *Thomas Merton: Essential Writings* (Maryknoll, NY: Orbis Books, 2000), 21–50.

In addition to young adults, Merton's writings have been having an impact in a variety of locations and among diverse populations. There are currently dozens of local chapters of the ITMS, and more continue to spring up, especially in Europe and the Global South. But perhaps the most unique chapter is the one located within the Massachusetts Correctional Institution in Shirley, Massachusetts. Founded in 2013 by the late educator and Merton enthusiast John Collins, the chapter is an outgrowth of a talk he gave about Merton at the inmates' request. In an interview with the *National Catholic Reporter,* several of the incarcerated men—some who have been in prison for decades—spoke about the significance of reading Merton. Joseph Labriola recalled being in solitary confinement, discovering a copy of Merton's *New Seeds of Contemplation* in his cell, and reading out of his cell's window to other convicts. One prisoner, Timothy Muise, said that the Merton group "affords men the opportunity to change, to re-evaluate their life in God's light."[9]

Young adults, US prisoners, and others who encounter Merton through new translations in foreign languages are not the only audiences with an appreciation for Merton's life and work, but the increasing diversity of this sort of reception only bolsters the claim that Merton is neither outdated nor irrelevant. It would seem that, a century after his birth, Merton still has much to offer the church and world, and fortunately there is no indication that the timeliness of his insight on matters of peacemaking, interreligious dialogue, and openness to lifelong conversion will be waning anytime soon. His wisdom speaks deep to the heart of those who encounter it. And given the ongoing inspiration and positive effects that continue in Merton's wake, one can only imagine the possibilities that another century of his influence may have in bringing us all closer to that "original unity" about which he speaks, helping to lead us to recognition that "what we have to be is what we are."

---

[9] Tanya Connor, "Merton Discussions Challenge Prisoners' Minds, Foster Their Prayer Life," *National Catholic Reporter,* November 22, 2014.

4

Friends of Merton

On November 10, 1958, Thomas Merton wrote a letter to Pope John XXIII in which the American monk shared with the new pope some reflections about the world and the church. In one part Merton describes how he had begun to understand that being a cloistered monk did not necessarily mean withdrawing from the world some absolute way. Instead, he discerned the Spirit calling him to another form of ministry from within the walls of the monastery by writing letters, connecting with women and men that he might never have had the opportunity to meet otherwise.

> It is not enough for me to think of the apostolic value of prayer and penance; I also have to think in terms of a contemplative grasp of the political, intellectual, artistic and social movements of this world—by which I mean a sympathy for the honest aspirations of so many intellectuals everywhere in the world and the terrible problems they have to face. I have had the experience of seeing that this kind of understanding and friendly sympathy, on the part of a monk who really understands them, has produced striking effects among artists, writers, publishers, poets, etc., who have become my friends without my having to leave the cloister. . . . In short, with the approval of my superiors, I have exercised an apostolate—small and limited though it be—within a circle of intellectuals from other parts of the world; and it has been quite simply an apostolate of friendship.[1]

[A version of this essay was originally published in *America Magazine* 210, no. 15 (April 28–May 5, 2014): 12.]

[1] Thomas Merton, "Letter to Pope John XXIII (November 10, 1958)," in *The Hidden Ground of Love: Letters*, ed. William H. Shannon (New York: Farrar, Straus, and Giroux, 1985), 482.

Merton came to realize that part of his religious vocation involved connecting with people of different backgrounds, experiences, and worldviews.

He corresponded with the writers Boris Pasternak, Czesław Miłosz, Ernesto Cardenal, and Evelyn Waugh; with activists Joan Baez, Daniel and Philip Berrigan; with theologians Paul Tillich, Karl Rahner, Abraham Heschel, and Rosemary Radford Reuther; with bishops, nuns, and religious leaders of other traditions, like Thich Nhat Hanh; and with so many others, including ordinary, unknown people.

I thought of Merton and his "apostolate of friendship" earlier this month while sitting at a pub one evening in England. I was in the company of a diverse collection of people: a middle-age father from Ireland, an Episcopalian priest from Scotland, and a man and a woman from England, both teachers. We were there enjoying some beer after a long but inspiring day of academic paper presentations and workshops on the life, thought, and legacy of this American monk. We were in Oakham in central Britain for the Thomas Merton Society of Great Britain and Ireland Conference, an event held every other year. The conference draws a varied group composed of top Merton scholars, those with a more casual interest in Merton, and all sorts of people in between. I was there to deliver a keynote address.

Strangers before this evening, those with whom I found myself at the pub began to exchange stories about how they came to discover the writings of Merton and what had led them to attend this three-day event. Most shared a version of the typical Merton story, which begins with reading *The Seven Storey Mountain*. However, the Irish man recalled a dramatic event that took place in a hospital room. Visiting his father, who was recovering from surgery, he was told that the man in the next bed was dying. The dying man happened to be reading a book, which led my new Irish friend to reflect: "If he's dying and is reading, it must be an amazing book! I need to know what it is."

The book was Merton's *The Seven Storey Mountain*.

Decades later this Irish man shared that Merton remained a major influence in his life ever since he read the book after that hospital encounter.

My own life has been blessed by Merton's ongoing apostolate of friendship. It is thanks to Merton that I met fellow Merton scholar David Golemboski more than fifteen years ago while we were both attending a Merton conference; he has subsequently become one of my best friends. I am grateful not only to know him, but grateful also to have his spouse and their children in my life. Last year I was privileged to have been invited to lecture around Southern Africa about Merton's ongoing relevance and wisdom. And for every one of the many wonderful people I met and the friendships I formed in those places, I am indebted to Merton. More recently an academic colleague launched a Merton reading group, where faculty from across disciplines meet monthly to discuss Merton's essays in *Raids on the Unspeakable*.

Merton has and continues to be a catalyst for relationship building, drawing together folks from various backgrounds, contexts, and social locations that find in his writings and thought something around which to build connections that might not otherwise have come to pass. It is a strikingly organic and yet mysterious experience, particularly when one considers how polarizing our contemporary society has become and how unlikely it is for those from different backgrounds to come together.

Few writers and thinkers have such an ability to bring people together. Even fewer so long after their death. Thomas Merton continues to exercise an apostolate of friendship, bringing people together across many divides. If you haven't met Merton and his friends yet, I encourage you to do so.

II

Thomas Merton on
Contemporary Christian Life

5

No Spouse Is an Island

Thomas Merton's Contribution
toward a Contemporary Spirituality of Marriage

It might at first seem counterintuitive to look at the work of a mid-twentieth-century American Trappist monk for insights in developing a theologically sound and pragmatically substantive spirituality of marriage. Yet the wisdom of Thomas Merton again demonstrates that to such a natural inclination there exist at least some significant exceptions to that rule. Although Merton did not construct a sustained or systematic treatment on the theology or spirituality of marriage as some scholars have since the Second Vatican Council's positive contributions to the subject in conciliar texts such as *Gaudium et Spes* and *Apostolicam Actuositatem*, his occasional reflections on marriage as sacrament and source of sanctity offers illuminative resources for those interested in developing a contemporary spirituality of marriage.[1] Merton's theological reflection on marriage is found in three primary forms: his book-length spiritual treatises, such as *No Man Is an Island*, *The New Man*, and *The Ascent to Truth*,[2] among others; his personal

---

[A version of this essay was originally published in *The Merton Annual* 25 (2012): 177–96. Used with permission.]

[1] All conciliar constitutions and decrees are taken from *The Documents of Vatican II with Notes and Index*, Vatican translation (Strathfield, Australia: St. Paul's Publications, 2009). Hereafter, all references to conciliar texts will include the document's Latin title and paragraph number with this edition's page number in parenthesis.

[2] See Thomas Merton, *No Man Is an Island* (New York: Harcourt Publishers, 1955); Thomas Merton, *The New Man* (New York: Farrar, Straus, and Giroux, 1961); and Thomas Merton, *The Ascent to Truth* (New York: Harcourt Publishers, 1951).

journal entries; and, perhaps in both the most diverse and pragmatic forms, in his extensive correspondence with a variety of people. While the explicit references to marriage in Merton's writing, journals, and correspondence offer a trove of valuable material, which has largely gone unexamined and without contemporary appropriation, his more broadly addressed work on the spiritual life also provides material valuable for the development of a spirituality of marriage today.[3]

The aim of this chapter is not to demarcate the definitive parameters of a spirituality of marriage according to Thomas Merton; instead I seek to highlight those areas of his writing fecund for appropriation in the contemporary theological enterprise of developing a spirituality of marriage, while also noting several trajectories worthy of further exploration. The dearth of scholarly engagement with Merton's thought in this area elicits a substantive treatment such as I propose below. It is my hope that this essay might provide the impetus for additional inquiry into what Merton's work might offer theologians and pastoral ministers today by way of resource and guidance.

The structure of this chapter is fivefold. First, we begin with a look at the current state of the development of a spirituality of marriage from the dual lens of helpful contributions and challenges to the process. Second, we examine Merton's contribution to the theological concept of vocation, particularly as it emerges in his writing with regard to marriage as a legitimate and holy vocation. Third, we consider the way in which Merton describes marriage as the place of divine encounter for spouses. Fourth, we explore Merton's understanding of marriage as the locus for Christian sanctity. And finally, we close with a summary of Merton's contribution to a contemporary spirituality of marriage.

---

[3] More than twenty-five years ago, before Merton's journals were edited and published, Lawrence Martone published an article titled "Merton's Insights Applied to Marriage," *Spiritual Life* 32 (1986): 105–10. Martone's article is helpful in that it is the first attempt to look at Merton's work as a serious resource for a spirituality of marriage, but it lacks a broad and sustained engagement with both the Mertonian corpus and the post-conciliar theological texts that frame the discussion of marriage as sacrament and the parameters of a marital spirituality today. The only other treatment of Merton's view of marriage is a short encyclopedia entry: Patrick O'Connell, "Marriage," in *The Thomas Merton Encyclopedia*, ed. William Shannon, Christine Bochen, and Patrick O'Connell (Maryknoll, NY: Orbis Books, 2002), 281–82.

Spirituality of Marriage: Seeds and Challenges

Thomas Merton often uses the image of seeds, a symbol frequently found in the gospel parables and Christian tradition, to refer to myriad dimensions of the Christian life of contemplation. The image is helpful insofar as we recognize the inchoate and, at times, unclear features of the *vita evangelica* ("gospel life") in its manifold forms. Like the mustard-seed-sized faith of those about whom Jesus speaks in the Gospel (Mt 13:31–32; Mk 4:30–32; Lk 13:18–19), there are aspects of our lives of prayer and Christian praxis that at once appear nascent yet bear potential for extraordinary growth. The metaphoric use of seed in such instances provides a multivalent image that relies on concurrent factors for its sustenance and growth, which could be taken to represent the liturgical life of the faithful, contemplative engagement with prayer, the support and participation of the community, and so on. A seed does not grow on its own but remains fragile and dependent on outside factors for its nurturing and development. The efforts to develop a contemporary spirituality of marriage, one that is not as restrictive or problematic as those found earlier in Christian history, culturally conditioned as they were, bear a resemblance to seeds: they are rich starting points that require assistance, support, and reflection to grow into a comprehensive and adoptable spirituality.

At the same time, while certain beneficial seeds of marital spirituality have been planted in recent decades, there also exist numerous challenges to the efficacious nurturing and harvesting of these spiritual seeds. Among the diverse challenges of contemporary experience, one might count the confluence of cultural and social views of marital normativity brought into conflict as a result of increased globalization; the absence of sustained theological reflection on the role of married life in the post-conciliar church; and the remaining specter, if not a reinvigorated reality in recent years, of a clericalism that subordinates so-called secular life, including marriage, in order to elevate clerical and religious life as objectively better or more holy.

In this section of the chapter, I wish to survey briefly both the seeds and challenges that emerged in recent years as theologians and others have consciously grappled with identifying sources for and the development of a spirituality of marriage.

Seeds of a Fruitful Spirituality of Marriage

Among the most important developments in the theology and spirituality of marriage in recent history is the way in which the Second Vatican Council addressed the subject of marriage in the document *Gaudium et Spes*. Whereas previous conceptualizations of marriage focused on the inferiority of that state of life when compared to other states such as religious life, as well as a nearly exclusive emphasis on the procreative end of marriage as the institution's subject and purpose, *Gaudium et Spes* presents a more expansive and theologically rich understanding of the source, purpose and end of marriage. The council explains: "For the good of the spouses and their offspring as well as of society, the existence of the sacred bond no longer depends on human decisions alone. For, God Himself is the author of matrimony, endowed as it is with various benefits and purposes."[4] The starting point for any reflection on marriage must begin with God as the source, the "author" as it is understood here, that bespeaks the inherent goodness and gift of this state of life.

Previous conceptions of marriage, many of which might unfortunately persist in our world today, understood marriage following the perspective offered by St. Augustine, namely, as a remedy for concupiscence.[5] This view considered the state of marriage as simply the least-bad option in response to the need for human sexual expressivity and the need for procreation. Furthermore, the operative understanding governing marriage for at least the four centuries prior to the Second Vatican Council was the notion of marriage as a contract.[6] This contract was the formal agreement between two parties—formerly between the groom and bride's father, if now between the bride and groom—that negotiated these two ends: procreation and the so-called bodily-sexual rights of the spouses.

In this regard, the council moved beyond the previously held notion of marriage and popular understanding of the contractual and subordinated nature of the state of life. It offered an image of marriage as primarily

---

[4] *Gaudium et Spes*, §48 (160).

[5] For an excellent historical study of the church's developing understanding of marriage during this time, see Philip Lyndon Reynolds, *Marriage in the Western Church: The Christianization of Marriage during the Patristic and Early Medieval Periods* (Leiden: Brill Publishers, 1994), esp. 259–79.

[6] Peter Jeffery, *The Mystery of Christian Marriage* (New York: Paulist Press, 2006), 37.

"a covenant of life and love."[7] However, as Peter Jeffery rightly notes, it seems that in the decades following the promulgation of *Gaudium et Spes* and the rest of the conciliar texts the covenantal and richly theological understanding of marriage has "been concealed."[8] One of the seeds of a fruitful spirituality of marriage is found within the conciliar conceptualization of marriage.

Another seed of a fruitful spirituality of marriage might found within the recent ressourcement efforts of theologians to identify trajectories within the Christian spiritual, theological, and historical traditions that might help inform a contemporary understanding of marriage in light of Christian discipleship and love.[9] There are rich resources available within the tradition to be reappropriated in such a way as to aid in the illumination of the sacrament of matrimony's meaning and relevance today. There is, perhaps more than ever, a need in our own time to elucidate a spirituality of marriage from a Christian perspective, especially considering the challenges that popular culture can present to spouses or would-be spouses in the church.

Challenges to Constructing a Spirituality of Marriage

During the fall of 2011 much media attention was paid to the story of the short-lived marriage of socialite-turned-celebrity Kim Kardashian and professional basketball player Kris Humphries. Their seventy-two-day-long marriage led to a media and internet frenzy of commentary and critique, much of which focused on the would-be scandal or abuse of the institution of marriage caused by the brevity and ostensibly flippant

---

[7] See *Gaudium et Spes*, §47–§52 (159–66); and Jeffery, *The Mystery of Christian Marriage*, 35–75.

[8] Jeffery, *The Mystery of Christian Marriage*, 35.

[9] For a helpful survey of recent literature, see Monica Sandor, "Contemporary Marital Spirituality: A Survey of the Principal Themes," *INTAMS Review* 11 (2005): 238–55. Some of the more notable later efforts to construct a contemporary spirituality of marriage in the English language include Richard Gaillardetz, *A Daring Promise: A Spirituality of Christian Marriage*, rev. ed. (Liguori, MO: Liguori Publications, 2007); Charles Gallagher, George Maloney, Mary Rousseau, and Paul Wilczak, *Embodied in Love: Sacramental Spirituality and Sexual Intimacy* (New York: Crossroad Publishers, 1994); and *Christian Marriage and Family: Contemporary Theological and Pastoral Perspectives*, ed. Michael Lawler and William Roberts (Collegeville, MN: The Liturgical Press, 1996), esp. 93–207.

treatment of this union.[10] The casual approach to marriage that this celebrity debacle represents, and it should be noted that this is simply one among many such instances, does not just affect the rich and famous but informs and reinforces elements of a popular cultural influence that reaches to the ends of an entire society.

The Second Vatican Council realized the various challenges that face marriage in our modern world. The council's most extensive treatment of the sacrament of marriage takes place under the heading of the second major section of the document titled "Some Problems of Special Urgency."[11] This particular section on marriage as it is understood within the hostile social climate of the world begins with the assertion that human dignity and the value of the individual are directly tied to the institution of marriage: "The well-being of the individual person and of human and Christian society is intimately linked with the healthy condition of that community produced by marriage and family."[12] Among those matters that the council decries as currently threatening marriage are counted polygamy, divorce, "so-called free love," and other "disfigurements," which the documents states all "have an obscuring effect."[13] It is difficult, we are told, for the wider culture to appreciate the sacredness of the bond and the sacramentality of the relationship of marriage due to these and other societal influences. Marriage is no longer presumed to be a lifelong and lasting institution, but, as demonstrated by the spectacle of the Kardashian and Humphries wedding and subsequent divorce, it is now popularly considered to be no more than a contractual agreement that might be dissolved whenever the contracting partners see fit. So prevalent are the misconceptions of the meaning and purpose of marriage that some like Ann Linthorst began to describe marriage as an "alternative lifestyle" more than forty years ago.[14] There are few social cues and cultural norms that overtly endorse a Christian view of marriage; this is indeed a great challenge today.

---

[10] See, for example, Monica Corcoran Harel, "I Do, Briefly," *The New York Times,* November 6, 2011.

[11] *Gaudium et Spes* §46–§52 (159–66).

[12] *Gaudium et Spes* §47 (159).

[13] Ibid.

[14] Ann Linthorst, *A Gift of Love: Marriage as a Spiritual Quest* (New York: Paulist Press, 1979), 1–16.

Another major challenge to marriage today identified by the Second Vatican Council is the notion of married love as having been "profaned by excessive self-love, the worship of pleasure and illicit practices against human generation."[15] Selfishness and the desire for immediate gratification play particularly insidious roles in the popular dissolution of the integrity of marriage. While these characteristics might not be limited to shaping a culture's understanding of marriage—for selfishness and the desire for immediate gratification also shape one's understanding of self, society, and all relationships in turn—they have inexorably shaped the popular understanding of why one enters into marriage and what the purpose of that relationship should be.

These are simply preliminary observations of just two of the many challenges that face both the maintenance of a Christian understanding of marriage and the construction of a contemporary spirituality of marriage in our own day. Having looked at both some positive seeds of a fruitful spirituality of marriage and samples of the challenges present to the efficacious nurturing and harvesting of those seeds, we now move to consider three ways in which the thought and writing of Thomas Merton offer us resources in moving toward a contemporary spirituality of marriage.

Marriage as a Legitimate Vocation

While the exclusive use of the term *vocation* to refer to clergy and consecrated religious has rightly been in decline since the Second Vatican Council's renewed emphasis on the place and dignity of the laity within the church, which is the body of Christ called people of God, there are some remnants of a disparity in dignity or value between the manifold expressions of Christian life in various states of living. One of the ways that Thomas Merton's work contributes to a contemporary spirituality of marriage rests in his broadening of the notion of vocation to extend beyond religious clerics such as himself to include marriage as a legitimate calling from God to live an authentically Christian life. His reflections about vocation, mostly written prior to the council, presage the more popular appropriation of the term in the contemporary and multivalent

---

[15] *Gaudium et Spes* §47 (159–60).

way. For this reason it might be helpful to return to Merton's insight to glean resources to aid people of today in understanding the divine invitation to enter the vocation of married life.

In his lesser-known book, *Life and Holiness*, Merton writes, "Every baptized Christian is obliged by his baptismal promises to renounce sin and to give himself completely without compromise, to Christ, in order that he may fulfill his vocation, save his soul, enter into the mystery of God, and there find himself perfectly 'in the light of Christ.'"[16] He makes the point early on in his writing that the term *vocation* should not be limited to the ministries and lifestyles of formal ecclesiastical roles. Instead, *all* Christians, all baptized persons, have a vocation, albeit this vocation varies from person to person. Writing as he was in the late 1950s and early 1960s, Merton does exhibit a vestigial preference at times for what he refers to as a "special vocation," by which he means consecrated religious life.[17] However, it should be noted that these comments are usually made in passing and take a subordinated place beside the expansive view of the Christian vocational horizon that Merton presents immediately afterward, as is the case in *Life and Holiness*. Shortly after naming the uniqueness of the religious vocation, Merton qualifies his statement, saying that all Christians are to take "the basic Christian vocation to holiness" seriously, something not reserved for just the clerics and religious. Nowhere does Merton make this as explicit as he does later in *Life and Holiness*:

> The way of Christian perfection begins with a personal summons, addressed to the individual Christian by Christ the Lord, through the Holy Spirit. This summons is a call, a "vocation." Every Christian in one way or other receives this vocation from Christ—the call to follow him. Sometimes we imagine that vocation is the prerogative of priests and of religious. It is true that they receive a special call to perfection. They dedicate themselves to the quest for Christian perfection by the use of certain definite means. Yet every Christian is called to follow Christ, to imitate Christ as perfectly as the circumstances of his life permit, and thereby to become a saint.[18]

---

[16] Thomas Merton, *Life and Holiness* (New York: Image Books, 1963), 12.
[17] Ibid., 13.
[18] Ibid., 34.

Every Christian has a vocation given by God to live in a particular way in the world, striving as it were at all times to follow Christ as a disciple. Merton advocates for what the Second Vatican Council would later call the "universal call to holiness" shared by all believers, an articulation of this a priori relational vocation of the baptized.[19]

Elsewhere Merton also discusses this universal notion of vocation within the context of contemplation and the Christian life. It appears as something resembling the Rahnerian conceptualization of an existential characteristic of human personhood.[20] In a similarly Rahnerian way, Merton presupposes the freedom that is integral to the idea of a universal Christian vocation. He suggests that it is our intentional response to a primordial and personal call that best constitutes what we mean when we talk about contemplation:

Hence contemplation is a sudden gift of awareness, an awakening to the Real within all that is real. A vivid awareness of infinite Being at the roots of our own limited being. An awareness of our contingent reality as received, as present from God, a free gift of love. This is the existential contact of which we speak when we use the metaphor of being "touched by God." Contemplation is also the response to a call: a call from Him Who has no voice, and yet Who speaks in everything that is, and Who, most of all, speaks in the depths of our own being: for we ourselves are words of His. But we are words that are meant to respond to Him, to answer Him, to echo Him, and even in some way to contain Him and signify Him.[21]

It is important to observe the inclusivity of Merton's reflection here. This experience of the divine in contemplation and subsequent response to

---

[19] See *Lumen Gentium* §39–§42 (52–57).

[20] See Karl Rahner, *Hörer des Wortes: Zur Grundlegung einer Religionsphilosophie,* in *Karl Rahner: Sämtliche Werke,* vol. 4, ed. Albert Raffelt (Freiburg: Herder and Herder, 1997).

[21] Thomas Merton, *New Seeds of Contemplation* (New York: New Directions Publishing, 1961), 3. For a comprehensive study of the development of Merton's thought in *New Seeds of Contemplation,* see Donald Grayston, *Thomas Merton's Rewritings: The Five Versions of Seeds/New Seeds of Contemplation as a Key to the Development of His Thought* (New York: Edwin Mellen Press, 1989).

God's call is not limited to a select few but is an offer extended to all humanity as a gift from God.

In other places Merton identifies this divine call and our free response as an explicit invitation to share in Christ's ministry to inaugurate the kingdom of God. In his popular book *No Man Is an Island*, Merton writes: "Each one of us has some kind of vocation. We are called by God to share in His life and in His Kingdom. Each one of us is called to a special place in the Kingdom."[22] Writing nearly a decade before the Second Vatican Council, Merton anticipates some of the conciliar texts' best expression of the dignity and place of *all* members of the body of Christ, described throughout *Lumen Gentium* as the people of God. It should be noted that Merton's inclusivity contrasts with the later post-synodal apostolic exhortation of Pope John Paul II, *Christifideles Laici*, in which the particular expressions of the vocation of the laity are relegated to the last part of the text and treated very superficially, drawing only on a single quote from St. Francis de Sales's *Introduction to the Devout Life*.[23] This articulation of the lay vocation, with only a passing reference to marriage in terms of Francis de Sales's text, is a very secularized and limited expression of what the meaning of a Christian calling by virtue of baptism means for all members of the body of Christ. Merton, by contrast, even despite his at times focus on religious life, does not relegate married spouses to a place of clerical subordination within the *ecclesia*. Instead, his emphasis is on the genuinely grace-filled reality of married life that is intrinsically holy and a particular invitation to Christian discipleship inasmuch as ordained priesthood or consecrated religious life is.

Merton asserts that the problem with the popular conception of vocation does not stem from any inherent inequality or inferiority of state of life but is instead engendered by something of a collective forgetfulness on the part of the church to support and recognize marriage as a "truly spiritual vocation." For this reason, I would assert, the writing of the late Pope John Paul II in this regard—namely, the continued subordination of married life to a "secular realm" and in a categorically inferior place to ordained priesthood and consecrated religious life—and those

---

[22] Thomas Merton, *No Man Is an Island* (New York: Harcourt Brace, 1955), 131.

[23] John Paul II, *Christifideles Laici*, §55–§56, December 30, 1988 (Washington, DC: USCCB Publishing, 1989), 166–71.

who follow a similarly antiquated and clerical trajectory of thought do violence to the integrity of vocation as a constitutive element of human existence, something given by God prior to any human demarcation or ranking. Merton explains:

> Hence we must not imagine that married life is "life in the flesh" and religious life alone is "life in the spirit." The married life is a *truly spiritual vocation*, though in many ways it is accidentally rendered difficult by the fact that married people do not recognize their spiritual opportunities and often find no one to guide them in the right direction.[24]

In an implicit way he goes on to discuss the failure of the church as a whole to support women and men in married life. The elevation of consecrated religious life has created what Merton calls a "tragedy," because it leads good women and men into thinking that they can never reach holiness, that they are in essence barred from a life of Christian perfection because they, naturally, "find it difficult or impossible to imitate the austerities, the devotions, and the spiritual practices of religious."[25] It is entirely understandable that they would feel such a way of life "difficult or impossible," because that is not the way of life that God has called spouses to live. Their vocation looks different, is affectively expressed in other ways, and is equally dignified and Christian. The problem lies with the church's tradition of silence about (at best) and subjugation of (at worst) married couples in the community of faith.

Another concern that Merton identified in the history of marital spirituality is the extreme idealization that could also take place of the relationship and sacrament from the perspective of celibate clerics and religious. One thinks of Augustine and his suggestion that marriage suffices to morally respond to natural human concupiscence. Yet, Merton notes in the correspondence with a woman named Mrs. Lytton, society also has its own idealization of marriage and what that type of relationship should look like and produce. Writing in the early 1960s, Merton describes his own take on his contemporary society's perpetuation of a certain view of marriage:

---

[24] Merton, *Life and Holiness*, 110, emphasis added.
[25] Ibid., 110.

I think that we live in a society which *makes* a problem out of love and marriage, whether one likes it or not. There is so much nonsense, explicit or otherwise, about sex: there is a myth of sex, it is glamorized, and impossible ideals are proposed, people get the idea that marriage is a failure unless one attains to utterly hopeless ideals of perfect adjustment, and so on. One has to face the fact that sex is both intoxicating and disconcerting, that it takes a person out of himself and leaves him in confusion. It is beautiful but it is also in some ways ugly. It is full of consolation and bliss, but it also arouses the power to hate. Love and hate go together, and sex is full of ambivalence. The real thing then is to learn to give oneself maturely, without futile idealization, accepting the unsatisfactory realities and the transient intoxications.[26]

Merton's frank approach to what he identifies as the problem of idealization of marriage and sex within his contemporary society sets the stage for him to offer his salient advice to Mrs. Lytton. He writes, "The great thing in Marriage is not an impossible ideal of fulfillment and exaltation but a mature rational Christian acceptance of the responsibilities and risks of human love."[27] Love plays a central role in Merton's understanding of the sacrament of marriage. Marriage is both authentically human and an expression of Christian discipleship. At one point Merton even suggests that a vocation to married life presupposes "the capacity for a deeply human love."[28] It is a legitimate vocation that should be neither subordinated nor elevated but embraced and lived as part of God's plan for humanity and salvation. In a 1965 letter to a woman named Edith, Merton responds to her news that she is engaged with yet another affirmation that marriage is indeed a vocation. He wrote: "I am happy to hear you have found someone you might marry. Certainly that is a most beautiful vocation, but a difficult one in these days when love is misunderstood so seriously."[29]

---

[26] Thomas Merton, "Letter to Mrs. Lytton (November 21, 1963)," in *Witness to Freedom: Letters in Time of Crisis*, ed. William Shannon (New York: Harcourt Brace, 1994), 309–10.

[27] Ibid., 310.

[28] Merton, *No Man Is an Island*, 99.

[29] Thomas Merton, "Letter to Edith (June 25, 1965)," unpublished correspondence, Thomas Merton Center, Bellarmine University (Louisville, KY).

Ahead of his time, Merton articulated well what the Christian tradition had long taught but so many had forgotten: *all* Christians have a vocation. Marriage, then, is not simply an external, contractual, or convenient way to live in the world, nor is it a subordinate form of life when compared to consecrated religious life, but it is inherently dignified, sacramental, and legitimately vocational. Spouses have been called by God and led by the Spirit into this way of expressing Christian love.

Marriage as the Place of Divine Encounter

The Second Vatican Council, in the *Pastoral Constitution on the Church in the Modern World (Gaudium et Spes)*, identified married love as the location where the two spouses primarily encounter God in Christ. "Authentic married love is caught up into divine love and is governed and enriched by Christ's redeeming power and the saving activity of the Church, so that this love may lead the spouses to God with powerful effect and may aid and strengthen them in the sublime office of being a father or a mother."[30] Within the covenant of marriage, both spouses experience the presence of God and are simultaneously brought into the life and love of the Trinity. This is something that Thomas Merton, years before the Second Vatican Council refocused the church's theology and spirituality toward the inherent dignity and vocation of the marriage covenant, identifies in his writings.

Perhaps one of the most succinct reflections that Merton offers on marriage as the place of divine encounter comes in what would eventually be posthumously published as *The Inner Experience*. This particular passage highlights Merton's understanding and presentation of the unique locus of trinitarian love in marriage and the privileged place the sacrament provides to the spouses for experiencing Christ:

> It follows from this that for the married Christian, his married life is essentially bound up with his contemplation. This is inevitable. It is by his marriage that he is situated in the mystery of Christ. It is by his marriage that he bears witness to Christ's love for the world, *and in his marriage that he experiences that love.* His marriage is a sacramental center from which grace radiates out into every

---

[30] *Gaudium et Spes* §48 (161).

department of his life, and consequently it is his marriage that will enable his work, his leisure, his sacrifices, and even his distractions to become in some degree contemplative. For by his marriage all these things are ordered to Christ and centered in Christ.[31]

Prompted by reflection on the mode and place of contemplation in the lives of lay women and men, Merton posits that it is precisely the married life itself that serves as that location, as that privileged place within which Christ is most immediately encountered. Merton goes so far as to suggest that married life provides the very condition for the possibility for all aspects of the spouse's work, relationships, and leisure. So too will married life provide the foundation and location for the spirituality of the spouses, a notion that flows directly from the recognition of the legitimacy and integrity of marriage as vocation.

At certain points in his writing Merton identifies by way of privation the meaning and purpose of marriage. As it concerns that privileged place of encounter with God, something oftentimes called contemplation, marriage should not be confused with a popular or "worldly" conception of marriage. Merton keenly notes, "The union of two in one flesh is not chiefly for consolation and mutual support," a view that is widely held by some.[32] As attributes of the relationship, consolation and mutual support are not inherently bad, but they are not the primary reasons why two people should enter into the covenant of marriage. There is also the temptation, if one fixates on those theses and other secondary aspects of marriage, to slip into a consumeristic or individualistically driven view of marriage. This is made more explicit in Merton's posthumously published book *Love and Living*: "The trouble with this commercialized idea of love is that it diverts your attention more and more from the essentials to the accessories of love. You are no longer able to really love the other person, for you become obsessed with the effectiveness of your own package, your own product, your own market value."[33] The flippancy and self-centeredness with which love is treated in popular

---

[31] Thomas Merton, *The Inner Experience: Notes on Contemplation*, ed. William Shannon (New York: HarperOne, 2003), 140, emphasis added.

[32] Thomas Merton, *The New Man* (New York: Farrar, Straus, and Giroux, 1961), 92.

[33] Thomas Merton, *Love and Living*, ed. Naomi Burton Stone and Patrick Hart (New York: Harcourt Brace, 2002), 30–31.

culture distracts, as Merton observes, from the essential properties of marriage and relationship. At the core, Merton claims, is this encounter with God through married life. Meanwhile, what popular culture and many modern people focus on are the accidental or incidental qualities of married life and love. Merton speculates that one reason marriages break up so rapidly (in his own day, and how much more so today) is this lack of recognition of the central reality of the encounter with the divine within married life. "For many people what matters is the delightful and fleeting moment in which the deal is closed. They give little thought to what the deal itself represents. That is perhaps why so many marriages do not last, and why so many people have to remarry."[34]

Merton situates marriage within the context of contemplative life to highlight the intrinsically spiritual nature of the covenant and sacrament. He describes marriage as inherently "creative and fecund," asserting that it is the intimate sharing and communication of marriage that "elevates marriage to that sublime spiritual level in which action and contemplation are capable of fusion in the brilliant darkness of mystery."[35] Too often marriage is seen through the Augustinian or clerical lenses that claim such a relationship prevents or distracts from an "authentic spiritual life." Certainly, this is an attitude reflected in Merton's own time in the pre-conciliar first half of the twentieth century. Yet Merton rejects this subordination and artificial demarcation to highlight that marriage itself is a locus of divine encounter:

> In the union of man and woman it is no longer words that are symbols of the mystery of God's holiness, but persons. God appears in them [the spouses] as sacred, not only in the sense that life itself seems sacred to us, because it is mysterious, but in the sense that the productive union of those who are humanly in love with each other is a sacred symbol of the infinite giving and diffusion of goodness which is the inner law of God's own life.[36]

Not only do the spouses experience God in married life, but they themselves reflect the image of God to each other. It is in the strictly theological sense that Merton uses the term *symbol* here. Instead of viewing the

---

[34] Ibid., 31.
[35] Merton, *The New Man*, 92.
[36] Ibid., 92.

spouses as mere signs that point to something other than themselves (God, in this case), they are understood to be symbols, realities that actualize that which they represent. The spouses help make God in Christ incarnate in their relationship and love. They do this for each other, and they do this for the world, as all Christians are called to do.

Another aspect of marriage as the place of divine encounter that Merton discusses in his writing is the physical, sexual relationship shared between the spouses. Certainly this is a topic that is usually avoided in most spiritual and theological literature over the centuries. Nevertheless, Merton takes this important component of married life very seriously and offers us a renewed and healthy Christian anthropological perspective that highlights the gift of sexuality and an opportunity for spouses to recognize God in their marital love. "The married love that is transfigured by the Church's sacrament reproduces something of this love by which Christ sanctified His Church, and the natural mystery of the communication of life by love becomes a supernatural mystery of the communication of holiness by charity."[37] Not only does marital sexual love reflect the love of God, but Merton claims it is an instantiation or "reproduction" of that divine love. He writes in *No Man Is an Island* that, "in married life, divine love is more fully incarnate than in the other vocations" and that married love "becomes a sign of divine love and occasion of divine grace.[38]

Merton feels strongly about the immanent presence of God in marriage. When spouses enter the covenant, they make a concrete, historical choice that is at one and the same time much more than a public commitment or contract. "When two [spouses] make this choice, this spiritual choice, with regard to one another, then a great mystery and transformation takes place in the world and God is present in this mystery."[39] They enter into a new way of living in the world and ministering the

---

[37] Ibid., 93. Additionally, in *No Man Is an Island*, Merton writes: "But it is clear that married life, for its success, presupposes the capacity for a deeply human love which ought to be spiritual and physical at the same time" (99). A recurring theme, Merton often ties the spirituality of married life to the physical and sexual expression of marital love.

[38] Merton, *No Man Is an Island*, 154.

[39] Thomas Merton, "Journal Entry on February 13, 1959," in *A Search for Solitude: The Journals of Thomas Merton, Volume Three 1952–1960*, ed. Lawrence Cunningham (San Francisco: HarperCollins, 1996), 259.

love of God in Christ to one another. They enter into the trinitarian life of God in a new way. They fulfill their baptismal call of Christian discipleship in a unique way.

Marriage as the Means by Which Spouses Become Saints

The journey for all baptized Christians is, ultimately, a pilgrimage toward sainthood. Thomas Merton does not claim, however, that everybody will necessarily enter the official canon of the saints, but that in the more Pauline sense of the term, we are all called or invited by God to be our truest selves, which, found in relationship with God, means striving to live who it is we were created to be. It is not at all unusual for many people to think that sanctity is something reserved for ordained priests and members of religious communities. However, Merton makes it very clear in his writing that such a restriction on the concept of sainthood is not helpful, nor is it supported by the Christian tradition. At one point, illustrating what he sees as the universal reality of human sanctification in Christ, Merton suggests that there will logically be many more married people that will become saints than those who are celibate priests and religious, because there are simply *more* married people in the world. He then asks the question, "How then can we imagine that the cloister is the only place in which men can become saints?"[40]

This notion that marriage provides the means by which spouses will become saints stems from the two previous points Merton makes about marriage, namely, that it is a legitimate vocation and that it is the privileged location for the spouses' encounter with God. For Merton, what is at the heart of what it means to be a saint is for a person to be *truly* himself or herself.[41] It is an intrinsic call that comes to be recognized more clearly through baptism and Christian discipleship, and the true self comes to be known only in knowing God. Because Merton holds that the privileged place for spouses to encounter God is in their marriage, where the love of each spouse for the other becomes the symbol of divine love made manifest in relationship, then the discovery of one's true self in

---

[40] Merton, *No Man Is an Island*, 99.

[41] Merton, *New Seeds of Contemplation*, 31: "For me to be a saint means to be myself. Therefore the problem of sanctity and salvation is in fact the problem of finding out who I am and of discovering my true self."

God is properly understood as recognizable in the sacramental nature of marriage. This response to God's invitation and encounter with God in marriage leads to a transformation in love, which offers an opportunity to discover one's true self and therefore move closer to sanctity. Merton explains the connection between God's love and becoming a saint:

I who am without love cannot become love unless Love identifies me with Himself. But if He sends His own Love, Himself, to act and love in me and in all that I do, then I shall be transformed, I shall discover who I am and shall possess my true identity by losing myself in Him. And that is what I called sanctity.[42]

Spouses, by virtue of their calling to the married life and the encounter of God experienced in love, help each other to discover their true selves and become saints. Merton explains, "We must come to recognize that the married state is also most sanctifying by its very nature, and it may, accidentally, imply sacrifices and self-forgetfulness that, in particular cases, would be even more effective than the sacrifices of religious life."[43] This notion of intrinsic means toward sanctity is true not only of typical forms of prayer and contemplation within the marital relationship, but in the physical and sexual exchange of love proper to the married life. Merton sees in the physicality of married life a gift from God that is a complementary characteristic or means to sanctity. He writes: "The existence of a sacrament of matrimony shows that the Church neither considers the body evil nor repugnant, but that the 'flesh' spiritualized by prayer and the Holy Ghost, yet remaining completely physical, can come to play an important part in our sanctification."[44] That's right, sexual expression of love within marriage is not only necessary (as a distorted Christian view might suggest because of the utility of procreation), but it is an actual contribution toward the spouses becoming saints. Elsewhere Merton reiterates this point, writing that "in authentic married love, two persons become not merely well-adjusted sexual partners, but they complete one another spiritually, they bring meaning and fulfillment to one another's lives by a unity which cannot be accounted for by the

---

[42] Ibid., 63.
[43] Merton, *Life and Holiness*, 14.
[44] Merton, *No Man Is an Island*, 99–100.

human and biological needs of the natural species."[45] In other words, marital sexuality is not simply the natural response of two adult human beings, but within the marriage precisely as *sacrament*, it becomes an expression of love and spirituality between the two mutually self-giving spouses. In effect, the physical expression of love shared by the couple is a symbol of God's unbounded love for humanity in creation.

Yet the physical, emotional and spiritual expression of sexual love shared by the married couple is not where the vocation of marriage and the encounter of God end. On the contrary, Merton believes that this love between spouses, emblematic of God's love for humanity in creation often illustrated theologically by Christ and the church, should spill over into the world in concrete and charitable actions. Christian spouses live out their vocation and invite others to experience the loving, compassionate, and self-giving face of God through their interactions in society and with others. This way of living in the world begins, however, within the marriage. Lawrence Martone picks up on this aspect of Merton's outlook in connecting marital commitment and relationship with that of the broader communal commitment that comes with baptism into the body of Christ: "[The] marital and communal commitment each demand an other-directed spirituality wherein one shares the cross of the other. By concentrating on another's needs, one loses sight of his or her own individual problems. Merton suggests that the burden of the cross in relationships is negligible compared to carrying around the weight of one's own problems."[46] Martone's reading of Merton's insight suggests that it is the day-to-day practice of Christian discipleship on the level of the spousal relationship that enables married individuals to develop what he calls "other-directed spirituality."

While the foundation of becoming a saint is located in the exhortation that "every Christian is therefore called to sanctity and union with Christ, by keeping the commandments of God,"[47] Merton makes it clear in *Life and Holiness,* as well as in other texts, that Christian life is not limited to an individualistic union of one person and God. Similarly, Christian life cannot be authentically lived in a union of a married couple and

---

[45] Thomas Merton, *Redeeming the Time* (London: Burns and Oates, 1966), 57.
[46] Martone, "Merton's Insights Applied to Marriage," 109.
[47] Merton, *Life and Holiness*, 13.

God alone, but as mentioned above, the love shared between the spouses should impel them to reach out in relationship to others.

The question naturally arises: *How* does one live out this life toward holiness? In what way or method can spouses reach out in relationship to others? Merton responds to this inquiry with some thoughts about the "methodology" of sanctity, noting from the outset that no concrete "method" exists (one, for example, can think of the myriad iterations of sanctity modeled by the canonized saints):

> The Christian "method" is then not a complex set of ritual obser-vances and ascetic practices. It is above all an ethic of spontaneous charity, dictated by the objective relationship between the Christian and his brother. And every man is, to the Christian, in some sense a brother. Some are actually and visibly members of the Body of Christ. But all men are potentially members of that body, and who can say with certainty that the non-Catholic or the non-Christian is not in some hidden way justified by the indwelling Spirit of God and hence, though not visibly and obviously, a true brother "in Christ?"[48]

In other words, there is no hard-and-fast method for Christian living other than charitably serving the needs of all with whom a Christian encounters. At a time when the general Catholic disposition to non-Catholics and non-Christians more broadly was incredulous if not dismissive, Merton sought to expand the horizon of Christian action, positing the gospel's universal law of love as the means to holiness in all places and when encountering all people:

> The will of God is therefore manifested to the Christian above all in the commandment of love. . . . This is the only ascetic "method" which Christ has given us in the Gospels: that all should show themselves his friends by being friends of one another, and by loving even their enemies (Mt. 5:43–48). If they should always behave in a spirit of sacrifice, patience, and meekness even toward the unjust and the violent, Christians are all the more strongly obligated to be charitable and kind to one another, never using vicious and insulting language toward one another (Mt. 5:20–26).[49]

---

[48] Ibid., 38–39.
[49] Ibid., 39.

Merton makes clear that his reading of the Gospel according to Matthew, as well as the rest of scripture, offers Christians a clear injunction toward living in the world, even if Christ does not make, and really could not make, explicit provisions for every instance a person might encounter on the pilgrimage of life.

At the heart of Christian life, then, is the realization that "we are all bound to seek not only our own good, but the good of others," and that "the whole Christian life is then an interrelationship between members of a body unified by supernatural charity, that is by the action of the Holy Spirit, making us all one in Christ.[50] The notion that one cannot save one's self is not only an anti-Pelagian warning, but a recognition that every Christian's journey toward becoming a saint is centered on relationship with and within the *entire* body of Christ, which Merton expands beyond the baptized to include all human persons.

In marriage the spouses recognize this command of love first and foremost with each other. As stated above, it is the love that is shared in the commitment to live out the vocation to which God has called the couple and the experience of the divine that takes place in the relationship that should lead toward the world and not simply end inwardly in marital isolation. Love and joy are naturally directed *ad extra*; their expression cannot be contained if it is a genuine experience of God's grace. What begins in marriage carries over to every aspect of the spouses' lives, which is how Merton explains the progression of Christian discipleship in the world. Merton writes that the Holy Spirit "leads us to the most perfect observance of [the law of love], to the loving fulfillment of all our duties, in the family, in our work, in our chosen way of life, in our social relationships, in civic life, in our prayer, and in the intimate conversation with God in the depths of our souls."[51] Therefore, every aspect of life is transformed by the law of love, which, in the case of two spouses, originates and is nurtured in the sacrament of marriage.

Spouses are called to minister to each other, encouraging and supporting the other along the journey while also being mindful to exhort and challenge the other when necessary. Just as the spouses are the ministers of the sacrament of matrimony, their ministry does not end after the exchange of vows but commences in that rite and continues through life.

---

[50] Ibid., 40.
[51] Ibid., 36.

Their goal is the same: to become saints. Their becoming saints begins and returns to their covenantal relationship, for it is the privileged place of encounter with God and the response to God's invitation to follow Christ in a unique way in the world.

No Spouse Is an Island

The title for this chapter is an adaptation of the title of Merton's best-selling book *No Man Is an Island*. His book's title, though, is explained only briefly in the text itself, and it is in that explanation that Merton's contribution toward a contemporary spirituality of marriage can best be understood. Merton writes:

> And since no man is an island, since we all depend on one another, I cannot work out God's will in my own life unless I also consciously help other men to work out His will in theirs. His will, then, is our sanctification, our transformation in Christ, our deeper and fuller integration with other men. And this integration results not in the absorption and disappearance of our own personality, but in its affirmation and its perfection.[52]

The contribution that Merton makes toward a contemporary spirituality of marriage is the threefold identification of the instantiation of the Christian life of discipleship and love experienced in the sacrament shared by two spouses. This spirituality of marriage begins with the recognition and embrace of a divine call, an invitation from God to live a certain way in the world. It includes the realization that God in Christ is most immediately and primarily encountered in the marital relationship and expressed in the love shared by the spouses for each other. It culminates in what Martone calls "other-directed spirituality" or the living of Christian discipleship of charity, service, forgiveness, and concern for all people. The whole flow of these three elements is not necessarily linear but instead represents an interrelated matrix that moves in and out from each aspect of the marital relationship.

At the core of any contemporary spirituality of marriage is the acknowledgment that indeed no spouse is an island. Marriage is not

---

[52] Merton, *No Man Is an Island*, 64.

something into which one person enters individually, but instead is a joint vocation to follow Christ in intimate partnership in the world. Marriage is not something devoid of or removed from God but is in fact the location where a spouse can encounter the divine most immediately. Marriage is not an end in itself, nor is it a self-enclosed partnership, but it is the very means by which two spouses become saints through the moving outward into the world to live a life of Christian love-in-praxis rooted in the shared spousal experience of Christian love.

There remains much work to be done in the area of developing a Christian spirituality of marriage that responds to the needs of spouses in our age. There are indeed seeds that we can discover planted deep within the Christian tradition and in the thought of contemporary spiritual writers and theologians. Thomas Merton offers us three themes the depth of each of which could not completely be examined in this chapter but have been introduced so as to offer a heuristic guide for further consideration of the twentieth-century Trappist monk's wisdom for a new time and audience. It is my hope that any future spirituality of marriage takes seriously Merton's insights, which lead to the assertion that marriage is a legitimate vocation, the privileged place for married couples to encounter the divine, and the primary means by which spouses become the saints God has called them to be.

6

Digital Natives and the Digital Self

The Wisdom of Thomas Merton for Young Adult Spirituality and Self-Understanding

In the years since I first suggested that the neologism the *digital self* might serve us well as a modern synonym for Thomas Merton's often-discussed *false self*, the technological and subsequently the spiritual context of our society has changed.[1] As a direct result of our fast-paced world, shaped as it is by our collective and increasing dependence on the internet, new social media, and digital communication technology, contemporary commentary on the state of our experience witnesses the rapidity with which the "latest" becomes "outdated," and the "tried and true" becomes "obsolete." In a sense, novelty is prized over pragmatism or even necessity, and a culture has been cultivated in which people are urged to update, upgrade, and upload not only their technology, but themselves as well. While this high-speed current of cultural and social transformation in our day might suggest that a term such as the *false self*, or the *digital self* (think *false self 2.0*), is no longer compatible with our contemporary operating systems and means of cultural navigation, I believe that the technological developments as well as the concurrent declivities of these last few years only

[A version of this essay was originally presented at the Contemplation in a Technological Era: Thomas Merton's Insight for the Twenty-First Century Conference, Bellarmine University, Louisville, Kentucky, September 23–24, 2022, and later published in *The Merton Annual* 24 (2011): 83–111.]

[1] See Daniel P. Horan, "Striving toward Authenticity: Merton's 'True Self' and the Millennial Generation's Search for Identity," *The Merton Annual* 23 (2010): 80–89.

increase the relevance of reflecting on Merton's insight as it relates to the intersection of technology, contemplation, and the discovery of the "true self." For this reason, I maintain that among the varied synonyms Merton himself used to describe the false self—among which are counted the exterior self, empirical self, outward self, shadow self, imaginary self, illusory self, masks, and so on—we should also count the digital self. Its aptness stems in part from the term's ability to capture the timely challenges of generations that have only known a technologically hegemonic world, a cohort of young people that must confront—in addition to myriad challenges to the spiritual life that all people of all ages must face—new and unanticipated realities that have significantly affected the way in which people go about the world, relate to one another, and develop their relationship with God.

Merton's writing on technology as an explicit theme has often been presented as a cautionary tale that verges on singular critique of technological reliance and appropriation. From automated farm equipment to the television, we read Merton's regularly incredulous take on the purported "advancement" new and emerging technologies offer society. I am not entirely convinced that such a reading of Merton adequately takes into account the true complexity of modern living, something in which Merton himself participated and something from which none of us—at least without extraordinary effort and intention—can escape. We, like Merton before us, are faced with the realization that we cannot critique technology or society's collective use of its varied forms from the outside or some rarefied space, because we are dependent on, complicit in, and inexorably shaped by—in countless known and unknown ways—the very thing we seek to critique. And this is perfectly fine. But, as with any honest engagement with a subject, we are called to acknowledge our hermeneutical biases. That so much of our experience is informed by the contemporary technology—which, unlike the domestication of horses, the creation of writing, or the invention of the automobile, occurs at previously unknown rates and has incredibly long-ranging impact—needs to be considered as we begin our reflection.

Due to the necessary limitations of time and scope, I wish only to return to the theme I first engaged several years ago: the insight of Merton's notion of the true self and its fecundity for aiding today's young adults in living authentically in relationship with themselves, with others and with God.[2] To do this we will first take a look at some of the challenges that face today's young adults in order to gain an appreciation for the context within which modern spiritual seekers live out their desire to better understand themselves and their God. Next, we will look at Merton's formulation of the true self and consider how the identity formation in a digital age might at times be considered a form of the false self. Finally, we examine some ways in which Merton's writing continues to be informative and offer wisdom to young people today.

Today's Spiritual Seekers

In his book *The Church of Facebook: How the Hyperconnected are Redefining Community*, Jesse Rice keenly notes that "at the root of human existence is our great need for connection: connection with one another, with our own hearts and minds, and with a loving God who intended intimate connection with us from the beginning. Connection is the very core of what makes us human and the very means by which we express our humanity."[3] What Rice is getting at here, in other words, is that at the core of our very humanity is the capacity and desire for relationship. How we understand ourselves, our world, other people, and God are all directly shaped by this need we share to be connected to others and to participate in a uniquely human experience of relationship. From a theological perspective this need and capacity for relationship is identified as an intrinsic or existential attribute of humanity. We are created *capax Dei*, that is, with the capacity for relationship with the divine, which serves as the ground upon which our human relationships stand. The Franciscan theological tradition emphasizes this aspect of theological anthropology further, serving as a spiritual exponent of the truth that our very createdness is itself a sign of our a priori or inherent relational quality. That we exist bespeaks an intentional and loving divine act of creation that is entirely contingent, therefore we are already always in

---

[2] While the primary focus of this essay was on the then-emergent Millennial Generation and the sociological research cited is centered on that group, what is said here may also be applicable to the now-emerging Generation Z and other generations affected by current and future technologies.

[3] Jesse Rice, *The Church of Facebook: How the Hyperconnected are Redefining Community* (Colorado Springs, CO: David C. Cook Publishers, 2009), 28.

relationship from the very moment of our existence.[4] We might recall the Hebrew Prophetic tradition, such as is found in the Book of Jeremiah when seeking to illustrate this theological truth: "Before I formed you in the womb I knew you, and before you were born I consecrated you" (Jer 1:5).

Recognizing our desire to enter relationship is a fundamental quality of our existence is therefore nothing new. However, the *way* in which we enter relationship today does present something new and for those who were born in or after 1982, the cohort popularly called the Millennial Generation (or simply "Millennials"), this feature largely defines the only world they have ever known. Adam Thomas, an Episcopal priest and member of the Millennial Generation, says as much in his book *Digital Disciple: Real Christianity in a Virtual World*, when he writes: "The new dimension of virtuality that Tech has added to our lives has brought new locations, new situations, and yes, new opportunities and dangers. . . . The lay of the land has changed, so to speak, and our new virtual environments are affecting us on multiple levels."[5] This is all the more true for the emerging young adults in Generation Z, who have never known a world absent of a concurrent digital or virtual dimension. How these changes are made manifest in the spiritual, emotional, and relational lives of today's young adults is what concerns us here, but before we look at some specific ways the "new virtual environments" have affected young adults, we need to examine briefly this first generation to collectively face this new context: the Millennials.

In what follows I offer a short overview of what I and other scholars mean by use of the term *digital natives* and how this moniker relates to our discussion of the place, value, and challenge of technology in the lives of Millennials. Then I very briefly introduce some of the scholarly discussion of Millennial identity formation. And to conclude this section, I propose five challenges to identity formation in a digital age.

Digital Natives

There are two types of people in this world, digital natives and digital immigrants, and the latter group is growing smaller each year. At least

---

[4] For more, see Daniel Horan, "Light and Love: Robert Grosseteste and John Duns Scotus on the How and Why of Creation," *The Cord* 57 (2007): 243–57.

[5] Adam Thomas, *Digital Disciple: Real Christianity in a Virtual World* (Nashville, TN: Abingdon Press, 2011), 7.

this is the view forwarded by John Palfrey and Urs Gasser in *Born Digital: Understanding the First Generation of Digital Natives.*[6] Palfrey and Gasser suggest that in today's society one can better understand the differences between the Millennial Generation—those born in or after 1982—and all those who were born before them by characterizing each cohort in terms of its respective relationship to technology. These authors explore the manifold ways technology has influenced, impeded, and reshaped adolescent identity formation over the years. Their research provides a helpful glimpse into the world of young adults who have only ever known a technologically advanced and digital world.

The Millennial Generation, unlike Generation X, the Baby Boomers, or any other cohort before, has grown up in a technologically hegemonic era. For example, most members of this generation have had access to computers, the internet, cable television, and cellular phones long before entering high school. Or, as one author says, "For many kids using the new technology is as natural as breathing."[7] This is especially true of Generation Z who have nearly universally had access to advance technological devices and platforms virtually from birth. Palfrey and Gasser summarize this world in which digital natives live and interact as a new dimension of reality. This dimension is not something completely distinct from the world as we have known it, but it is unlike that which has come before.

> Unlike most Digital Immigrants, Digital Natives live much of their lives online, without distinguishing between the online and the offline. Instead of thinking of their digital identity and their real-space identity as separate things, they just have an identity (with representations in two, or three, or more different spaces). They are joined by a set of common practices, including the amount of time they spend using digital technologies, their tendency to

---

[6] John Palfrey and Urs Gasser, *Born Digital: Understanding the First Generation of Digital Natives* (New York: Basic Books, 2008; rev. ed. 2011).

[7] Don Tapscott, *Growing Up Digital: The Rise of the Net Generation* (New York: McGraw-Hill, 1998). See also Tapscott's subsequent study, published more than a decade after the first, in which he revisits the Millennial Generation's relationship to technology as a larger portion of the cohort has come of age. For more see Don Tapscott, *Grown Up Digital: How the Net Generation Is Changing Your World* (New York: McGraw-Hill, 2009).

multitask, their tendency to express themselves and relate to one another in ways mediated by digital technologies, and their pattern of using the technologies to access and use information and create new knowledge and art forms. For these young people, new digital technologies—computers, cell phones, Sidekicks—are primary mediators of human-to-human connections.[8]

Furthermore, with electronic books, virtual worlds, GPS navigation systems, and so forth, there is hardly anything exempt from its duplicate electronic or virtual counterpart. To say that young adults take technology for granted is an understatement. Millennials and members of Generation Z live in and have, for the most part, only ever known a technologically advanced and digital world.

Palfrey and Gasser suggest that young adults face two challenges in identity formation that are heightened by this digital world. The first is the instability of identity that results from frequent changes and, increasingly, from non-volitional acts of the person whose identity is at stake.[9] Concerning the frequent changes, the authors point out that "a Digital Native's identity is context-specific; its expression depends on who's asking, what environment they're in, and what day it is. [Therefore, there are multiple identities.] These multiple identities complicate matters in terms of how Digital Natives think of themselves and present themselves to the world."[10] This superfluidity is complicated further when one considers that a Millennial faces a decrease in his or her ability to control identity as others perceive it.[11] Whereas teenagers in the Agrarian or Industrial Age might be able to form their identity in a manner that allows them to present their "self" in a social setting with some sense of how they are perceived through personal interaction, digital natives almost constantly define and redefine their personal and social self-image while being simultaneously removed from the interpreters who perceive those images. Such a disconnection

---

[8] Palfrey and Gasser, *Born Digital,* 4; also see Michael Thomas, *Deconstructing Digital Natives: Young People, Technology, and the New Literacies* (New York: Routledge, 2011).

[9] Palfrey and Gasser, *Born Digital,* 31.

[10] Ibid., 27.

[11] Ibid., 31.

often leaves Millennials and members of Generation Z vulnerable to identity manipulation and falsification.[12]

In addition to the challenge of instability there is also that of the insecurity of young-adult identities today. As Palfrey and Gasser note: "It is hard for a sixteen-year-old girl in a wired society to control who can access or make changes to her identity. It would be impossible for her to secure her digital identity at any given moment, even if she wanted to."[13] So while experimenting with one's identity and self-image is a normal process of adolescent and young adult development, the digital age complicates the traditional process through the media used, the public forum it is presented in, the frequent changes that one experiences, and the lack of control the young person has over his or her perceived identity. The consequences of this new phenomenon have taken a particularly deleterious toll on members of Generation Z, as noted in a recent study published by the Surgeon General of the United States in the wake of the COVID-19 pandemic.[14]

David Buckingham presents another way to look at these two challenges of instability and insecurity of identity raised by Palfrey and Gasser. He suggests that instead of viewing these as two separate problems, we should consider them under one context that has both potentially positive and negative dimensions. Buckingham writes:

> On the one hand, it could be argued that the internet provides significant opportunities for exploring facets of identity that might previously have been denied or stigmatized. . . . Such arguments presume that media can be used as a means of expressing or even discovering aspects of one's "true self," for example, in relation to sexuality. Yet on the other hand, these media can also be seen to provide powerful opportunities for identity play, for parody and subversion. . . . Here, the emphasis would lie not on honesty and truth, but on the potential for performance and even for deception.[15]

---

[12] Ibid., 32. Also see Julie M. Albright, *Left to Their Own Devices: How Digital Natives are Shaping the American Dream* (New York: Prometheus Books, 2019).

[13] Palfrey and Gasser, *Born Digital*, 33.

[14] See "Protecting Youth Mental Health: The US Surgeon General's Advisory" (2021), https://www.hhs.gov.

[15] David Buckingham, "Introducing Identity," in *Youth, Identity, and Digital Media*, ed. David Buckingham (Cambridge, MA: MIT Press, 2008), 8–9.

No matter how one characterizes the new landscape of identity formation, it remains clear that the context has changed and the process has become more complicated, if not dangerous.

The complexity of identity formation for young adults reaches its climax with the paradox that as digital natives are able to more easily create multiple identities online and experiment with how they present themselves, they are also more bound to a single identity—a sprawling, morphing, shifting, and public identity—than ever before.[16] Whereas a young adult in the pre-digital era could simply pack up and move to another location, meet a new group of people, and essentially recreate his or her identity, today's young adults are more tightly linked to the digital representations of their identities that can be accessed at nearly any time and from nearly any location, and which never go away.

Identity Formation in a Digital Age

One of the hallmarks of identity formation for young adults growing up in a digital age, as we have already seen, is its fluidity. Scholars like Zygmunt Bauman and David Buckingham have suggested that, unlike the way in which identity was understood or formed in the pre-digital age, digital natives engage a personal (and perhaps even a collective) identity that is "almost infinitely negotiable."[17] As Buckingham has noted elsewhere, this fluidity or negotiability is both positive and negative, carrying with it both advantageous and problematic implications. On the positive side, such fluidity offers a seeming freedom that young people may have never known in a previous era. This freedom to "explore oneself" is heightened by the speed of communication and the sharing of ideas, cultures, and experiences across the normative borders of society and language. On the negative side, such fluidity presents an omnipresent challenge of instability, uncertainty, and confusion in terms of one's ability to relate to oneself, others, and ultimately, God.

Sharon Daloz Parks has described the process of young adult identity formation as like one's journey toward becoming "at home" in the universe:

---

[16] Palfrey and Gasser, *Born Digital*, 34–35.

[17] See Buckingham, "Introducing Identity," 2; and Zygmunt Bauman, *Identity* (Cambridge: Polity Press, 2004).

It has become increasingly clear that there is value and healing in incorporating into our understanding of human development an imagination of becoming at home. A part of becoming at home in the universe is discovering our place within it, in the new global commons in which we now find ourselves. We are beginning to recognize that this becoming is not so much a matter of leaving home as it is undergoing a series of transformations in the meaning of home. We grow and become both by letting go and holding on, leaving and staying, journeying and abiding—whether we are speaking geographically, socially, intellectually, emotionally, or spiritually. A good life and the cultivation of wisdom require a balance of home and pilgrimage.[18]

The metaphor of becoming at home in one's life does align comfortably with the notion that young adults can fabricate or develop a personal identity through social media, technology, or self-narration. On the contrary, the dual poles of home and pilgrimage suggest a dialectic tension that suggests a different journey of discovery and recognition. One "finds," as it were, one's "place," rather than constructing something *ex nihilo*. The imagery from Parks draws on language much more in line with Christian notions of vocation and philosophical concepts of inherent individuation than it does with the malleable content of the digital self.[19] What role new and emerging technologies play in the self-understanding or identity formation of young adults remains a pressing question. Framed with the perspective of digital native identity and spirituality formation in mind, is technology intrinsically good or bad?

The sociological, psychological, and demographic reports vary by scholar and study as to the pull of the positive and negative aspects of digital-age identity formation for young adult generations. On the one hand is someone like Mack Hicks, whose book title reveals his position, *The Digital Pandemic: Reestablishing Face-to-Face Contact in the Electronic*

---

[18] Sharon Daloz Parks, *Big Questions, Worthy Dreams: Mentoring Young Adults in Their Search for Meaning, Purpose, and Faith* (San Francisco: Jossey-Bass Publishers, 2000), 51.

[19] For more on this notion of inherent individuation, see Daniel Horan, "Praying with the Subtle Doctor: Toward a Contemporary Scotistic Spirituality," *The Cord* 58 (2008): 225–42.

Age.[20] On the other hand is a much more optimistic reading of contemporary young-adult identity formation in the works of authors such as Neil Howe, William Strauss, John Palfrey, Urs Gasser, and others.[21] Still others, like Jesse Rice, David Buckingham and Sherry Turkle, the founder and director of MIT's Initiative on Technology and Self, offer something of a middle-of-the-road approach that acknowledges both the positive effects of newfound freedom and the challenges inherent in the hyperactivity and disconnection consistently present to the young people of this age.

Turkle has used the term *tethered self* to illustrate how she sees the Millennial Generation's constant engagement with communication technology influencing how young adults have come to understand themselves. They have come to expect others and are now expected themselves to always be "on and available" for those with whom they regularly communicate; texting, DMing, SnapChatting, and the like have made accessibility an expectant constant. Therefore, there is no end to the workday, no escape from friends, and no time for solitude as one's identity becomes more and more reflective of the so-called tethered self. As nice as it is to be able to be reached and to reach others quickly, it is also a burden that was previously unknown. Such behavior moves from innovative novelty to smart-phone addiction as one can no longer imagine oneself without this ever-present technology. Rice explains:

> The cultivation of a healthy self-concept is being subtly undermined by the tendency toward always-on behavior. By way of example, Turkle mentions the fact that many kids are getting cell phones at a younger age, a reality that is having an impact on their development. The new phone is enabling parents and children to be in touch with one another, but it can prevent the child from having to face certain difficult tasks on their own. "With the on-tap parent," Turkle observes, "tethered children think differently about their own responsibilities and capacities. These remain potential, not proven." Likewise, when a young person jumps on Facebook [or

---

[20] Mack Hicks, *The Digital Pandemic: Reestablishing Face-to-Face Contact in the Electronic Age* (Far Hills, NJ: New Horizon Press, 2010).

[21] See Palfrey and Gasser, *Born Digital*; and Neil Howe and William Strauss, *Millennials Go to College*, 2nd ed. (Great Falls, VA: Life Course Associates, 2007).

other social networking sites] as soon as they cross the minimum age of twelve, they are newly connected to a vast and growing network of "others" from whom they can receive guidance, comfort, and camaraderie. While this is often a positive experience—teens need access to a widening circle of voices in order to make sense of themselves and their world—it can also be potentially harmful. Young people can come to so fully depend on the advice and opinions of others—including parents—that they become stunted in their ability to navigate life on their own.[22]

It is also important to remember that there are indeed positive aspects to this shifting digital context that bolster creativity, access, and connectivity among the digital natives who engage new technologies. But given the modern digital parallels to what Merton identified as the false self, it is worth focusing on some of the challenges that this digital world presents to young adult identity formation.

Five Challenges to Young Adult Identity Formation

Drawing on what we have already examined in the work of Palfrey, Gasser, Buckingham, and Parks while developing their insight further, we can identify several challenges to Millennial and Generation Z identity formation in a digital age.

1. *Affective Instability.* Palfrey and Gasser suggest that the public identity—or *identities*—of digital natives are highly fluid, reflecting the shifting adaptations, experimentations, and expressions by young adults in digital spaces. With real-time updates to public profiles, news feeds, live-streaming accounts, and other forms of digital affectivity, young adults are constantly adjusting and readjusting the way their identities are presented to others. The theologian Ilia Delio has described this fluidity as a sort of mask that covers up the fear of authentic human interaction, of getting to know another person, thereby encouraging a world of superficial interactions and anonymity. She writes: "The prevalence of anonymity marks our culture today; hence the desire for some people to be identified either by dress, tattoos, or sculptured hair. We are wired

---

[22] Rice, *The Church of Facebook*, 143–44.

together on the internet, on our Droids, iPhones, and video screens, but face to face we are like marble statues."[23] Fred Herron picks up on this same phenomenon and writes that it is like young people today are paralyzed by the confusion of their own being.[24]

2. *Lack of Interpretative Control.* It is true that all identities are subject to interpretation and evaluation by others. The way in which others perceive us is not something we can ever fully control. But scholars warn that the increasingly public nature of identity formation matched with the ease in accessibility made possible with smart-phone technology and other tools make manipulation and misrepresentation of one's identity in electronic formats a more acute risk for Generation Z and younger Millennials than for any other cohort.[25] Such identity abuse was witnessed over the last decade, for example, with tragic events involving gay teenagers who were "outed" by others who manipulated their public identities through social media. This sort of behavior is not always as extreme as those instances leading to the suicides of these young people, but daily public negotiations or anxiety around the need to maintain control of one's digital self draws energy away from other pursuits in life, which raises concerns about long and short-term impacts on young adult identity formation and socialization.

3. *The Prioritization of Instant Gratification.* Another concern that arises from the challenges present to young people in the digital age is the prioritization of instant gratification as the modus operandi of all things from information acquisition to communication. As Rebekah Willett has observed, today's young adults increasingly are viewed and view themselves as consumers who demand immediate response and return in both the public square of the marketplace and in the private realm of personal relationships.[26] Those things that require time, patience, and long-term commitment may become more challenging for Millennials because they have become accustomed to the immediacy

---

[23] Ilia Delio, *Compassion: Living in the Spirit of St. Francis* (Cincinnati: St. Anthony Messenger Press, 2011), xiii.

[24] Fred Herron, *No Abiding Place: Thomas Merton and the Search for God* (Latham, MD: University Press of America, 2005).

[25] For more, see Palfrey and Gasser, *Born Digital*, 31–37.

[26] Rebekah Willett, "Consumer Citizens Online: Structure, Agency, and Gender in Online Participation," in *Youth, Identity, and Digital Media*, ed. David Buckingham (Cambridge, MA: MIT Press, 2008), 49–70.

of return afforded by communications technology, social networking, online search engines, and the like.

4. *A Loss of Recognized Embodiment.* Although a human being can never lose the experience of embodiment (at least not yet), this reality that stands at the heart of theological anthropology becomes less recognized with those who spend more time in front of a computer monitor or smart-phone screen. Some scholars have observed that digital natives have a very different perception of self, especially their physicality, than their generational predecessors. Much more of their day-to-day experiences and social interactions take place "in the head" and by way of digital mediation than it does in the typified human experience of embodied relational engagement or physical and tactile activity. This technologically ubiquitous context has led to a loss in the realization or recognition of digital natives' embodiment, thereby affecting the ways in which they understand themselves as fully embodied, corporeal, interdependent human creatures.

5. *Diminished Emphasis on Vocation.* There is little scholarship currently available that explores the relationship between Millennial and Generation Z engagement with technology and their understanding of personal (or collective) vocation as an identity or calling created by God. The ease with which today's young people can create, manipulate, and recreate a digital identity appears to diminish any attempt of the Christian community to emphasize a person's unique and individual vocation created by God. Instead of striving to enter into a relationship with one's Creator in order to better understand oneself, Millennials and members of Generation Z might come to devote their energy instead toward becoming whomever they desire or wish to be instead of pursuing deeper knowledge of the person God has called them to be.

The challenges outlined here, in addition to the numerous areas of concern that continue to be uncovered, suggest there is an emergent meta theme that is found throughout the process of identity formation for young people today. At the risk of oversimplifying a complex issue, I believe that what is lost in a technologically hegemonic experience of personal and social development such as that experienced by digital natives today is the communal or relational sense of identity formation that may have been easier in previous generations.

Jesse Rice creatively describes this transformative and problematic shift that leads to distraction and confusion rather than elucidation and self-understanding for so many:

Our lives unfold, moment by moment, and the only way we can truly experience them is in the moment. Being always-on can thwart awareness of the present moment, keeping our attention ever focused on the new rather than the now. Endless Facebook-checking, email-checking, texting, updating, posting—it all serves in keeping us "disembodied," unable to get a tangible grip on ourselves in relation to those around us.[27]

There has been a long tradition, particularly within Christianity, of recognizing that who we are is discovered in large part through the living out of relationships—with others, ourselves, and God. This relational dimension of human existence is particularly emphasized in Thomas Merton's understanding and presentation of the true self. It is only in relationship with God—and not through our personal constructs of "self"—that we can first discover and subsequently embrace who we are in an existential way as beloved children of God.

Merton, Technology, and the True Self

In this section of the chapter I address the way in which Merton broadly critiques technology as it concerns the contemplative life and suggest that perhaps we might accept his concerns with some qualification. I believe that Merton's critiques of technology provide us with some resources for engaging the concerns about confronting the digital self as today's young adults seek a more substantive spiritual life and authentic self-understanding. I also offer a brief review of what Merton means by the true self.

Merton's Critique of Technology vis-à-vis Contemplation

The way about which Thomas Merton writes of technology, particularly later in his life, bears a style and orientation that would have made the Western Enlightenment philosopher Jean-Jacques Rousseau

---

[27] Rice, *The Church of Facebook*, 149.

proud.[28] In Merton's now-famous and posthumously published work *The Inner Experience: Notes on Contemplation*, we read of the twentieth-century monk's lamentation that modern life in general, and technologically advanced societies in particular, have lost something of an original disposition toward the contemplative life. While Merton's concern for what he sees as the decreasing time and space appropriated for prayer and contemplation in his contemporary culture is legitimate, we should note that he moves beyond reasonable critique to romanticize an age and people that no longer exist. Merton writes: "In the preindustrial ages and in primitive societies that still exist, man is naturally prepared and disposed for contemplation. In such a world we find men who, though perhaps not all literate, possess traditional artistic and technical skills and are in a broad sense 'artists' and 'spiritual men.'"[29]

Merton continues this praise of the "preindustrial man" for some time, striving as he does to illustrate an image he will later use in contrast to those citizens of the contemporary technological age:

> They are formed by their tradition and their culture. Even though such men may not be able to read and write, they are not necessarily "ignorant." On the contrary, they possess a certain very important and vital kind of knowledge, and *all of it* is integrated into their lives. They have a wholeness and a humanity, and therefore a poise, a simplicity, and a confidence, which have vanished from a world in which men are alienated, enslaved to processes and to machines. Preindustrial man is therefore all ready to become a contemplative. . . . There was no special difficulty for individuals to find their way into a monastery or to a hermitage and there devote themselves spontaneously to a life centered on the Presence and Infinite Reality of God.[30]

---

[28] Here, of course, I am alluding to Rousseau's famous treatise *Discourse on Inequality* (1754), in which the early modern philosopher posits the state of "natural man," from which we have inherited contemporary iterations the likes of the "noble savage," or, as in the case of Thomas Merton's *The Inner Experience*, the "preindustrial man." See Thomas Merton, *The Inner Experience: Notes on Contemplation*, ed. William H. Shannon (New York: HarperOne, 2003), 128 and throughout.

[29] Merton, *The Inner Experience*, 127.

[30] Ibid., 128.

How Merton could claim to know authentically any of what he claims here as fact, writing as he did from within the confines of a Trappist monastery in the mid-twentieth century, is never explained. But Merton has convinced himself that there was a problem in his own day with the way people "in the world" showed an ostensibly decreasing ability to engage in contemplation.[31]

There are several reasons Merton finds technology to be problematic. One is the universal obsession with improvement and the rapidity with which things must change in a technological society.[32] Another concern is the lack of ethical reflection when it comes to matters of technology. In a talk given at the Abbey of Gethsemani on June 5, 1966, Merton said: "Another thing technology doesn't ask is, 'Is this right?' The individual engaged in dealing with technology may ask this question too, but technology as such doesn't."[33] During the same presentation Merton raises a concern that is partnered with his ethical question, namely, the philosophical value of technology and its apparent disinterest in things of permanence, identity, and meaning. Merton contrasts technology's focus on questions like "what does this do?" with a philosophically significant question such as "what is this?" or "what does this mean for the salvation of my soul?" To which he adds, "You can save your soul in a technological environment, but there is no machine for saving your soul."[34]

There is much reason to be sympathetic to Merton's critique of technology and the way it impedes or distracts from an active spiritual life. We have seen this dynamic reflected in the academic literature as it concerns today's young adults and identity formation. However, it seems more than appropriate to approach Merton's critique of technology in modern society with the proverbial grain or two of salt. This qualification is necessary for two reasons. The first is that Merton's romantic notion of "preindustrial" or "natural" humanity, men and women who once existed as utopian contemplatives or might currently exist as endangered aboriginals in some remote community, bears the marks of an outdated and controversial Rousseauian concept of so-called primitive human nature.

---

[31] Ibid., 142.

[32] Thomas Merton, "The Christian in a Technological World," in Paul Dekar, *Thomas Merton: Twentieth-Century Wisdom for Twenty-First-Century Living* (Eugene, OR: Cascade Books, 2011), 210.

[33] Ibid., 212.

[34] Ibid., 211.

The second need for qualification centers on Merton's value judgment and assignment of moral culpability for those who find themselves in situations, whether of their choosing or otherwise, that create contexts hostile to contemplation. Merton's critique reads at times as not geared at technology per se, but at the technophiles that emerge in the digital age and uncritically embrace the latest, greatest technologies. "The tragedy of modern man is that his creativity, his spirituality, and his contemplative independence are inexorably throttled by a superego that has sold itself without question or compromise to the devil of technology."[35] As we see, there is little sensitivity or pastoral concern expressed in Merton's admonition of modern people enveloped in a continuum of technological existence. While some people certainly embrace nearly all technology without qualification, others are more discerning and even skeptical of such developments but might have no other choice, due to work or other external factors, than to engage with new technologies.

Yet in other instances Merton makes explicit attempts to acknowledge that he does not wish to extend a blanket judgment of condemnation on all technology. Such is the case in his letter to the moral theologian Bernard Haring on December 26, 1964, in response to the preparatory schema that would eventually become Vatican II's *Gaudium et Spes* (*The Pastoral Constitution on the Church in the Modern World*). Merton writes:

> I am not of course saying that technology is "bad," and that progress is something to be feared. But I am saying that behind the cloak of specious myths about technology and progress, there seems to be at work a vast uncontrolled power which is leading man where he does not want to go in spite of himself and in which the Church, it seems to me, ought to be somewhat aware of the intervention of the "principalities and powers" of which St. Paul speaks.[36]

While Merton vacillates about the inherent goodness or evil of technology, such that one is unable to pinpoint precisely his position due to his at times whimsical pronouncements of technology as "good" and "bad" at different points, we might choose to interpret this as merely

---

[35] Merton, *The Inner Experience*, 129.

[36] Thomas Merton, "Letter to Bernard Haring, December 26, 1964," in *The Hidden Ground of Love*, ed. William H. Shannon (New York: Farrar, Straus, Giroux, 1985), 383–84.

symptomatic of the great complexity technology plays in the lives of modern people. This is something even Merton understood at some level. It is important to remember that Merton's own life was filled with the comforts and advantages of a technological society, even if he did lament his unavoidable complicity as he did in the talk he gave on June 5, 1966: "Technology is revolutionizing the monastic life. And when I say that I'm not screaming, or yelling, or anything. I'm just stating a fact. It is revolutionizing the monastic life. And you have to take into account the fact that the monastic life is now deeply influenced by technology."[37]

Nevertheless, while it is important to state plainly that a reading of Merton's critique of technology as unmitigated by several significant factors is untenable, his critique presaged the second half of the twentieth and first decades of the twenty-first centuries. As we have already seen and also know through experience, there are indeed far-reaching concerns about the role technology plays in the lives of young adults today. Even in his day Merton saw the specter of something problematic emerging in the collective experience of young people. He writes:

> The crisis of identity which is everywhere normal in adolescence has become a grave problem in America extending far beyond adolescence and through young adulthood. Possibly there are many who never really resolve this problem in our society. One of the characteristics of "mass society" is precisely that it tends to keep man from fully achieving his identity, from operating fully as an autonomous person, from growing up and becoming spiritually and emotionally adult.[38]

His concern about the identity of young adults, those we could categorize as digital natives today, reverberates with those who remain concerned about the identity and spiritual lives of the Millennials and Generation Z. To consider the ways in which Merton offers contemporary spiritual seekers—whether young adults themselves or those tasked with their spiritual or social mentoring—a model by which to discover one's true self, we must first review what the Trappist monk meant by the term.

---

[37] Merton, "The Christian in a Technological World," 207.

[38] Thomas Merton, *Contemplation in a World of Action* (Notre Dame, IN: University of Notre Dame Press, 1998), 61.

The True Self: An Overview

"The secret of my identity is hidden in the love and mercy of God," Thomas Merton famously wrote in *New Seeds of Contemplation*.[39] Immediately following his equally well-known exposition on the existential presence of the false self (or, perhaps more accurately, the false *selves*) of each person, Merton locates the reality of our true identity in God. This is done within the context of his reflections on contemplation. That it is through prayer and not through our own fabrication that our identity is *discovered* (and I use that term deliberately to diminish any constructive notion of the true self that might be read into Merton's exposition) is an important detail to recall.[40]

In his introduction to Merton's notion of the true self, William Shannon explains that one of the most consistent aspects of Merton's varied

---

[39] Thomas Merton, *New Seeds of Contemplation* (New York: New Directions, 1961), 35.

[40] There have been some discussions about a passage in *New Seeds of Contemplation* in which Merton writes: "Our vocation is not simply to *be*, but to work together with God in the creation of our own life, our own identity, our own destiny. We are free beings and sons of God. This means to say that we should not passively exist, but actively participate in His creative freedom, in our own lives, and in the lives of others by choosing truth. To put it better, we are called to share with God the work of *creating* the truth of our identity" (32). Some have suggested, in what I assess to be a combination of eisegesis and isolated reading, that *New Seeds of Contemplation* offers evidence that Merton's notion of the true self is, at least in part, a human construct that we help shape. This is clearly not the case. Merton, even within the passage cited above, is introducing and addressing the variance in vocational responsibility that exists among creation. Unlike trees or birds, human beings have been granted free will and have, by virtue of their divine image and likeness, a responsibility or share in whether to discover and embrace their true identity. There is work involved in this, something to which Merton alludes in this chapter of *New Seeds of Contemplation*, noting the difficulty of the task at hand. The work is a matter first of (a) "choosing truth," which is the recognition that who we are is found in God alone; and then (b) living out our true self in contradistinction to the false self or selves of our own personal or social construction. In this respect we "co-create" with God through our exercise of free will and our conscious and active response to reject the false self. This and similar isolated passages, when read outside the context of Merton's continuous reflection on the true self elsewhere in *New Seeds of Contemplation* and in other texts, can be misrepresented. It is important, if tangential to the rest of this chapter, to highlight this interpretive error—an admittedly infrequent yet existent line of thinking—lest a misunderstanding of the distinction Merton draws between the false and true selves persist.

reflections on the subject has to do with his insistence that whatever the true self may be, it is not found on the surface or appear within the realm of the exterior. "There is a huge difference between what we appear to be and what we are, between our exterior self and our inner self."[41] Shannon offers this description of what he understands Merton to mean when describing the true self:

> The true self . . . is the self that sleeps silently in my depths, waiting to be awakened by the power of the Spirit. It is the openness in us to the call of God to become one with God (or rather to discover that we are and always have been one with God). It is what Daniel Walsh, Merton's onetime teacher and friend, called "man's capacity for divinity," and what the distinguished German Catholic theologian, Karl Rahner, called human "openness to the Transcendent." Merton describes it as "the white-hot point of mystical receptivity" which is present in all of us, but dormant in most of us.[42]

I am particularly fond of Shannon's way of describing the true self in these terms. He continues his elucidation with an unreferenced description of John Duns Scotus's notion of the formal distinction as it relates to the medieval Franciscan theologian's principle of individuation known as *haecceitas*, which happens to be one of the most important influences in Merton's development of the true self.[43] While the details of this medieval influence on Merton's thought are not germane to this overview of the true self, suffice it to say that the emphasis in Shannon's description and in Merton's writing centers on the reality that one's truest identity, one's

---

[41] William H. Shannon, *Thomas Merton: An Introduction* (Cincinnati: St. Anthony Messenger Press, 2005), 87.

[42] Ibid, 89–90. For an interesting study on the influence of Dan Walsh on Merton's understanding of the true self, see Robert Imperato, *Merton and Walsh on the Person* (Brookfield, WI: Liturgical Publications, 1987).

[43] Imperato notes that Walsh's doctoral dissertation was on John Duns Scotus ("The Metaphysics of Ideas according to Duns Scotus," unpublished dissertation, Medieval Institute, Toronto, 1933). For more on this, see Daniel Horan, "Sparks of *Haecceitas*: A Scotist Reading of Thomas Merton," *The Merton Journal* 17 (2010): 15–21; idem, "Thomas Merton the 'Dunce': Identity, Incarnation, and the Not So Subtle Influence of John Duns Scotus," *Cistercian Studies Quarterly* 47 (2012): 149–75; and idem, *The Franciscan Heart of Thomas Merton: A New Look at the Spiritual Inspiration of His Life, Thought, and Writing* (Notre Dame, IN: Ave Maria Press, 2014).

"true self," is intrinsic, inherent, and really identical with that person's very existence.

Because the true self is only known perfectly to God, Merton often discusses his understanding of this identity in contrast to the so-called false self. The false self—what we have come to identify in this chapter among Millennials and members of Generation Z as the digital self—is oftentimes likened to a mask or a shell. Take, for example, Merton's description of this contrast in his essay, "Rain and the Rhinoceros":

> Now if we take our vulnerable shell to be our true identity, if we think our mask is our true face, we will protect it with fabrications even at the cost of violating our own truth. This seems to be the collective endeavor of society: the more busily men dedicate themselves to it, the more certainly it becomes a collective illusion, until in the end we have the enormous, obsessive, uncontrollable dynamic of fabrications designed to protect mere fictitious identities—"selves," that is to say, regarded as objects. Selves that can stand back and see themselves having fun (an illusion which reassures them that they are real).[44]

There is something of a gravitational attraction emitted by the false self that draws a person deeper and deeper into what might be considered a narcissistic spiral of self-obsession and limited focus. In a technologically hegemonic age, and for digital Natives especially, the attraction to work and rework one's digital self becomes nearly hypnotic. Most Millennials and members of Generation Z can attest to the "black hole" of time that social networking sites like Facebook, Twitter, Instagram, and TikTok present to the already overscheduled days of today's youth. Yet, this is often the locus of the contemporary person's energy and self-understanding. How one presents oneself in the digital realm becomes the privileged location for the manifestation of the false self.

One's true self is only found in God, and one finds God in prayer. In his reflections on the meditative and contemplative practice of prayer that leads to finding one's true self, Merton recalls that the Christian mystical tradition teaches that one cannot find one's innermost self—and therefore find God—as long as one remains preoccupied by the activities

---

[44] Thomas Merton, "Rain and the Rhinoceros," in *Raids on the Unspeakable* (New York: New Directions, 1966), 15.

and desires of the outward and false self.[45] The true self only *appears* elusive because we are too concerned with our false self (selves) to turn toward God. We are held back from our own authentic self-discovery by our dependence on self-gratification; pleasure seeking; love of comfort; proneness to anger, pride, vanity, greed; and so on.[46] While Merton confirms the challenge of discovering one's true self, at times speaking metaphorically of it as a "shy, wild animal,"[47] it still remains an ever-present reality possible of being "discovered" and "awakened" through contemplation.[48] Merton sums this up well when he writes: "Therefore there is only one problem on which all my existence, my peace and my happiness depend: to discover myself in discovering God. If I find Him I will find myself and if I find my true self I will find Him."[49]

The Wisdom of Merton for Young Adults

To address the particular ways in which Merton's work and insight might serve as a heuristic or at least inspirational model for Millennials in a concrete manner, I now offer a brief reflection on each of the five themes presented above that highlight some key challenges to young adult identity formation in a digital age. While these five areas are not exhaustive, it is my hope that they help to situate the contemporary relevance and application of Merton's work for another generation and cultural context.

Affective Instability

We begin with a look at the fluidity of identity in the digital age. In some sense this is a problem that is the most clearly correlative with the work of Thomas Merton. At the heart of any iteration of the false self exists the problem of instability. Because the false self, whether we call it the digital self or something else, is a human construction; it is necessarily fleeting and finite. Such constructions of identity are merely masks or shells that

---

[45] Merton, *The Inner Experience*, 15.

[46] Ibid, 15.

[47] Ibid., 5.

[48] Mark O'Keefe, "Merton's 'True Self' and the Fundamental Option," *The Merton Annual* 10 (1997): 242.

[49] Merton, *New Seeds of Contemplation*, 36.

cover over our insecurities and present to the world an affect created in the image and likeness of our own desires, insecurities, or fears. This type of self-understanding is therefore predictably malleable and subject to the passing interest and immediate distractions of a given moment.

Merton's approach to discovering one's most authentic identity, one's true self, can aid digital natives in the search for the grounding and authenticity that they seek or will come to seek when the affective instability of the digital self comes to be understood for what it is: a manifestation of the false self. While those attuned to the spiritual life and the transcendent quality of existence may already be sensitive to the difference between the true and false selves, young adults are often much more confused about the distinction. Fred Herron has written about this in the lives of his high school and college students:

> Wrenched or released from the secure moorings of childhood, ado-
> lescents are cast adrift and must begin to search for their pearls of
> great price, for a treasure [that] merits all their hopes and dreams.
> Those who minister to adolescents may choose to use these op-
> portunities to challenge them to reflect more deeply upon the
> meaning of their existence and the goal of the journey. Those who
> accept this challenge will find themselves grappling, in a variety of
> ways, with the meaning of the false and true selves and with the
> challenge of on-going integration.[50]

The challenge posed by the lure of the digital self calls us to pause and reevaluate the ways in which we are engaging in identity formation. Toward what end do we direct our energies and efforts in lifelong self-understanding? For digital natives, mentorship and guidance is especially needed in this regard.

This instability can oftentimes take the form of identity fragmenta-tion. Merton writes in *The Inner Experience*:

> The first thing that you have to do, before you even start thinking
> about such a thing as contemplation, is to try to recover your basic
> natural unity, to reintegrate your compartmentalized being into a
> coordinated and simple whole and learn to live as a unified human

---

[50] Herron, *No Abiding Place*, 75.

person. This means that you have to bring back together the fragments of your distracted existence so that when you say "I," there is really someone present to support the pronoun you have uttered.[51]

The way to respond to the instability of the digital self and the lure of the false self is to refocus on the unification of our very human existence. While the exterior world appears disconnected, fragmented, disordered, and confused, the true self remains protected from the fleeting quality of individuals constructing their identities. Although such an understanding of identity might bear too many Neoplatonic undertones for the contemporary hearer, instead of associating one's true self with the static or immutable quality of personal identity, one should instead locate the consistency of the true self within God, as Merton does. For Merton, the stability of the true self is found not within its own Platonic idealism but within the love of God. Just as God remains already always in relationship with creation, so too one's true self remains already always present at the core of each person's unique existence.

Lack of Interpretative Control

The challenge faced by digital natives regarding the potential for identity manipulation and abuse vis-à-vis new social media and electronic communication is a serious and omnipresent threat. Not long ago I heard a sponsorship advertisement on NPR for an internet company whose sole purpose is to safeguard and defend its clients' online reputations. The need for serious professionals and digital native youth alike to be aware of the way in which their now public identities are presented and received introduces a new layer to the discussion of the false self in Merton's writing. For Merton, what makes the false self possible arises from our human limitedness, finitude, and sin. Everybody is, as Merton writes, "shadowed by an illusory person: a false self."[52] While we have, it would seem, always been plagued by the temptation to focus our energies and efforts on the construction and representation of our false selves, it is not entirely clear that the third-party manipulation of those identities was as present a threat as it is today.

---

[51] Merton, *The Inner Experience*, 4.
[52] Merton, *New Seeds of Contemplation*, 34.

In contrast to the false self, Merton writes the true self or "the inner self is precisely that self which cannot be tricked or manipulated by anyone."[53] Because the true self is identical with our very existence and not our own construction, and because the true self is found in God alone, it is, practically speaking, sheltered from redaction and distortion both by us and by others. Merton explains further:

> The inner self is not *part* of our being, like a motor in a car. It *is our entire substantial reality itself*, on its highest and most personal and most existential level. . . . The inner self is as secret as God and, like Him, it evades every concept that tries to seize hold of it with full possession. It is a life that cannot be held and studied as object, because it is not "a thing." It is not reached and coaxed forth from hiding by any process under the sun, including meditation.[54]

Unlike the pseudo-identities of our own construction, the true self is not fabricated and is not an object to be observed, examined, reshaped, or represented. One cannot, therefore, find the true self anywhere but in relationship with God. One important lesson that comes through Merton's writing on this quality of the true self is that we should focus our efforts not in the false establishment of ourselves "out there," as if we had to colonize society, culture, and technology to assert our own existence. Instead, we ought to work to free ourselves from the strictures of the false self's limitedness in order to be free of the burdens of distraction and self-centeredness and therefore enter more deeply into relationship with God and so come to know ourselves.

The Prioritization of Instant Gratification

Things happen today in rapid succession. Just as digital natives have come to expect everything from news delivered immediately by electronic media to food prepared in a matter of minutes at fast-food restaurants, there is a sense in which coming to know oneself and then relate that identity to others emerges with force for young people today. Speed is the name

---

[53] Merton, *The Inner Experience*, 5.
[54] Ibid., 6–7, emphasis added.

of the game, and immediacy is what is expected, if not demanded. Yet, as Merton explains time and again, contemplation and the journey to know God does not happen overnight (let alone in the time it takes to download an iPhone app!). This focus on instant gratification by young people today poses a real challenge to Millennials seeking authentic and substantive engagement within themselves, with God, and with others. Merton warns us of the temptation to acquiesce in matters of self-indulgence while journeying on the pilgrimage of life and prayer. He writes: "Freedom to enter the inner sanctuary of our being is denied to those who are held back by dependence on self-gratification and sense satisfaction, whether it be a matter of pleasure-seeking, love of comfort, or proneness to anger, self-assertion, pride, vanity, greed, and all the rest."[55] One of the most pressing issues Merton sees in what he calls the "technological revolution" is the effect of the speed with which everything evolves and moves ahead, oftentimes without proper reflection:

> I am not concerned with what [technology] does, but in the effects on people, on life, and on outlook. This profoundly challenges one's whole outlook on life. And for us, the huge problem is this: what do you mean by "a contemplative view of life" in this intensely active concern with moving ahead as fast as possible?[56]

There is an entire lifestyle shift that is demanded by those who wish to move away from the false self and seek God through contemplation. "In seeking to awaken the inner self we must try to learn how this relationship is entirely new and how it gives us a completely different view of things."[57] Precisely because this focus on the need for instant gratification is so deeply ingrained in the false self, Merton explains that real and substantial changes in the way one relates to others and sees the world must become a priority.

And this takes time. Contemplation, which is the relationship with God in prayer that Merton identifies for us as the path toward "awakening" or "discovering" one's true self, is not susceptible to the demands and urgency of an instant-gratification culture. Space and time are needed within which we can direct our attention to our relationship with God,

---

[55] Ibid., 15.

[56] Merton, "The Christian in a Technological World," 211.

[57] Merton, *The Inner Experience*, 19.

which is always already present. Merton's insight for Millennials and members of Generation Z may appear as an admonition, an exhortation for today's young people not to become swept up and distracted by the sheer quantity of information and activity always awaiting them. What is lasting, valuable, and true does not come delivered to us in a text message or appear in an overnight delivery box. The true self is simply not subject to the whims of digital natives' cultural expectations. To put it another, more colloquial way, when it comes to the discovery of the true self, it's all in God's time.

A Loss of Recognized Embodiment

As acknowledged earlier, one is never able to "lose" one's embodiment as such, but one can certainly lack real recognition of what it means to be an embodied person. In a way that resembles what I might call a "digital Manichaeism," young people can appear less concerned and aware of their own creatureliness or embodiment because of the dissociated effects of increased technological engagement. The more time young people spend playing video games, surfing the internet, texting, scrolling social-media feeds, and otherwise constructing their digital selves, the less connected they are likely to become to creation and the empirical reality of life.

Merton said in another Gethsemani lecture: "Now if technology is for man, there are perhaps problems arising from a certain dehumanization in life, as a result of a too Faustian concept of man. I'm not just talking about machines, but this completely technological view of life where the important thing is efficiency."[58] This seems to address the concern about self-gratification and the speed of technology. What often emerges from an increased focus on technology is what Merton describes as a concurrent depersonalization in life. What does this look like? Merton offers a response:

> What is depersonalization? . . . The way I conceive it, it's the idea of a person being cut off from his internal resources, his creative self, spontaneity, direct contact with life. In my language, a depersonalized is person when he has no direct contact with anything. . . . He has reactions that are dictated for him by everyone else.[59]

---

[58] Thomas Merton, "Marxism and Technology," in Dekar, *Thomas Merton*, 217.
[59] Ibid., 218.

As Paul Dekar summarizes well, "Merton doubted that technology could deliver what people expected, a new world of progress, prosperity, and peace. Rather, technology would usher in a kind of new jungle."[60] It is precisely within this jungle—not a physical jungle the likes of Vietnam but an intellectual, psychological, emotional, and spiritual jungle—that digital natives often lose an integrated sense of embodiment.

In an essay that first appeared in *Commonweal* magazine, titled "Poetry and Contemplation," Merton again highlights the conflict inside of which contemporary people find themselves as the lure of technology depersonalizes and encourages the conditions of a decreased sense of embodiment:

> In an age of science and technology, in which man finds himself bewildered and disoriented by the fabulous versatility of the machines he has created, we live precipitated outside ourselves at every moment, interiorly empty, spiritually lost, seeking at all costs to forget our own emptiness and ready to alienate ourselves completely in the name of any "cause" that comes along.[61]

Merton goes on to explain that at first glance, it seems absurd to talk about contemplation in such a world. Yet, this is precisely the remedy for the depersonalization and disembodiment that are symptomatic of an emphasis on the digital self and the move away from the prayerful journey to God in the discovery of one's *real* identity.

Who we are in our truest sense is not a disembodied mind or collection of ideas, thoughts, and questions. Nor is our body a simple machine for which we could substitute another machine or nothing at all. Instead, we are created out of divine love, with intentionality and a unique, incommunicable, and unrepeatable identity. As the German theologian Karl Rahner says, our bodies are the sacrament or symbol of who we are; they actualize and make present that which they represent.[62] To live in a way that diminishes this reality or seeks another experience of identity is to

---

[60] Dekar, *Thomas Merton*, 104.

[61] Thomas Merton, "Poetry and Contemplation: A Reappraisal," in *The Literary Essays of Thomas Merton*, ed. Patrick Hart (New York: New Directions, 1981), 339.

[62] Karl Rahner, "Theology of Symbol," in *Theological Investigations*, vol. 4, trans. Kevin Smyth (Baltimore: Helicon Press, 1966), 221–52.

be complicit in our own alienation from others, from God, and from ourselves. Authentic contemplation, the quest to awaken or discover the true self by deepening our relationship with God, does not separate us further from empirical selves but helps us to recognize the inherent glory and holiness granted to all of creation—including our creaturely bodies—through God's loving will that we should exist.

Diminished Emphasis on Vocation

Stemming from the popular notion that we are the fabricators of our own identity is the notion that what we become—individually, collectively, and professionally—is simply the product of our own choosing or the result of cosmic chance. The Christian tradition has maintained for centuries that human beings each receive a vocation from God (from the Latin verb *vocare*, "to call") that reflects who a person is at his or her deepest level. A vocation, popularly understood as something reserved for those such as Thomas Merton who are members of religious communities, actually is intended in a much broader sense. Merton explains what a vocation means:

> Each one of us has some kind of vocation. We are all called by God to share in His life and in His Kingdom. Each one of us is called to a special place in the Kingdom. If we find that place we will be happy. If we do not find it, we can never be completely happy. For each one of us, there is only one thing necessary: to fulfill our own destiny, according to God's will, to be what God wants us to be.[63]

In other words, what Merton is saying to us is that we are not created simply to fabricate a future shaped by our fantasies or to go forward in life unaided by the Creator. He intends quite the opposite. Through prayer and discernment one comes to recognize that God has given each person certain gifts, including skills, talents, dispositions, interpersonal abilities, intellect, personality, emotional and other forms of intelligence, and the like. Merton asserts that we are most happy when we deploy

---

[63] Thomas Merton, *No Man Is an Island* (New York: Harcourt Brace, 1955), 138.

those God-given gifts within the state of life we find ourselves and come to live our true self in community.

This is certainly a challenge for digital natives, who have been reared in a context in which identity is so unstable. Today's young adults look around and see a context that encourages ways of going about the world that are far from the image of self-understanding and spirituality present in Merton's explanation of what it means for everyone to have a vocation given by God.

The Quest for the True Self for Digital Natives

In some sense each of these five challenges represents a particular aspect or symptom of the complex environment that digital natives face today. On the one hand, the inertia of contemporary culture and the hyperactivity of a technocratic context lend themselves to creating a complex situation from which one finds it increasingly difficult to escape, which is very different from previous generations. Yet, on the other hand, we are only naming the reality of living in the twenty-first century, calling to mind the truths about who we are and who God is that are in need of renewed attention so that we might come to know our true selves.

Indeed, it is not easy to live in today's complex world. God only knows how dramatically the cultural, social, and technological environments of our contemporary existence have changed from the time I typed these words not that long ago until the time you encountered them in this moment. God only knows how things will change in decades and centuries to come.

What Thomas Merton offers young people today—those we acknowledge as digital natives in a technological world—is a reminder about the existence of and a path toward understanding their true self. While technological advances are not inherently bad, they do not alone provide a way to discover one's true self, because technology alone is not the way to discover God. As Merton reminds us, who we are is in God, and it is through contemplation that we must journey on such a pilgrimage of spiritual self-discovery and self-understanding.

7

Inspiration and Guidance
from Thomas Merton for Priests

For reasons that have always remained a mystery to me, some Catholic
Christians have viewed Thomas Merton with suspicion. Any remaining
cloud of doubt was unequivocally lifted on September 24, 2015, when
Pope Francis addressed a historic joint session of the United States Congress during his first apostolic visit to North America. In that now-famous
address the holy father named four "great Americans" whom he held
up as models of Christian living for contemporary disciples: Abraham
Lincoln, Martin Luther King, Jr., Dorothy Day, and *Thomas Merton*.

Pope Francis introduced Merton as someone who "remains a source
of spiritual inspiration and a guide for many people." He added that
"Merton was above all a man of prayer, a thinker who challenged the
certitudes of his time and opened new horizons for souls and for the
church. He was also a man of dialogue, a promoter of peace between
peoples and religions." It is very likely that this latter point was one of
the greatest sore subjects for the Merton naysayers in recent decades;
that is, some took issue with the fact that Merton was unafraid to risk
relationship across ecumenical and interreligious boundaries, thereby
both anticipating the pastoral call of the Second Vatican Council and
then, later, living out that very same call.

Although Pope Francis highlights the life and legacy of Merton as a
source of inspiration and guidance for the whole church, I explore in this
chapter some of the ways that Merton offers ministerial priests insight,
wisdom, and guidance in today's world. I believe that the four categories

---

[A version of this essay was originally published in *The Priest Magazine* (2018):
14–19. Used with permission.]

Pope Francis names as key characteristics of Merton's legacy serve us well as a helpful framework and are worthy of greater examination. These themes are prayer, challenging certitudes, dialogue, and peacemaking.

Prayer

Thomas Merton is best known for his early writings on prayer and contemplation. After his surprise best-selling spiritual autobiography, *The Seven Storey Mountain* (1948), his next best-known book is *New Seeds of Contemplation* (1949; 1961). This book, along with others like *Thoughts in Solitude* (1958) and *No Man Is an Island* (1955), offers reflections on the Christian life of interiority and faith. While today we recognize that all women and men have what *Lumen Gentium* describes as a "universal call to holiness," few Catholics in the American church of the 1940s, 1950s, and early 1960s would have assumed that a personal prayer life was something that pertained to anyone who wasn't a priest or religious sister or brother. Merton upended that presumption, suggesting that the world in which all people find themselves was in fact a world in which God seeks connection and relationship with all people.

Rather than imagine that prayer is something that operates according to our terms, Merton invited all people to consider God as the one who *seeks us first* and that we can cultivate practices of attunement to that loving presence of God already always near us. "We must learn," Merton writes in *New Seeds of Contemplation*, "to realize that the love of God seeks us in every situation, and seeks our good. His inscrutable love seeks our awakening."

Even as professional ministers we can at times slip into old habits of viewing prayer as something we control. We are the ones who open up the Breviary, we are the ones who preside at the Eucharist, and we are the ones who run the show. Among other insights about prayer, Merton reminds us that God is in control and that it is in fact God who runs the show. Theologically, this is something we learned in seminary and might know intellectually. It is not we who consecrate the Eucharist, but Christ in the Spirit. It is not we who forgive sins, but God who forgives sin. It is not we who heal the broken and brokenhearted, but the Holy Spirit who heals through our ministry. So, too, is this the case with prayer.

Rather than convince ourselves that we must seek God out in particular circumstances and in special locations, can we come to recognize the relationship that God has inaugurated with us? That relationship is the very grounding and source of our ministry and life. And our working on that relationship, that response to God of communication and presence, is an action on our part that acknowledges the God who is always closer to us than we are to ourselves, as St. Augustine noted.

Merton's most famous contribution to the Christian spiritual tradition was the notion of the "true self." The true self is our real identity: who it is we are before God and who it is that God intends us to be. It stands in contrast with the many false selves we attempt to construct, the result of seeking acceptance and validation externally, which so often arises from our insecurity or unwillingness to believe that we are already loved as we are by our Creator. Merton writes in *New Seeds of Contemplation* that we can only discover our true self in discovering God. It is within the context of our relationship with the Creator—within the context of prayer—that we come to know who we really are, which is necessary for being effective ministers. As priests, we know well that we cannot give to others what we do not have ourselves, and this especially includes spiritual inspiration and guidance. Merton's writings offer us an opportunity for renewal on this front, allowing us to return to the basics of discovering ourselves in the act of discovering God in prayer.

Challenging Certitudes

One of the things that has made Pope Francis extraordinarily popular with most people, as well as unpopular with a small handful of others, is his willingness to forego the "we have always done it this way" attitude so commonplace in leadership structures of the church. For Pope Francis, the priority must always be the gospel. This was also the case with Merton, who, in the face of pressing social issues and concerns of his day, preferred to draw inspiration and grounding from the gospel and Christian tradition rather than simply retreat from a difficult situation.

In addition to challenging the presumed elitism of a personal spiritual life previously viewed as the exclusive domain of priests and vowed religious, Merton also challenged some of the certitudes about where the boundaries of the so-called "sacred" and "profane" rested in the modern world. In a way that anticipated Vatican II's *Gaudium et Spes*, Merton had an inherent appreciation for the fact that the body of Christ, which is the church, did not exist in isolation apart from the realities of others—Christian and non-Christian alike. Merton felt drawn to correspond and enter into relationship with many kinds of people, believers and unbelievers, intellectuals and ordinary people from around the world. Rather than stay locked in a kind of hermetically sealed religious cloister, Merton was open to engaging with the broader world from within the monastery. He recognized his deep ties to all people years before *Gaudium et Spes* would be promulgated and open with the line: "The joys and hopes, the griefs and anxieties of the men and women of this age, especially those who are poor or in any way afflicted, these are the joys and hopes, the griefs and anxieties of the followers of Christ." Whereas a major certitude of religious life in his time was that he should *fuga mundi* ("flee the world"), Merton instead saw a ministerial opportunity to *turn to the world* and help preach the gospel in whatever way he could. On November 10, 1958, Merton wrote to Pope John XXIII and described this way of ministry, writing that "with the approval of my Superiors, I have exercised an apostolate—small and limited though it be—within a circle of intellectuals from other parts of the world; and it has been quite simply an apostolate of friendship."

A potential "certitude of our time" remains a sense of ministerial identity that keeps us apart from others. The notion of a cultic model of priesthood places a significant value on a kind of priestly isolationism; you don't have to be a monk to live a kind of *fuga mundi* existence. Merton's "apostolate of friendship" allowed him to remain true to his vows of obedience and stability, while also being open to the experiences, insights, challenges, and wisdom of others. He also learned of the "joys and hopes, griefs and anxieties" of people he would otherwise never have met or have the opportunity to know.

One of the ways Merton provides us with guidance and a challenge today is by encouraging us to step outside our comfort zones to engage with the concerns of those around us locally and those throughout the world. Whereas Merton had to rely on the letter-writing technology of his time, our age presents us with almost instantaneous access to news and information from around the globe. Pope Benedict XVI regularly spoke about the need Christian ministers have to evangelize what he called the "digital continent" of the internet and social media where so many people "live" most of their lives today. Merton's insight allows us to reconsider the presuppositions we have about what is or is not off limits in terms of engaging the cultures and realities of the world around us with the gospel of Jesus Christ. We would do well to develop our own "apostolate of friendship."

Dialogue

A key element of Merton's "apostolate of friendship" was his openness to learning about and dialoguing with people of other religious traditions and worldviews. He recognized that he did not have some apodictic answer to every question life presented him with and that those outside the usually circles of mid-twentieth-century Catholicism in America might have some insight to share. He wrote in *Conjectures of a Guilty Bystander* (1966): "If I can understand something of myself and something of others, I can begin to share with them the work of building the foundations for spiritual unity. But first we must work together at dissipating the more absurd fictions which make unity impossible."

Merton was no supporter of syncretism or relativism. He believed that one could only pursue honest and real interreligious or ecumenical dialogue by first being deeply grounded in one's own tradition. On Easter 1965 Merton wrote to a student named Marco Pallis and explained this point:

> One cannot supplement his own tradition with little borrowings here and there from other traditions. On the other hand, if one is genuinely living his own tradition, he is capable of seeing where other traditions say and attain the same thing, and where they are different. The differences must be respected, not brushed aside, even and especially where they are irreconcilable with one's own view.

Merton challenges us today to be more open to dialogue with those of differing religious traditions, political perspectives, cultural commitments, and the like. Whereas some shy away from such openness, Merton's invitation is for contemporary priests to be truly men of relationship and mercy who must first be deeply grounded in their own

Catholic Christianity so as to take part in fruitful discussions with others. As Vatican II reminds us in *Nostra Aetate*, there is nothing true or good in other religions and traditions that the Catholic Church rejects. The question is whether or not we are committed enough to our faith to be open to learning from the wisdom and experiences of others.

Promoters of Peace

Merton's commitment to peacemaking is well known among scholars of his writings but not widely known by the general public. This is in part because Merton's superiors censored much of his writings on topics like racism and war, peace and violence, during his lifetime, fearing they be scandal for those people who did not feel it appropriate for a Catholic monk to write on such pressing and, at times, controversial subjects. Fortunately, he did receive permission to circulate his writings among a small group of Catholic leaders and intellectuals. And since his death, Merton's writings have become widely accessible.

For Merton, the vocation of peacemaking was not something reserved for a few but a requirement of all the baptized who bear the name Christian. In his posthumously published book *Passion for Peace: The Social Essays of Thomas Merton* (1997), Merton writes:

> Christians must become active in every possible way, mobilizing all their resources for the fight against war. First of all there is much to be studied, much to be learned. Peace is to be preached, nonviolence is to be explained as a practical method, and not left to be mocked as an outlet for crackpots who want to make a show of themselves.

While Merton envisions Christian peacemaking a gospel mandate for all disciples, the last point he makes here is aimed at us: ministerial priests. He challenges us to do our research, know the circumstances of our time, familiarize ourselves with the tradition of Catholic social teaching, preach peace and nonviolence to our congregations, and model peacemaking by our words and deeds. Indeed, this is no easy task. But it is our task, as Pope Francis continually reminds us. In the same book Merton later writes that this pastoral ministry of peacemaking "is the great Christian task of our time." Fortunately for us, Merton has left us volumes of insight to aid us in preparing for this task, such as in his books *Faith and Violence* (1968), *Seeds of Destruction* (1964), *Peace in the Post-Christian Era* (2004), and *The Cold War Letters* (2006), among others.

At a time when global tensions are on the rise, the threat of terrorism always looms large, the rhetoric of politicians and public figures offends and divides, and physical violence is an all-too-familiar reality for many people, Merton points us in the direction of our fundamental vocation as priests and ministers: always to be men of prayer, dialogue, and peacemaking who are not afraid to challenge the certitudes of our time.

III

Insights about Key Christian Virtues

8

Kyrie Eleison

_____

Mercy at the Heart of Thomas Merton's Theology of Revelation

At the core of foundational theology is the notion of revelation, which is reflection on the means by which God reveals God's self to humanity and the rest of creation. Though he was not an academic theologian by training, Thomas Merton's writing and teaching nevertheless reflect the work of a thinker whose deep familiarity with the Christian tradition, life of contemplative prayer, and ever-growing engagement with the signs of his time converged to inform his own foundational theology.[1] While scholars have explored numerous dimensions of Merton's work across various theological loci, little work has been published so far about Merton's theology of revelation as such.

_____

[A version of this essay was originally published in *The Merton Annual* 30 (2017): 78–87. Used with permission.]

[1] On the subject of Merton as theologian see, for example, Michael A. Yonkers, "Man, the Image of God: The Theological Anthropology of Thomas Merton," MA thesis, Loyola University of Chicago, 1976, esp. 1–10; Lawrence S. Cunningham, *Thomas Merton and the Monastic Vision* (Grand Rapids, MI: Eerdmans, 1999), esp. 187–89; William H. Shannon, "Theology," in *The Thomas Merton Encyclopedia*, ed. William H. Shannon, Christine M. Bochen, and Patrick F. O'Connell (Maryknoll, NY: Orbis Books, 2002), 470–71; Christopher Pramuk, *Sophia: The Hidden Christ of Thomas Merton* (Collegeville, MN: The Liturgical Press, 2009); and Daniel P. Horan, *The Franciscan Heart of Thomas Merton: A New Look at the Spiritual Inspiration of His Life, Thought, and Writing* (Notre Dame, IN: Ave Maria Press, 2014); see also Daniel Rober, "Was He a Theologian?" *Commonweal Magazine* (September 26, 2011), book review of Pramuk's *Sophia*.

My primary aim here is simple. This chapter is a preliminary exploration of how the theme of mercy is found at the heart of and throughout
Merton's theology of revelation as it appears in several of his texts. It is
striking how Merton's frequent discussions about mercy are intertwined
with consideration of God's revelation, a characteristic of his theology
that presciently anticipates the work of modern theologians and religious
leaders such as Cardinal Walter Kasper and Pope Francis.

I have organized this chapter into three parts. First, in order to appreciate Merton's distinctive reflections on mercy within the context of
revelation, we look at what is meant by a theology of revelation, especially
since the reforms of the Second Vatican Council in the Roman Catholic Church. Second, we survey Merton's writings on mercy, noting he
frequently describes mercy in revelatory terms that both anticipate and
then reflect the ressourcement theology of Vatican II. Finally, I propose
that Merton's writings on mercy offer us an underappreciated resource
for theological reflection on the nature of divine revelation.

Theology of Revelation

As the late Jesuit theologian Avery Cardinal Dulles rightly noted, for
the first eighteen hundred years of Christianity the doctrine of revelation was not treated with the systematic precision of questions related
to Christology or Pneumatology. Instead, early and medieval theologians approached revelation indirectly, oftentimes in apologetic or
polemical modes: Christians sought to situate what appeared to others
as their "novel" beliefs within the context of divine disclosure.[2] Thinking etymologically, this nascent understanding of revelation was aptly
descriptive, given that the term's Latin root, *revelatio,* means simply "the
removal of a veil" (Latin: *velum*), and therefore fundamentally pertains
to "dis-closure."[3] It was only in the seventeenth century, during the rise
of the European Enlightenment and increasing incredulity of all things
transcendent, that rationalists "began to deny or minimize revelation,"

---

[2] See Avery Dulles, *Revelation Theology: A History* (New York: Herder and Herder,
1969), 31.
[3] Avery Dulles, "Faith and Revelation," in *Systematic Theology: Roman Catholic
Perspectives,* ed. Francis Schüssler Fiorenza and John P. Galvin, 2nd ed. (Minneapolis:
Fortress Press, 2011), 80.

thereby inviting—or better, *necessitating*—a theological response.[4] This response is most succinctly seen in chapter 2 of Vatican I's *The Dogmatic Constitution on the Catholic Faith* (*Dei Filius*) (1870). Here we see the council fathers building upon the work of the Council of Trent and making concrete a particularly narrow description of what constitutes divine revelation:

> Now this supernatural revelation, according to the belief of the universal church, as declared by the sacred council of Trent, is contained in written books and unwritten traditions, which were received by the apostles from the lips of Christ himself, or came to the apostles by the dictation of the holy spirit, and were passed on as it were from hand to hand until they reached us.[5]

What is laid out here is what many theologians have described as a "propositional view" of divine revelation, which means that when we speak about revelation we are primarily discussing something akin to a collection of discrete truths. As theologian Richard Gaillardetz explains, at this moment in church history "revelation was seen according to the analogy of verbal communication in which God literally 'spoke' to the biblical prophets and apostles. . . . In like manner church teaching was often viewed according to the model of human speech."[6]

Since the European Enlightenment revelation has been viewed in terms of divine decrees, concrete statements, or a canon of divinely authored texts. This reactive position, shaped as it was by the defensive posture of the church in the wake of the reformations and the emergence of modernity, held fast until the Second Vatican Council (1962–65). Key conciliar *periti* (theological experts) such as Yves Congar, Joseph Ratzinger, Henri de Lubac, and Karl Rahner had already been working since the early 1950s on reexamining the nature and meaning of divine revelation as it appeared, admittedly indirectly, in the biblical witness and the writings of early Christian theologians. The fruit of their rigorous

---

[4] Ibid. Also see Charles Taylor, *A Secular Age* (Cambridge: Harvard University Press, 2007).

[5] Vatican I, "*Dei Filius*," in *Decrees of the Ecumenical Councils*, ed. Norman P. Tanner (Georgetown: Georgetown University Press, 1990), 2:806.

[6] Richard R. Gaillardetz, *By What Authority? A Primer on Scripture, the Magisterium, and the Sense of the Faithful* (Collegeville, MN: Liturgical Press, 2003), 3.

scholarship was Vatican II's *Dogmatic Constitution on Divine Revelation* (*Dei Verbum*). This short though important text presents a renewed understanding of revelation that is not limited to written or verbal communication alone but instead explains that the meaning of divine revelation is primarily about relationship. The opening paragraphs of *Dei Verbum* show that *revelation* is a term used to express that "fellowship" God desires to extend to all human persons, which was most fully expressed through the incarnation, life, death, and resurrection of Christ.[7]

> In His goodness and wisdom God chose to reveal Himself and to make known to us the hidden purpose of His will by which through Christ, the Word made flesh, man might in the Holy Spirit have access to the Father and come to share in the divine nature. Through this revelation, therefore, the invisible God out of the abundance of His love speaks to men as friends and lives among them, so that He may invite and take them into fellowship with Himself.[8]

Christ is the center of Christian revelation because it is by means of the incarnate Word that God most fully reveals—*unveils* or discloses— God's self and invites us into relationship. Put another way, Jesuit theologian Roger Haight has suggested that we understand divine revelation as "personal encounter." This encounter consists of three dimensions: First, it is an experience of "intersubjective communication," meaning that neither we nor God relate to each other as objects but only as full subjects; second, it is an experience of transcendence for God is nevertheless wholly (Holy) other; and third, this relationship we call revelation is pure gift that reflects God's gratuity.[9] This last point in particular anticipates our exploration of Merton's own association of revelation with divine mercy.

The shift from what Bernard Lonergan called the "classicist mindset" to "historical consciousness" as exemplified in the Second Vatican Council's teaching on divine revelation set the stage for greater exploration of what exactly revelation *looks like* in light of this theological

---

[7] Vatican II, *Dei Verbum*, in Tanner, *Decrees of the Ecumenical Councils*, 2:971–81.

[8] Vatican II, *Dei Verbum*, no. 2.

[9] Roger Haight, *Dynamics of Theology* (Maryknoll, NY: Orbis Books, 2001), 73–74.

ressourcement.[10] As Lonergan elsewhere writes, "For revelation is God's entry and His taking part in man's making of man."[11] And so theology not only has to reflect on revelation, but also it has somehow to mediate God's meaning into the whole of human affairs. And this is precisely what Thomas Merton sought to do.

Mercy at the Heart of Revelation

Merton lived during this liminal period and was writing as the renewal of the Catholic theology of revelation was taking place. His outlook on revelation was not solely propositional but primarily relational. As we see him explain in *New Seeds of Contemplation*:

> Too often our notion of faith is falsified by our emphasis on the statements about God…It is of course quite true that theology can and must study the intellectual content of revelation and especially the verbal formulation of divinely revealed truth. But once again, this is not the final object of faith. Faith goes beyond words and formulas and brings us the light of God Himself.[12]

He added a caution, warning those tempted to fall back on exclusively propositional understanding of revelation that we cannot be satisfied simply with doctrinal statements in understanding what we mean by revelation. "Therefore we must make every effort to believe the right formulas," Merton writes, "but we must not be so obsessed with verbal correctness that we never go beyond the words to the ineffable reality which they attempt to convey."[13]

We see Merton grapple with this "ineffable reality" of divine revelation most clearly in his writings in those instances in which he is reflecting on

---

[10] See Bernard Lonergan, "The Transition from a Classicist World-View to Historical-Mindedness," in *A Second Collection: Papers by Bernard J. F. Lonergan, SJ*, ed. William F. J. Ryan and Bernard J. Tyrell (Toronto: University of Toronto Press, 1974), 1–9.

[11] Lonergan, "Theology in Its New Context," in *A Second Collection,* 62.

[12] Thomas Merton, *New Seeds of Contemplation* (New York: New Directions Publishing, 1961), 128–29.

[13] Ibid., 129.

divine mercy. This shouldn't be surprising for, as Merton scholar Christine Bochen noted in her 2001 ITMS presidential address, "Mercy was a thread woven into the very fabric of Merton's life and theological vision." In fact, she added, in some way "mercy informs all his writings."[14] Here we will look at just a few illustrative examples of how Merton's writings on mercy present us with a theology of revelation that is distinctively relational and constructive.

In his book *No Man Is an Island*, Merton opens his chapter explicitly titled "Mercy" with the exclamation: "How close God is to us."[15] His reflections on mercy begin with the claim that God is not known in "abstract consideration," which he likens to a "presence in which we dress Him in our own finery," but instead God is known within the context of the mercy God has shown us in Christ.[16] Through the incarnation, God has revealed a preferential pattern of relational disclosure that we might understand as solidarity, that is, the compassionate relating to those in our midst who suffer. Merton explains, "If we want to know God, we must learn to understand the weaknesses and sins and imperfections of other men as if they were our own. We must feel their poverty as Christ experienced our own."[17] The way God reveals God's self to us is by means of showing us mercy and showing us how then to love one another in precisely this manner. Merton describes the event of the incarnation in an almost pedagogical way, noting that part of Christ's ministry was to show us how to live, in addition to showing us who God is. He writes:

> Jesus descended into the abyss of our degradation in order to forgive us after He had, in a sense, become lower than us all. It is not for us to forgive others from lofty thrones, as if we were gods looking down on them from Heaven. We must forgive them in the flames of their own hell, for Christ, by means of forgiveness, once again descends to extinguish the avenging flame. . . . God Who is infinitely rich became man in order to experience the poverty and misery of fallen man, not because He needed this experience but

---

[14] Christine Bochen, "'Mercy within Mercy within Mercy': Presidential Address—ITMS Seventh General Meeting," June 7, 2001, Bellarmine University, 3.

[15] Thomas Merton, *No Man Is an Island* (New York: Harcourt Brace, 1955), 206.

[16] Ibid., 206.

[17] Ibid., 212.

because we needed His example. Now that we have seen His love, let us love one another as he has loved us. Thus His love will work in our hearts and transform us into Himself.[18]

As Merton elaborates in his essay "The Good Samaritan," the life and teaching of Christ are more than abstract ideas or "philosophical answers" to the questions of our existential reality.[19] Instead, God provides a *relational* answer in the form of God's very self-made-flesh. Merton explains that, in Jesus's response to the lawyer asking about who constitutes his neighbor in the Gospel, God's "answer is a divine revelation, not a natural ethical principle. It is a revelation of the mystery of God. Hence in revealing truth, it remains mysterious and in some sense hidden. Yet if we get as close as we can to the source of revelation, we can gain deeper insight into the mystery."[20]

For Merton, what Jesus Christ reveals in the Gospel—by both his life and his deeds—is an embodiment of the ancient Hebrew notion of *hesed* proclaimed by the Old Testament Prophets who announced the character of God to the people called to covenantal relationship. While the magnitude of the meaning of *hesed* is often lost in English translation, Merton attempts to articulate a more capacious rendering in noting that *hesed* "is something more than mercy. But it contains in itself many varied aspects of God's love which flash forth in mercy and are its fountain and its hidden source. . . . The [*hesed*] of God is truth. It is infallible strength. It is the love by which He seeks and chooses His chosen, and binds them to Himself."[21] Merton ties this understanding of *hesed*, of God's incomprehensible mercy, to the theophany in which God reveals God's self to Moses on Sinai. When God shows God's self to humanity, what is seen is *hesed*.

In an essay titled "The Climate of Mercy," first published in the Franciscan journal *The Cord* in 1965 and later posthumously collected in the book *Love and Living*, Merton makes his most direct connection between divine mercy and revelation.

---

[18] Ibid., 214–16.

[19] Thomas Merton, "The Good Samaritan," in *Seasons of Celebration* (New York: Farrar, Strauss, Giroux, 1965), 175.

[20] Ibid.

[21] Ibid., 177–78.

Mercy is, then, not only forgiveness, but life. It is more than that. It is the epiphany of hidden truth and of God's redeeming Love for man. It is the *revelation of God Himself*, not as an infinite nature, as a "Supreme Being," and as ultimate, absolute power, but as Love, as Creator and Father, as Son and Savior, as Life-giving Spirit. Mercy is, then, not simply something we deduce from a previously apprehended concept of divine Essence ("If he is the Supreme Being, then it follows that he is supremely loving, etc. . . ."), but *an event in which God reveals himself to us* in His redemptive love and in the great gift which is the outcome of this event: our mercy to others.[22]

Clearly stating that "the revelation of God" and the "event in which God reveals himself to us" are not mere deductions or abstractions but a relational experience of God's very nature, Merton locates his own theological view in line with what Vatican II makes official in *Dei Verbum*, namely, that God's disclosure to humanity is fundamentally relational and that at the heart of that relationship stands divine mercy. Who God is, what God does, and how God thinks are all governed by the divine principle of *hesed* announced by the prophets and embodied in Christ.

For Merton, the realization of the nature of divine revelation shaped not only his theological outlook but also his own spiritual practice and self-understanding. Christine Bochen's reflections on this theme pick up here, noting that what I call Merton's "theology of revelation" can also be understood as "epiphanies of mercy" in the sense that "an epiphany is a manifestation of the divine in our midst."[23] Bochen keenly notes that "Merton experienced epiphanies of mercy throughout his life and that, in the course of these experiences he learned, firsthand, the reality and meaning of mercy."[24] Given that Merton's insightful writings on discovery of the true self insist at each turn that one discovers who one is in the discovery of God, we can assert that Merton discovered his own identity in ever-more-profound ways as he recognized the experience of God's mercy in his own life.

---

[22] Thomas Merton, "The Climate of Mercy," in *Love and Living*, ed. Naomi Burton Stone and Patrick Hart (New York: Harcourt Brace, 1979), 203, emphasis added.

[23] Bochen, "Mercy within Mercy within Mercy," 4.

[24] Ibid.

Merton as a Resource for Thinking about Revelation and Mercy

As in so many other areas of Merton's prodigious reflections and writings, his work on mercy and its essential relationship to divine revelation anticipated much of the best dogmatic theology to come. Several of his writings on mercy at the heart of revelation predate the Second Vatican Council's promulgation of *Dei Verbum* as well as its placement in the center of contemporary Christian reflection by Pope Francis. In closing this chapter I look briefly at how Merton's approach to mercy at the heart of revelation both anticipates and complements the masterful work of theologian Walter Cardinal Kasper, whose 2013 book *Mercy: The Essence of the Gospel and the Key to Christian Life* inspired Pope Francis's intentional focus on the theme throughout his ministry as bishop of Rome.[25] I cannot here do justice to the richness and profundity of Kasper's book, particularly in all of its dimensions. However, it is worth noting that following his exposition of scriptural passages about divine mercy (including those pertaining to the life and ministry of Jesus), Kasper asserts that mercy is not merely one divine attribute among others: "According to the testimony of all of scripture, the Old as well as the New Testament, God's mercy, however, is the attribute, in God's self-revelation in the history of salvation, that assumes first place."[26] In fact, so essential is this for Kasper that he reiterates: "Mercy expresses God's essence, which graciously attends to and devotes itself to the world and to humanity in ever new ways in history. It is God's *caritas operativa et effectiva.* Therefore, we must describe mercy as the fundamental attribute of God."[27]

Kasper expounds on the significance of mercy as the central illustrative attribute of God in a number of ways. Like Merton before him, Kasper insists that this truth of God's revelation is not merely a theoretical contribution to an esoteric discussion but instead a profound tenet of faith that has significant and practical implications. To highlight two such implications, it is worth considering how the revelation of God

---

[25] See Walter Cardinal Kasper, *Mercy: The Essence of the Gospel and the Key to Christian Life*, trans. William Madges (New York: Paulist Press, 2014). The earliest German text, *Barmherzigkeit,* was published in Germany in 2012 and expanded in 2013; it then served as the source for this English translation.

[26] Ibid., 88.

[27] Ibid., 89.

who is mercy influences (a) our understanding of salvation, and (b) our understanding of God's *pathos* as it concerns our experience of sin, suffering, and injustice.

On the first point, Kasper insists that, "God's mercy is the primordial presupposition and ground of creation and of all of salvation history."[28] This leads to reflection on the nature of salvation, particularly as it concerns the entirety of the human family. Whereas thinkers throughout the centuries have circumscribed salvation by means of a number of categories and, frequently enough, by means of insisting on cognitive assent to certain propositional claims, Kasper reads scripture and the tradition in such a way as to insist on the possibility of universal salvation. On the second point, Kasper reads the tradition in a way departing from so-called traditional Scholastic theology, which persistently denied the capability of God to suffer (that is, divine impassibility).[29] On returning to patristic and scriptural resources, Kasper contends that the tradition has been all too binary, pitting, as it were, divine omnipotence against divine mercy. In response, Kasper asserts:

> Therefore, God cannot be affected and overpowered, passively and involuntarily, by pain or harm. But in his mercy, God allows himself, in sovereign freedom, to be affected by pain and suffering. In his mercy, God is shown to be masterfully free. His mercy is not induced by human need or woe. God graciously chooses to be affected and moved by the pain and suffering of humankind. Thus, many theologians today in the Catholic, Orthodoxy, and Protestant traditions speak of the possibility of God suffering vicariously with us.[30]

These two points bring us back to Merton's understanding of God who reveals God's self as mercy. Merton likewise recognized the role of divine mercy in understanding who God is and how God acts regarding salvation. Returning to the Hebrew notion of *hesed*, Merton explains that it "is a gratuitous mercy that considers no fitness, no worthiness, and no return. It is the way the Lord looks upon the guilty and with His look

---

[28] Ibid., 97.
[29] Ibid., 117.
[30] Ibid., 119.

makes them at once innocent."[31] It is according to God's very nature as revealed to us through divine self-disclosure that God intends the salvation of all, those we might deem justified and those we might otherwise dismiss. Furthermore, this extends not only to humanity, but, anticipating Kasper's ressourcement, Merton writes that the "Christian concept of mercy is, therefore, the key to the transformation of a whole universe in which sin still seems to reign."[32] In a Pauline key (see Romans 8), Merton appears to extend God's mercy to the entirety of creation.

Merton's framing of the revelation of divine mercy within the event of the whole paschal mystery of life, death, and resurrection of Jesus Christ focuses our attention on what God does for us in the kenotic movement of the Logos in taking on our weakness, frailty, and sin, and then the suffering on the cross. So important is the experience of the God who suffers for and with us that Merton goes so far as to say in one place that the event of divine revelation of mercy is "the saving event of the Cross, which alone enables us to enter into a true spiritual harmony with one another, seeing one another not only in natural fellowship but in the Spirit and mercy of Christ, who emptied Himself for us and became obedient even to death (Philippians 2:2–8)."[33]

What Cardinal Kasper and Pope Francis provide us with is contemporary insight and voice, which hearken not only to the Christian tradition of centuries past but also to the wisdom of our brother Thomas Merton of the last century. Reading Kasper and Francis helps to contextualize the insights of Merton for a new generation and a new era, while reading Merton allows us to expand our appreciation for the development of Christian theologies of revelation in recent years and the role divine mercy plays in that doctrinal consideration. I do not think it merely coincidental that Pope Francis publicly cites both Merton and Kasper as significant spiritual and theological influences. Together, all three offer us companionship in Christian reflection on the experience of God and mercy in our world.

---

[31] Merton, "The Good Samaritan," 178.
[32] Merton, *No Man Is an Island*, 207.
[33] Merton, "The Climate of Mercy," 203.

9

Learning from a "Saint Next Door"

The Pursuit of Holiness
in Thomas Merton and Pope Francis

The widely known Jesuit author James Martin concluded his 2006 best-selling book *My Life with the Saints* with the affirmation that "the universal call to holiness is an invitation to be ourselves. . . . The invitation to holiness is a lifelong call to draw closer to God, who wants nothing more than to encounter us as the people we are and the saints we are meant to be."[1] This is not an insight unique to him, for as he explains earlier in his book, Thomas Merton was a significant influence on his understanding of holiness and identity. What Martin summarizes well is the central conviction that Merton wrote about and discussed over the course of his monastic career. As Merton explains in *New Seeds of Contemplation*, "For me to be a saint means to be myself"; the only way to discover who we really are is to discover ourselves in God.[2] Sanctity—holiness—is not about becoming something or someone that we are *not*, but striving to be more authentically who it is God created us to be—in our particularity, uniqueness, and distinctive contexts.

On April 9, 2018, more than half a century after Merton wrote about holiness and what it means to be a saint, Pope Francis released a surprise apostolic exhortation titled *Gaudete et Exsultate (Rejoice and*

[A version of this essay was originally presented at the Sixteenth Annual International Thomas Merton Society Conference, Santa Clara University, California, June 27–30, 2019, and later published in *The Way* (2021): 9–19. Used with permission.]

[1] James Martin, *My Life with the Saints* (Chicago: Loyola Press, 2006), 390.

[2] Thomas Merton, *New Seeds of Contemplation* (New York: New Directions, 1961), 31.

Be Glad), On the Call to Holiness in Today's World.[3] While he does not mention Merton by name in this document, as he did three years earlier during his address to the joint session of the United States Congress, Pope Francis nevertheless lays out a pattern of Christian holiness that evokes the life and writing of the late Trappist monk. In this chapter I engage in a double reading of Pope Francis's exhortation on holiness and some of Merton's mature writing on holiness. I say *some of Merton's writing* because he writes about holiness and sanctity throughout his broad corpus. I have selected to narrow my focus to Merton's 1963 book *Life and Holiness*, which contains essays originally published in 1961 and 1962, and which reflects a period of Merton's own thinking on contemplation, faith, and sanctity that notably intersects with his "turn to the world" around this same time.[4] My intention is to highlight how Merton's writings anticipate the nature of Christian discipleship presented in Pope Francis's magisterial teaching, and I do so according to three headings: (a) holiness is a universal call; (b) sanctity is particular; and (c) there are false forms of holiness. After examining these themes in Merton and Francis, I will conclude this short chapter by suggesting that Merton is precisely the kind of non-canonical "saint next door" Pope Francis describes, and therefore worthy of broader appreciation and veneration.

Holiness Is a Universal Call

The bulk of Thomas Merton's writings on the topic of holiness were completed before the Second Vatican Council. In this way his affirmation of a "universal call to holiness," as Vatican II's *Lumen Gentium* (*The Dogmatic Constitution on the Church*) would put it, anticipates what would become formalized in that document. Nearly a full decade before the promulgation of *Lumen Gentium*, Merton dedicates a lengthy chapter in *No Man Is an Island* to the concept of vocation as a universal attribute.[5] He begins that essay with the following reflection:

---

[3] Future references to this document will be with in-text citations: *GE*, followed by the respective paragraph numbers.
[4] Thomas Merton, *Life and Holiness* (New York: Doubleday, 1963).
[5] Thomas Merton, *No Man Is an Island* (New York: Harcourt Brace, 1955), 131–63.

Each one of us has some kind of vocation. We are all called by God to share in His life and in His Kingdom. Each one of us is called to a special place in the Kingdom. If we find that place we will be happy. If we do not find it, we can never be completely happy. For each one of us, there is only one thing necessary: to fulfill our own destiny, according to God's will, to be what God wants us to be.[6]

He later adds: "All vocations are intended by God to manifest His love in the world."[7] Wherever we find ourselves, in whatever time, no matter who we are or what we do, each of us has received a call to follow God's will and present the love of God to others in our distinctive contexts.

Years later Merton picks up this theme in his books *New Seeds of Contemplation* and *Life and Holiness*, among other places. In the latter book, which we focus on here, Merton explicitly uses language that will later appear in the conciliar debates and the final texts of Vatican II.[8] He writes in *Life and Holiness* that "every Christian is therefore called to sanctity and union with Christ."[9] He explains: "The way of Christian perfection begins with a personal summons, addressed to the individual Christian by Christ the Lord, through the Holy Spirit. This summons is a call, a 'vocation.' Every Christian in one way or other receives this vocation from Christ—the call to follow him."[10] The language we find in *Lumen Gentium* reads: "Fortified by so many and such powerful means of salvation, all the faithful, whatever their condition or state, are called by the Lord, each in his own way, to that perfect holiness whereby the Father Himself is perfect."

Pope Francis takes this line from *Lumen Gentium* as the starting point in his exhortation *Gaudete et Exsultate*. In a way that echoes Merton's own concerns that too many people reduce the striving after Christian holiness as an activity reserved for consecrated religious or the ordained

---

[6] Ibid., 131.

[7] Ibid., 153.

[8] This is not to suggest in a causal sense that Merton directly influenced the formation of *Lumen Gentium*. Rather, it merely shows in a correlative manner that Merton was thinking alongside some of the *periti* of the council and other leading theological voices of the age. It also affirms Merton's status as entirely orthodox, contrary to what his contemporary or later naysayers would suggest.

[9] Merton, *Life and Holiness*, 13.

[10] Ibid., 34.

ministers of the church, Pope Francis states bluntly: "To be holy does not require being a bishop, a priest, or a religious. We are frequently tempted to think that holiness is only for those who can withdraw from ordinary affairs to spend much time in prayer" (*GE*, no. 14). He unequivocally affirms Merton's insights, stating: "This is not the case. We are all called to be holy by living lives with love and by bearing witness in everything we do wherever we find ourselves" (*GE*, no. 14). Reiterating the universality of the call to holiness, the pope ties this vocation to baptism, exhorting Christians to "let the grace of your baptism bear fruit in a path of holiness" (*GE*, no. 15).

But what is the holiness that all Christians are called to seek? This is another dimension of the universality of sanctity that Merton and Pope Francis share in common. Both make clear that authentic Christian holiness has absolutely nothing to do with individual perfection or sinlessness. To claim otherwise is to contravene doctrinal statements on the consequences of original sin and our ecclesial status as a church always already holy and sinful.[11] Merton warns us that we should "not therefore delude ourselves with easy and infantile conceptions of holiness," which are too often reduced to the hagiographic tales of superhuman heroism.[12] Merton rejects this otherworldly perspective of holiness. He adds:

> Hence sanctity is not a matter of being *less* human, but *more* human than other men. . . . It follows that a pretended 'way of perfection' that simply destroys or frustrates human values precisely because they are human, and in order to set oneself apart from the rest of men as an object of wonder, is doomed to be nothing but a caricature. And such caricaturing of sanctity is indeed a sin against faith in the Incarnation."[13]

Merton puts forth a great deal of effort to combat this mistaken understanding of holiness as personal perfection. He writes: "That is why it is perhaps advisable to speak of 'holiness' rather than 'perfection.' A 'holy' person is one who is sanctified by the presence and action of God in him. He is 'holy' because he lives so deeply immersed in the life, the

---

[11] See Brian P. Flanagan, *Stumbling in Holiness: Sin and Sanctity in the Church* (Collegeville, MN: Liturgical Press, 2018).

[12] Merton, *Life and Holiness,* 19.

[13] Ibid., 24.

faith, and the charity of the 'holy Church.'"[14] And herein lies the clue about what sanctity and holiness means: "The true saint is not one who has become convinced that he himself is holy," Merton explains, "but one who is overwhelmed by the realization that God, and God alone, is holy."[15] Sanctity is marked by participation in *God's holiness*, a welcome surrender to the transcendent sign of love and peace working through us because of God, and not because of us. In this way Merton articulates what it means to be a saint. "The saint, then, seeks not his own glory but the glory of God. And in order that God may be glorified in all things, the saint wishes himself to be nothing but a pure instrument of the divine will. He wants himself to be simply a window through which God's mercy shines on the world."[16] Merton later elaborates on this point, making a sound trinitarian argument for the participation in God's holiness as conformity to Christ in the Spirit.[17]

This sense of authentic Christian holiness as participation in the singular holiness of God, conforms to the ancient Hebrew understanding of sanctity witnessed to in the Old Testament. Theologian Elizabeth Johnson argues for the retrieval of this understanding of sanctity in *Friends of God and Prophets*.[18] Like Merton and Johnson, Pope Francis emphasizes authentic sanctity as participating in God's holiness and does so in a particularly christological valence. He explains: "At its core, holiness is experiencing, in union with Christ, the mysteries of his life. It consists in uniting ourselves to the Lord's death and resurrection in a unique and personal way, constantly dying and rising anew with him" (*GE*, no. 20). Invoking Merton's most famous spiritual contribution, the pope writes: "Sooner or later, we have to face our *true selves* and let the Lord enter" (*GE*, no. 29). Given that the only real holiness that exists is God's holiness, the universal call to participate in the life of God necessarily leads to reflection on the church for, as Pope Francis reiterates in this exhortation and elsewhere, Christianity always implies community—the community of believers, the communion of saints. Or,

---

[14] Ibid., 20.

[15] Ibid., 26.

[16] Ibid., 26.

[17] For example, see Merton, *Life and Holiness*, 58–59.

[18] See Elizabeth A. Johnson, *Friends of God and Prophets: A Feminist Theological Reading of the Communion of Saints* (New York: Continuum, 1998).

as Merton says, "The whole Christian life is then an interrelationship between members of a body unified by supernatural charity, that is by the action of the Holy Spirit, making us all one in Christ."[19]

Sanctity Is Particular

Merton has a telling passage in *Life and Holiness* about saints and the particularity of holiness, which is often overlooked in our narratives about exemplary Christian models of living. He writes:

> The popular idea of a "saint" is, of course, quite naturally based on the sanctity which is presented for our veneration, in heroic men and women, by the Church. There is nothing surprising in the fact that the saints quickly become stereotyped in the mind of the average Christian, and everyone, on reflection, will easily admit that the stereotype tends to be unreal. The conventions of hagiography have usually accentuated the unreality of the picture, and pious art has, in most cases, successfully completed the work. In this way, the Christian who devotes himself to the pursuit of holiness unconsciously tends to reproduce in himself some features of the popular stereotyped image. Or rather, since it is fortunately difficult to succeed in this enterprise, he imagines himself in some sense obliged to follow the pattern, as if it were really a model proposed for his imitation by the Church instead of a purely conventional and popular caricature of a mysterious reality—the Christlikeness of the saints.[20]

Merton goes out of his way to deconstruct the false narrative of cookie-cutter sanctity too often depicted in the rote lives of the saints that are nothing more than a misleading caricature of holy mendacity. Since holiness is participation in the life of God, and each person experiences God in distinctive times and places, Merton asserts that "it is in the ordinary duties and labors of life that the Christian can and should develop his spiritual union with God."[21] Later he adds: "Each one becomes perfect,

---

[19] Merton, *Life and Holiness*, 40.
[20] Ibid., 22.
[21] Ibid., 9.

not by realizing one uniform standard of universal perfection in his own life, but by responding to the call and the love of God, addressed to him within the limitations and circumstances of his own particular vocation."[22]

In this way Merton's reflections on the true and false selves offer a profound gift to those discerning how best to understand the pursuit of Christian holiness. As inspiring and important as the lives of the saints are, they do not offer a how-to guide for Christian living in every context. This is where attention to one's prayer life and ongoing and deepening discovery of who we are in God is the foundation for Christian holiness. Pope Francis spends a fair amount of time addressing this topic. He writes:

> We should not grow discouraged before examples of holiness that appear unattainable. There are some testimonies that may prove helpful and inspiring, but that we are not meant to copy, for that could even lead us astray from the one specific path that the Lord has in mind for us. The important thing is that each believer discern his or her own path, that they bring out the very best of themselves, the most personal gifts God has placed in their hearts, rather than hopelessly trying to imitate something not meant for them. (*GE*, no. 11)

In so many ways this is much easier said than done, a fact that both Merton and Pope Francis acknowledge. A life pursuing Christian holiness, then, requires discernment, prayer, and action rather than unreflective repetition of hagiographic caricature. Pope Francis states directly that participation in the life of Christ, that is God's holiness, ought to lead to concrete actions, actions that do not necessarily obtain to the miraculous or incredible. He says: "This holiness to which the Lord calls you will grow through small gestures" (*GE*, no. 16). Reiterating *Lumen Gentium's* teaching and Merton's insistence on the particularity of sanctity, Pope Francis explains that how we live our lives, interact with those around us, and choose to spend our time, energy, and resources all contribute to a life of Christian holiness in keeping with the tradition.

---

[22] Ibid., 29.

There Are False Forms of Holiness

Another aspect of a theology of holiness shared by both Merton and Francis is the reality of false forms of holiness. I've already mentioned the problematic of romanticizing caricatures of heroic sanctity and personal perfection. Additionally, both Merton and Francis are concerned with a limited scope of who qualifies as *potentially* holy—namely, ordained ministers and consecrated religious alone. Merton anticipates and Pope Francis reiterates Vatican II's affirmation that *all* are called to holiness, regardless of their state of life, social location, education, or context.

While these are indeed illustrations of what we might call false forms of holiness, at least by omission if not by description, there are two other kinds that troubled both Merton in the 1960s and Pope Francis today. The first is a reduction of faith to propositional claims. This is an intellectualizing of faith that Pope Francis calls "contemporary gnosticism" (*GE*, nos. 36–46). Pope Francis warns about the tendency to mistake what one knows (or thinks one knows) *about* faith claims *for* authentic Christian faith. He explains that such people think holiness is about having all the right answers, memorizing catechetical statements, having the most compelling apologetic response in an argument. He says: "A healthy humble use of reason in order to reflect on the theological and moral teaching of the Gospel is one thing. It is another to reduce Jesus's teaching to a cold and harsh logic that seeks to dominate everything" (*GE*, no. 39).

While Merton does not address this particular form of false holiness directly in *Life and Holiness*, he does spend a fair amount of time in *New Seeds of Contemplation*, in his chapter on faith, considering this matter. He writes: "Too often our notion of faith is falsified by our emphasis on the statements *about* God which faith believes, and by our forgetfulness of the fact that faith is a communion with God's own light and truth."[23] He highlights the dangerous effect that results from this amnesia of authentic faith, noting: "If instead of resting in God by faith, we rest simply in the proposition or the formula, it is no wonder that faith does not lead to contemplation. . . . Faith goes beyond words and formulas and brings us the light of God Himself."[24] Holiness is not measured by

---

[23] Merton, *New Seeds of Contemplation*, 128.
[24] Ibid., 129.

how much one knows or how often one wins an argument or theological dispute (however one might adjudicate such a showdown), and yet in an age of increased fear and polarization, wherein communications technology and scientific discovery affect culture and experience on a daily basis, a gnostic or intellectual reduction of the faith can seem secure and appealing. But it is not reflective of Christian holiness.

The second form of false holiness is a restrictive or legalistic view of Christian faith, or what Pope Francis describes as "contemporary Pelagianism" (*GE*, nos. 49–62). In *Life and Holiness* Merton contrasts Christian charity, truly a sign of active participation in the life and holiness of God, with forgetfulness about the real purpose of the church's organizational discipline, rituals, teaching authority, and hierarchy. He explains: "If we forget that the laws and organization of the Church are there only to preserve the inner life of charity, we will tend to make the observance of law an end in itself."[25] Sadly, for many today, this is what it means to strive for holiness. Pope Francis likens this sort of attitude and behavior to the various forms of the ancient Pelagian heresy, which basically describes a radical sense of self-sufficiency that precludes the need for grace or the work of God in our lives. If Christian holiness is signified by participation in the holiness of God in Christ through the Spirit, then one can see the immediate problem. And yet, so many self-identified Christians become obsessed with rules and procedures, rubrics and canonical norms, that they miss the whole point of the faith. Merton says that for these sorts of folks, "the Christian life becomes externalized," and such a person "may eventually become so absorbed in the externals of law and of organization that he loses a real sense of the importance of charity in the Christian life."[26] Pope Francis affirms this sentiment of Merton, writing, "Some Christians spend their time and energy on these things, rather than letting themselves be led by the Spirit in the way of love" (*GE*, no. 57).

Learning from a "Saint Next Door"

It's rare to find such congruence between a modern magisterial document and the insights of anybody, including our own Thomas Merton, writing

---

[25] Merton, *Life and Holiness,* 43.
[26] Ibid.

sixty years earlier. But in terms of their theology of holiness, Merton and Pope Francis are on precisely the same page. As I conclude my reflections here, I wish only to draw attention to one logical consequence of the insights both Merton and Francis offer; namely, that if authentic Christian holiness is a universal call, always particularly situated, and does not fall into the trap of false holiness, then there are far more saints than we typically count in the church's liturgical calendar. Pope Francis opens his exhortation acknowledging this under-considered truth that there are countless women and men of faith over the centuries that we might rightly call the "saints next door." These are not folks who draw the attention of the church universal; oftentimes they are not affiliated with wealthy religious orders or have prelates lobbying on their behalf. They are the ordinary, everyday, largely anonymous people who strive to life their faith in love, thereby signifying participation in the divine life—that is God's holiness—to those they encounter. They are our neighbors, friends, fellow parishioners, family members, mentors, teachers, and strangers. They reveal the compassionate face of God without fanfare and without the acclaim they might deserve, but their lives and work bespeak the truth Christ's life, death, and resurrection sought to reveal to us. These are people who are our companions on the pilgrim journey of faith; they are members of the "great cloud of witnesses" the Letter to the Hebrews describes; they are our models for what it means to walk in the footprints of Jesus Christ and to take the gospel seriously.

I believe that Thomas Merton is one such "saint next door." This is not to claim that he should be formally canonized; I'm of several minds about that possibility. But it is to claim that we do not need such ecclesiastical affirmation to venerate his life and legacy and to be inspired by his words and deeds. Thomas Merton was, in Beth Johnson's borrowing from the Book of Wisdom, a true "friend of God and a prophet." In this way he is already a saint, someone whose whole humanity was and is on display; someone who struggled to make sense of the gospel call in *his particular* location and time and context; and someone who continues to call us to likewise discern through the struggle, so that each of us may too participate in the holiness of God and share in the divine life.

10

The Heart of Christian Discipleship

Evangelical Poverty
in Thomas Merton and Pope Francis

Since his election as bishop of Rome on March 13, 2013, Pope Francis has continuously captured the attention of the world by the simplest of gestures and statements that convey the profound witness, challenge, and timelessness of the Gospel. Among the recurring themes at the center of his proclamation of the gospel is the universality of evangelical poverty as a constitutive dimension of the vocation to Christian discipleship. At every turn Francis articulates the mandate that all the baptized must embrace this way of living in the world after the example of Jesus Christ, this way of *poverty* that is exemplified in the life and ministry, death and resurrection of Christ. Thanks to his simple yet charismatic leadership, Francis has made it commonplace for us to hear exhortative messages such as the following:

> It is important that the generosity with which Christians give to good causes be not lowered to a kind of automatic and formal routine, a mere reaching into the pocket to shut up an importunate preacher. There is money given, but is there sufficient thought of the need of the poor? At the present time, it would seem that Christian charity ought to take on a somewhat different dimension. By giving money to an organization, we can fulfill in theory the obligations of Christian charity, but in actual fact we can remove

---

[A version of this essay was originally presented at the Fourteenth Biennial International Thomas Merton Society Conference, Bellarmine University, Louisville, Kentucky, June 4–7, 2015.]

ourselves and insulate ourselves against the problems and suffering of our fellow man. We turn over a few dollars to an organization that "takes care of the poor," and this sets our minds at rest. We have no further responsibility now. But today, with the immense resources of technology and the things that can be done to improve living conditions, Christian charity demands something more than just working to enrich myself and then sharing the surplus with others through the medium of an organization. Today we need to emphasize once again the importance of *work* in the context of Christian charity: work not just to make our living and have something to share, but work in order to *make a better world,* to *abolish poverty* or to make it less terrible.[1]

This kind of challenge, this clarion call to take seriously the deep demands of Christian charity beyond the superficial contributions of philanthropy and respond to the systemic injustices of our day, is par for the course in the age of Francis of Rome.

But note that this quotation isn't from Pope Francis during the last few years, but rather from Thomas Merton's writings more than fifty years ago! What is striking, particularly at this time in the church, is the deep resonance between the wisdom of Thomas Merton and the spirit of renewal ushered in by Pope Francis as he embodies the call of the Second Vatican Council. There are many ways that Merton's insight and writings anticipate the social justice commitments of the current bishop of Rome, but it seems fitting to explore Merton's understanding of evangelical poverty in light of the centrality of this theme in Pope Francis's teachings and example. In addition to highlighting yet another one of the many ways Merton continues to be relevant today, this brief exploration of the meaning and place of evangelical poverty in Merton and Pope Francis also offers a contribution to a previously overlooked dimension of Merton scholarship. Few have directly considered the subject of poverty in Merton's thought and writing so far.

In this chapter I proceed according to a few thematic headings that help organize our consideration. These themes are (a) the meaning of evangelical poverty; (b) the universal call of evangelical poverty;

---

[1] Thomas Merton, *The Life of the Vows,* ed. Patrick F. O'Connell, Initiation into the Monastic Tradition, vol. 6 (Collegeville, MN: The Liturgical Press, 2012), 437.

(c) evangelical poverty as protest; (d) evangelical poverty as solidarity; and (e) evangelical poverty at the heart of Christian discipleship.

The Meaning of Evangelical Poverty

One of the more striking parallels is not only between the thinking of Thomas Merton and Pope Francis on the subject of poverty, but also the way both thinkers parallel the tenets of Latin American liberation theology on this subject. Merton anticipates the work of Gustavo Gutiér-rez, whose *A Theology of Liberation* would be published in Spanish three years after Merton's death, and Pope Francis aligns with it too. Given the equivocal quality of the term *poverty,* Gutiérrez offers a helpful demarcation according to three categories: (1) abject or material poverty; (2) so-called spiritual poverty; and (3) evangelical poverty.[2]

The first meaning of poverty is what most people think of when they hear the term. Abject or material poverty is the condition in which people do not have the fundamental necessities for basic human flourishing. Here we can think of food, clothing, shelter, affection, healthcare, and the like. Material poverty is an evil, says Gutiérrez; it is something against which to protest.

The second meaning of poverty—so-called spiritual poverty—is often-times misunderstood and therefore poses a temptation for self-professed Christians to intentionally or unwittingly compartmentalize their lives such that they view their "internal prayer life" or "individual relationship with God" as having little or nothing to do with the other aspects of their life. This approach to poverty typically arises from a misreading of Matthew 5:3: "Blessed are the poor in spirit, for theirs is the kingdom of heaven." An erroneous reading renders this beatitude a justification for the wealthy, the powerful, and oppressors to pay little or no attention to the real-life consequences of their actions and lifestyles. This way of thinking and being-in-the-world is certainly not what the gospel is about.

To mistake the poverty of authentic Christian discipleship for *either* romanticizing of material poverty *or* this distorted view of spiritual poverty is to miss the point entirely. In both cases it is a matter of taking

---

[2] See Gustavo Gutiérrez, *A Theology of Liberation: History, Politics, and Salva-tion*, trans. Caridad Inda and John Eagleson (Maryknoll, NY: Orbis Books, 1973, 1988).

part of the picture and confusing it for the whole, emphasizing the wrong points and projecting our own desires into our understanding of the gospel call. Evangelical poverty is about *both* material poverty and a correct reading of spiritual poverty.

Gutiérrez offers us helpful insight into the meaning of *evangelical poverty.* This third approach is that of intentional poverty arising from the gospel commitment to discipleship as both a form of solidarity and protest (more about each of these later). Gutiérrez, drawing on God's own example of kenotic impoverishment through the incarnation, explains how we might understand this poverty:

> Poverty is an act of love and liberation. It has a redemptive value. If the ultimate cause of human exploitation and alienation is selfishness, the deepest reason for voluntary poverty is love of neighbor. Christian poverty has meaning only as a commitment of solidarity with the poor, with those who suffer misery and injustice. The commitment is to witness to the evil which has resulted from sin and is a breach of communion. It is not a question of idealizing poverty, but rather of taking it on as it is—an evil—to protest against it and to struggle to abolish it. As Paul Ricoeur says, you cannot really be with the poor unless you are struggling against poverty. Because of this solidarity—which one must manifest itself in specific action, a style of life, a break with one's social class—one can also help the poor and exploited to become aware of their exploitation and seek liberation from it.[3]

Poverty in the terms that Jesus understands them in the gospel is never an end in itself; rather, it is a means toward protesting the unjust systems that perpetuate material poverty and moving toward solidarity with our sisters and brothers. At the core of the gospel message and the kind of poverty that Christ calls his disciples to embrace is always at the service of relationship; this relationship isn't superficial, it isn't typically easy or pleasant, but instead it demands something of us and calls us out of a place of blindness, comfort, and complacency toward a realization of solidarity with others. This is what Jesus was all about; this is what the Gospels are all about. And both Merton and Pope Francis seem to get it.

---

[3] Ibid., 172.

Preparing his lectures to the monks in formation, Merton likewise affirms the meaning of evangelical poverty as a means toward an end. His starting point is first the religious context of the vow of poverty (which is really a way of talking about the vow of conversion of life within the Trappist rule). Merton initially addresses the subject of the technical aspects of the young monks' vow, but then shifts to dedicate a significant portion of his reflections on evangelical poverty in general. He writes: "Poverty is a necessary means to an end—religious perfection is charity in union with Christ. . . . Possession of goods is not in itself evil, and poverty is not good as such, but only in relation to love of Christ."[4]

Here Merton names the tension that Gutiérrez also recognized in the gospel call to embrace evangelical poverty. It's not simply a matter of "giving everything up" for the sake of a romanticized material poverty; nor can we be indifferent to our material reality. Instead, there must be a goal in mind, and the goal is modeled in Christ. Possessions get in the way of relationship with others and have a tendency to establish hierarchies that include some and exclude others. Merton affirms that Christ came to exclude no one, but paid particular attention to the poor, the *anawim* (Hebrew for "little poor ones"), which after Merton's death would come to be known in Catholic social teaching as "the preferential option for the poor."[5] Merton writes: "Christ came to preach the Gospel to the poor. This was not only part of his personal mission or the manifestation of a personal preference of his. It was a specific fulfillment of the prophecies of the Old Testament which pointed to the messianic time as the age when justice would be done to the poor and injustice rectified—a time of peace and new order."[6] In looking to Jesus as the model of Christian discipleship, Merton explains that "the Lord loved the poor, was Himself poor, and wanted His disciples to be poor. In fact, the apostles remained poor men, working with their hands. The rich who became Christians distributed their good to the poor, and the whole community lived a common life, not of destitution but of simplicity, proper to the poor."[7]

In ways that should be immediately apparent, Merton's identification of poverty with Christian living and the model of Christ anticipates Pope

---

[4] Merton, *The Life of the Vows*, 383.

[5] For more, see William O'Neil, *Catholic Social Teaching: A User's Guide* (Maryknoll, NY: Orbis Books, 2021).

[6] Merton, *The Life of the Vows*, 429.

[7] Ibid., 430.

Francis's apostolic exhortation *The Joy of the Gospel* (*Evangelii Gaudium*), in which we read: "Our faith in Christ, who became poor, and was always close to the poor and the outcast, is the basis of our concern for the integral development of society's most neglected members."[8] Pope Francis has made it clear in his daily homilies and in the general tenor of his pastoral teaching that evangelical poverty is something embraced for the sake of the kingdom of God as a means and not as an end in itself.[9] Again, in *The Joy of the Gospel*, he writes: "It is essential to draw near to new forms of poverty and vulnerability, in which we are called to recognize the suffering Christ, even if this appear to bring us no tangible and immediate benefits. I think of the homeless, the addicted, refugees, indigenous peoples, the elderly who are increasingly isolated and abandoned, and many others."[10] Like Merton and Gutiérrez, Pope Francis has a deeply christological understanding of evangelical poverty.

An understanding of evangelical poverty as not an end in itself, but as a means to something greater in terms of relationship modeled after Christ's example also gestures to the inherent power relations at play in the way that the world operates. In discussing with his novices the rationality or even necessity of the religious vow of poverty, Merton remarks:

> If it were easy and common to keep to these rational norms [reasonable and ordinate possession], and if everybody could keep his possessive instincts within these limits, there would be no need for a vow of poverty. The vow is necessary because *it is easier and surer* to give up all possessions than to strive to strike the right balance in ordinary, legitimate forms of proprietorship. In actual practice, normal and licit proprietorship is rather uncommon. *Too much is possessed by too few.* We easily delude ourselves that inordinate needs are really necessities, or we love possessions inordinately and for inadequate reasons. As a result of our greed, others have to suffer.[11]

While God intends us to share our material possessions with one another in order to facilitate a just and equitable society, in reality we see the

---

[8] Pope Francis, *Evangelii Gaudium* (2013), no. 186.

[9] See Pope Francis, *Morning Homilies*, trans. Dinah Livingstone (Maryknoll, NY: Orbis Books, 2015).

[10] Pope Francis, *Evangelii Gaudium*, no. 210.

[11] Merton, *The Life of the Vows*, 414.

effects of sin made manifest in selfishness and greed. Merton contends that what is at the heart of this desire for inordinate possessing is in fact the desire for *power*, which appears under several guises including conspicuous waste, the paternalism of philanthropy, and the fear of deprivation that leads to acquisitiveness, among others.[12]

Similarly, as the Brazilian liberation theologian and former Franciscan friar Leonardo Boff has written that Pope Francis "has something of the spirit of Saint Francis of Assisi; he is for poverty, simplicity, and total stripping away of power."[13] Pope Francis writes that, "The thirst for power and possessions knows no limits. In this system [of our societies], which tends to devour everything which stands in the way of increased profits, whatever is fragile, like the environment, is defenseless before the interests of a deified market, which become the only rule."[14]

The embrace of evangelical poverty, the surrender of inordinate possessiveness in order to enter into closer relationship with others is the only solution, which is the universal responsibility of all Christians that should lead to both protest and solidarity.

The Universal Call of Evangelical Poverty

It can be easy to set apart the world of the consecrated religious and ordained ministers from the world of everybody else, the world of popes and monks from the everyday reality of the laity. For many centuries prior to the Second Vatican Council it was commonplace to see a two-track system of Christian discipleship—the religious were the real deal, the "active duty" equivalents, whereas the laity were akin to the National Guard or part-time practitioners of the gospel. This was an erroneous way of viewing the church, one that had seemingly forgotten about the "universal call to holiness" that came with baptism. It was a commitment to recognize and respond in light of the truth that, "the joys and the hopes, the griefs and the anxieties of the men of this age, especially those who are poor or in any way afflicted, these are the joys and hopes,

---

[12] Merton, *The Life of the Vows*, 414–18.

[13] Leonardo Boff, *Francis of Rome and Francis of Assisi: A New Springtime for the Church*, trans. Dinah Livingstone (Maryknoll, NY: Orbis Books, 2014), 70.

[14] Pope Francis, *Evangelii Gaudium*, no. 56.

the griefs and anxieties of the followers of Christ."[15] *The Dogmatic Con-stitution on the Church* (*Lumen Gentium*) and the *Pastoral Constitution on the Church in the Modern World* (*Gaudium et Spes*) irrevocably call the church to its roots, its universal kinship shared beyond orders and offices, beyond race and gender, beyond state of life.

In sync with the spirit of the council, Thomas Merton instructed his young brothers in a similar perspective, striving to situate the voca-tion of the modern monk within the communion of believers called the church. Evangelical poverty, while lived out differently among the various charismatic iterations of consecrated and secular Christian life, is nevertheless a universal call and part of the life baptism inaugurates. Discussing how we so often blindly follow an inordinate "need to pos-sess," which leads us to a place of selfishness, Merton explains that "it is not only that each one is prohibited from being personally attached, but also there is a basic obligation for every Christian to use material things in a way that takes account of the needs and opportunities of others."[16] Merton illustrates this with the following example:

> For instance, if I have a farm on high ground in an area where my neighbors are flooded out by a river, I owe them shelter and assistance. For me to selfishly keep supplies that would normally be legitimate, and not share with those in need, would be a sin. Possessions that would be perfectly legitimate when all others have about the same, in the same situation, cease to be legitimate when others are in grave need and I can assist them.[17]

Just as the Word made flesh among us let nothing get in the way of lov-ing, forgiving, healing, and entering to relationship with others, so too we must take down those barriers that prevent us from sharing freely with others and entering into genuine communion. The need to possess, especially in the face of others' suffering or plight, is simply another way of describing our turning away from our baptismal vocation.

This need to possess has become even more apparent in our own day. More than fifty years after Merton taught the universality of evangelical

---

[15] Vatican II, *Gaudium et Spes*, no. 1.
[16] Merton, *The Life of the Vows*, 410.
[17] Ibid., 411.

poverty to his novices, Pope Francis points out that we have become numb to the truth of our call:

> The great danger in today's world, pervaded as it is by consumerism, is the desolation and anguish born of a complacent yet covetous heart, the feverish pursuit of frivolous pleasures, and a blunted conscience. Whenever our interior life becomes caught up in its own interests and concerns, there is no longer room for others, no place for the poor. God's voice is no longer heard, the quiet joy of his love is no longer felt, and the desire to do good fades.[18]

Like Augustine, who described our state of sin as like those bent over unable to see anything but ourselves, like one keenly attuned to the message of *Gaudium et Spes*, Pope Francis identifies again the perennial temptation we face to be deaf to the griefs and anxieties of our sisters and brothers. Our call is to scrutinize "the signs of the times" and to interpret "them in the light of the Gospel."[19]

This response is not the limited domain or the restricted responsibility of priests and nuns alone, but as Pope Francis makes clear, it is the vocational duty of *everybody*. He writes: "Each individual Christian and every community is called to be an instrument of God for the liberation and promotion of the poor, and for enabling them to be fully a part of society. This demands that we be docile and attentive to the cry of the poor and to come to their aid."[20]

Echoing the teaching of Pope John XXIII in his encyclical *Mater et Magistra*, both Merton and Pope Francis implicitly express a mode of being Christian disciples that intends us to "see, judge, and act." This is how Pope John XXIII taught that the social teaching of the gospel should be enacted in the world.[21] The way we come to be better followers of the gospel is by *seeing* the needs of those around us, the privilege we may have, and the barriers to relationship we place within and without; *judging* the ways we can do something about abject or material poverty in the world around us; and *acting* in response. In our actions as a result of this process we should work to protest or "fight" abject or material

---

[18] Pope Francis, *Evangelii Gaudium*, no. 2.

[19] Vatican II, *Gaudium et Spes*, nos. 1, 4.

[20] Pope Francis, *Evangelii Gaudium*, no. 187.

[21] See John XXIII, *Mater et Magistra*, esp. no. 287.

poverty as well as strive toward deeper solidarity with all our sisters and brothers.

Evangelical Poverty as Protest

In the preface to his 1964 book *Seeds of Destruction*, Merton writes as a Christian called to scrutinize the "signs of the times" in light of the gospel. He asserts that it is his job as a Christian and even more so as a monk to take the *action* of denouncing the evil he *sees* and *judges* in the world. This is not his task alone, but he asserts that it is both his moral obligation and that of all Christians:

> Therefore it seems to me to be a solemn obligation of conscience at this moment of history to take the positions which are indicated in the following pages [of this book]. These positions are, it seems to me, in vital relation with the obligations I assumed when I took my monastic vows. To have a vow of poverty seems to me illusory if I do not in some way identify myself with the cause of people who are denied their rights and forced, for the most part, to live in abject misery. To have a vow of obedience seems to me to be absurd if it does not imply a deep concern for the most funda-mental of all expressions of God's will: the love of His truth and of our neighbor.[22]

Beginning with his own social location as a Catholic monk, Merton ties his particular monastic vocation to the broader reality of injustice in the world.

Pope Francis continues the Second Vatican Council's return to the roots of discipleship when he announces, "We also evangelize when we attempt to confront the various challenges which can arise" today.[23] The action we are called to perform in the face of this need, in our effort as church to relieve the suffering of the poor, in response to the call to protest poverty, is articulated by Pope Francis in *The Joy of the Gospel* according to

---

[22] Thomas Merton, *Seeds of Destruction* (New York: Farrar, Straus, and Giroux, 1964), xv–xvi.

[23] Pope Francis, *Evangelii Gaudium*, no. 61.

a fourfold "no!" This should lead us to say "no" in the following ways: "no to an economy of exclusion, in which people are pushed to the margins and are discarded; no to the idolatry of money and the ideology of the absolute autonomy of the markets; no to money, which rules rather than serves; and no to social inequality, which incites violence."[24] Elsewhere Pope Francis speaks of the various ways we can and must work to protest the suffering of others in the world, including in terms of the care of immigrants, the elderly, the young, and even the rest of creation.

Evangelical Poverty as Solidarity

In addition to protesting actively to the injustices of our day, evangelical poverty should serve as a means toward the end of increased relationship best articulated in terms of solidarity. In his conferences to the young monks Merton addresses the goal of solidarity in two ways. First, within the context of the distinctive manifestation of Christian living found in monastic life, solidarity is understood as the binding together of the individual monks with the experience of the whole body of Christ. Key to this is recognition of the role of sin in our individual and collective lives. Merton writes: "The life of vows is, therefore, a *life of reparation* in which we consciously and freely assume the obligation, binding the whole race, to repair the disorder caused by sin, to reorient out own souls and all of mankind to God, its last end."[25]

But this solidarity is not simply spiritual or removed from the realities of everyday life. Merton also asserts a pragmatic dimension of solidarity, one that applies to all women and men of faith. Merton says:

> This notion of solidarity is most important to give our idea of charity a correct and genuinely Christian orientation. If we merely think of charity as an "affective" or interior thing, we will tend to cultivate a delusion. The affective charity which is indeed most important is measured by and nourished by exterior and effective

---

[24] Summarized in Walter Kasper, *Pope Francis's Revolution of Tenderness and Love: Theological and Pastoral Perspectives*, trans. William Madges (New York: Paulist Press, 2015), 77. For the full texts, see Pope Francis, *Evangelii Gaudium*, nos. 53–60.

[25] Merton, *The Life of the Vows*, 42.

charity, and all depends on union with Christ in His Mystical Body, the Church.[26]

In a sense Merton is welding together the pragmatic and the relational, the elements of protest and the solidarity together. He enumerates some ways in which this form of loving (*caritas*) solidarity can be manifested, including "ardently desiring the spiritual and temporal good of our brother as we desire our own" and "desiring *everything* that in *any* way is for the good of my brother and of the church—and of mankind as a whole."[27] Though his particular state in life limited the physical dimensions by which he could enter into solidarity with women and men outside the cloister, his emphasis on the necessity of fostering those relationships by whatever means—physical *and* temporal—helps to lay out an example of Christian living.

Pope Francis takes Merton's intuition a step further, not only affirming the positive dimension of our call to embrace evangelical poverty as a means toward solidarity, but also the negative dimension of our continued willful ignorance, which not only places barriers to human relationships but also affects our relationship with God. Pope Francis writes that a lack of solidarity toward the needs of the materially poor will directly affect our relationship with God.

> The Church has realized that the need to heed this plea is itself born of the liberating action of grace within each of us, and thus it is not a question of a mission reserved for a few. . . . it means working to eliminate the structural causes of poverty and to promote the integral development of the poor, as well as small daily acts of solidarity in meeting the real needs which we encounter. The word "solidarity" is a little worn and at times poorly understood, but it refers to something more than a few sporadic acts of generosity. It presumes the creation of a new mindset which thinks in terms of community and the priority of the life of all over the appropriation of goods by a few.[28]

---

[26] Ibid., 89.
[27] Ibid.
[28] Pope Francis, *Evangelii Gaudium*, no. 187–188.

This new mindset is what Merton alludes to when challenging those of us "guilty bystanders" who content ourselves with good intentions or theoretical positions, but who never leave the self-imposed cloister of our lives to consider, to be influenced by, or to inter into relationship with others.[29] Pope Francis notes in *The Joy of the Gospel*:

> Sometimes we prove hard of heart and mind; we are forgetful, distracted, and carried away by the limitless possibilities for consumption and distraction offered by contemporary society. This leads to a kind of alienation at every level, for "a society becomes alienated when its forms of social organization, production, and consumption make it more difficult to offer the gift of self and to establish solidarity between people."[30]

As if we needed an additional indictment, Pope Francis magnifies the universal call of evangelical poverty as a means toward solidarity when he says:

> No one must say that they cannot be close to the poor because their own lifestyle demands more attention to other areas. This is an excuse commonly heard in academic, business or professional, and even ecclesial circles. While it is quite true that the essential vocation and mission of the lay faithful is to strive that earthly realities and all human activity may be transformed by the Gospel, none of us can think we are exempt from concern for the poor and for social justice.[31]

Evangelical Poverty at the Heart of Christian Discipleship

It is striking how keenly Merton and Pope Francis reflect each other in their respective articulations of the meaning, goal, and universal call of evangelical poverty. Because the gospel, the good news of Christ, is all

---

[29] The phrase is taken from Thomas Merton, *Conjectures of a Guilty Bystander* (New York: Image Books, 1965).

[30] Pope Francis, *Evangelii Gaudium*, no. 196. The quotation at the end of the passage is from Paul II, *Centesimus Annus*, no. 41.

[31] Pope Francis, *Evangelii Gaudium*, no. 201.

about relationship, it should come as no surprise that the call to embrace evangelical poverty after the example of Christ himself stands at the heart of Christian discipleship. Having been asked to help form the next generation of monks in the Trappist way of life, Merton tied together the particular charismatic call of conversion of life to the universal call of evangelical poverty. Through his reflections we can glean insights pertinent not only to consecrated religious, but to all the baptized and all women and men of good will. Having been chosen as the bishop of Rome nearly fifty years after Merton's death, Pope Francis—perhaps without a single direct reference to or thought about the late American monk—carries on the tradition of scrutinizing the "signs of the times in the light of the gospel" for our age. A beneficiary of the work of liberation and contextual theologians whose scholarship and wisdom only surfaced with full force after Merton's earthly life prematurely ended, Pope Francis has in a way honed the message of the gospel, distilling it to its most fundamental or radical compositional parts: gospel poverty and divine mercy. There are what matter most. All else in our lives of faith fall under these headings. My intention in this chapter has been to plant a seed, one both ancient and new, of curiosity and reflection that leads to more of us reading Merton and Pope Francis alongside one another. I have argued elsewhere that Thomas Merton can be said to have had something of a "Franciscan heart," given his affection for the saint from Assisi and the strong influence of the theological tradition of the Franciscan movement in his writings.[32] I believe that this Franciscan heart can be understood to extend beyond the *poverello* from Assisi to the pope who bears the saint's name. At the very least, I have little doubt that had Merton lived to be more than one hundred years old, he would have been very pleased with the current bishop of Rome, this other man named Francis.

---

[32] See Daniel P. Horan, *The Franciscan Heart of Thomas Merton: A New Look at the Spiritual Inspiration of His Life, Thought, and Writing* (Notre Dame: Ave Maria Press, 2014).

11

True and False Love

Thomas Merton's Spirituality of the Restless Heart

In the December 24, 1966, issue of *Ave Maria* magazine, published by the Congregation of Holy Cross at the University of Notre Dame, Thomas Merton published an essay titled, "A Buyer's Market for Love?" The essay was later collected in the posthumously published volume *Love and Living* under the title "Love and Need: Is Love a Package or a Message?"[1] In it, Merton writes: "Love is our true destiny. We do not find the meaning of life by ourselves alone—we find it with another. We do not discover the secret of our lives merely by study and calculation in our own isolated meditations. The meaning of our life is a secret that has to be revealed to us in love, *by the one we love*." These are the words of the mature Merton, one who had lived, loved, and learned a tremendous amount over the course of what would be a life cut tragically short, for he would die suddenly two years to the month after this essay was published.

Interestingly, this essay was also written as one of Merton's most significant experiences of love was shifting in real time and an important relationship was coming to an end. It all began in March 23, 1966, when

---

[A version of this essay was first presented in the "Tuesdays with Merton" lecture series on September 13, 2022 at Saint Mary's College in Notre Dame, Indiana.]

[1] See Thomas Merton, "A Buyer's Market for Love?" *Ave Maria* 104 (December 24, 1966): 7–10, 27; and Thomas Merton, "Love and Need: Is Love a Package or a Message?" in *Love and Living*, ed. Naomi Burton Stone and Brother Patrick Hart (New York: Harcourt Brace, 1979), 25–37.

Merton left his hermitage to have back surgery in Louisville, Kentucky. Christine Bochen summarizes:

> A week later he met M., a student nurse assigned to care for him, and they fell in love. In the weeks and months that followed, as spring turned to summer, they exchanged letters, talked on the phone when Merton was able to call, and spent some time together at Gethsemani and in Louisville. Their visits were few, hours alone fewer still. But, almost from the beginning, Merton knew that the relationship could not endure. He was, after all, a monk.[2]

By the time the essay appeared in print, Merton and M. had effectively ended their relationship and all but stopped communication by letter and phone. And yet, I note this significant moment in Merton's life and its proximity to the publication of this essay because I believe they are related. The Merton who could so clearly and confidently proclaim that "love is our true destiny" and "the meaning of our life is a secret that has to be revealed to us in love, *by the one we love*" is one who had himself lived what he writes, had practiced what he now preaches.

What we find in Merton's mature writing on love is wisdom for us all. It is, I believe, a reflection of someone who finally knew what it was to love and be loved in a way that he had not previously experienced, but that we all long for in some manner. As the late Benedictine Sister and psychologist Suzanne Zuercher once wrote about the relationship between Merton and M., "In my opinion, it was Margie, more than any other person or any other experience, who brought the spiritual master to embrace the fullness of his humanity."[3] The renowned scholar of spirituality Cynthia Bourgeault expressed a similar sentiment in a 2002 essay in which she wrote that "Merton's love can be seen not as a fall from a monastic ideal of purity, but as having its own intrinsic beauty and coherence."[4] This is what, in part, makes Merton such an important

---

[2] Christine M. Bochen, "Introduction," in *Learning to Love: Exploring Solitude and Freedom*, vol. 6, ed. Christine M. Bochen (San Francisco: HarperSanFrancisco, 1997), xvi.

[3] Suzanne Zuercher, *The Ground of Love and Truth: Reflections on Thomas Merton's Relationship with the Woman Known as "M"* (Chicago: In Extenso Press, 2014), 12.

[4] Cynthia Bourgeault, "Merton in Love," *The Merton Seasonal* 27 (Summer 2002): 21.

and attractive spiritual teacher: he is not speaking from some place of inaccessible perfection or ascetic distance, but from an embodied, fully human, beautiful, and familiar location of good but flawed reality. And it took a lifetime for him to arrive at the wisdom he leaves us today.

Merton's writings on love, in all its forms—from theological virtue to poetic ideal to experiential reality and beyond—developed over time. It is a theme that appears in his journals, correspondence, essays, and books. It is a subject that, as he regularly notes, is unavoidable if one takes seriously the centrality of *agapic* love in the Christian tradition and the inherent capacity and need for love as a fundamental human experience. But Merton's own understanding of love shifted, developed, and grew over time. It is well known that in his youth his relationships with women were at best superficial, reflecting an inadequate—even *false*—sense of love. At worst, as we know, such romantic relationships led to neglect and abandonment; such was the case while he was a student at the University of Cambridge. Some scholars have speculated that a contributing factor in this understanding of love and relationship was the loss of his mother at age six and his father at age sixteen.[5] Others have reflected on this youthful naivete and sexist socialization in the context of the early twentieth century. Whatever the constellation of external and internal factors were that led to Merton's early immature understanding of love, he came to a deeper appreciation for both love of God and love of neighbor as time moved on.

This chapter is neither a narrow examination of Merton's romantic experience of love with M.,[6] nor is it a comprehensive survey of Merton's writings on human and divine love (such an exercise would take several volumes). Instead, what follows is a more modest attempt at lifting up some of Merton's wisdom on the topic of authentic love. Merton frequently contrasts authentic, real, *true* love with what is untrue, selfish, or *false* love, as we might say. While this distinction is seen variously throughout Merton's extensive written corpus, I want to focus on two illustrative essays where we can see him teasing out the contrast and the challenge of knowing and living true love. The first was originally

---

[5] Among others, this is reflected in John Moses, *Divine Discontent: The Prophetic Voice of Thomas Merton* (London: Bloomsbury, 2014).

[6] See Zuercher, *The Ground of Truth and Love*; Bochen, "Introduction"; and Bourgeault, "Merton in Love," 20–25.

published in two parts in the fall of 1960 and was later collected in the volume *Disputed Questions* with the new title, "The Power and Meaning of Love."[7] The second is the essay "Love and Need: Is Love a Package or a Message?" from which the quotation I shared at the outset was taken. From these two important essays we glean insights about the real meaning of true love and the corruptions that lead to false love. But before that, I explore what I am tentative calling Thomas Merton's *spirituality of the restless heart,* inspired by the famous Augustinian line: "You stir us to take pleasure in praising you, because you have made us for yourself, and our heart is restless until it rests in you."[8] After that we will look at some of the variations of false love Merton describes and then what the characteristics of true love are before presenting a brief conclusion.

Merton's Spirituality of the Restless Heart

Thomas Merton was never content. His life always seemed to reflect an embodied sense of restlessness. From an early age he was constantly on the move: from France to the United States to Bermuda back to France then to England, first at Oakham then at Cambridge, then back to the United States. He was also intellectually on the move as a young man and a university student, enrolling first in modern languages at Cambridge then English literature at Columbia; he was intrigued by intellectual and social movements of his time, found himself captivated by Catholic Christianity, entered the church, and then immediately began vocational discernment to religious life. He went first to the Franciscans, which did not pan out (although for more complicated reasons than most typically realize),[9] and ultimately to the Cistercians. But before that he would teach English for three semesters at St. Bonaventure University in Western

---

[7] Originally published in a Benedictine journal of spirituality as Thomas Merton, "Love and Person," *Sponsa Regis* 32, no. 1 (September 1960): 6–11; and "Love and Maturity," *Sponsa Regis* 32, no. 2 (October 1960): 44–53; and later as Thomas Merton, "The Power and Meaning of Love," in *Disputed Questions* (New York: Harcourt Brace, 1960), 97–126.

[8] Augustine, *Confessions*, trans. Henry Chadwick (New York: Oxford University Press, 1998), 3.

[9] See Daniel P. Horan, *The Franciscan Heart of Thomas Merton: A New Look at the Spiritual Inspiration of His Life, Thought, and Writing* (Notre Dame, IN: Ave Maria Press, 2014), esp. 55–78.

New York State, bouncing back and forth in his mind and heart about where to go next; for example, living and discerning for a summer with Catherine de Hueck Doherty and her Madonna House community in New York City.[10] Even after entering the Abbey of Gethsemani, Merton was still constantly on the move, longing for more solitude in a hermitage on the abbey grounds, or another monastery in South America, or another monastic Order like the Camaldolese. Even in the last few months before his untimely death in 1968 Merton traveled on his way to Asia through the American West—including Alaska—to scout out possible sites for a remote site on which to establish a new hermitage.[11]

The fruits of Merton's struggles and spiritual restlessness are found in the wisdom and insights that he leaves us today. Whether resulting from the challenges of personality or context, or some combination of both, Merton's restlessness informed his own prayer life and religious discernment. When we read his writings on the spiritual life, we see not only instructions for the reader, but a reminder to himself about the need for spiritual reorientation and anchoring in God rather than the peripatetic quest for stability, affirmation, acceptance, recognition, or worth from without. Such is the case when we read in *New Seeds of Contemplation*: "When humility delivers a man from attachment to his own works and his own reputation, he discovers that perfect joy is possible only when we have completely forgotten ourselves. And it is only when we pay no more attention to our own deeds and our own reputation and our own excellence that we are at last completely free to serve God in perfection for His own sake alone."[12] Merton writes this within the context of discussing the spiritual journey toward perfection and sanctity, which follows his lengthy reflections on the true and false selves.

Merton then succinctly notes: "To say that I am made in the image of God is to say that love is the reason for my existence, for God is love. Love is my true identity. Selflessness is my true self. Love is my true character. Love is my name."[13] And, as if channeling St. Augustine's reflections on

---

[10] For more, see Robert A. Wild, ed., *Compassionate Fire: The Letters of Thomas Merton and Catherine de Hueck Doherty* (Notre Dame, IN: Ave Maria Press, 2009).

[11] See Thomas Merton, *Thomas Merton in Alaska: The Alaskan Conferences, Journals, and Letters* (New York: New Directions Publishing, 1989).

[12] Thomas Merton, *New Seeds of Contemplation* (New York: New Directions, 1961), 58.

[13] Ibid., 60.

the restless character of his heart, Merton writes: "To find love I must enter into the sanctuary where it is hidden, which is the mystery of God."[14] Near the end of *New Seeds of Contemplation*, in a chapter simply titled "Pure Love," Merton writes about what he considers to be our "alienated condition," separated from God and therefore from our true selves. Like "prodigals in a distant country, the 'region of unlikeness,'" we come to recognize that we are on a journey that is often characterized by restlessness, by a hunger or a longing.[15] Elsewhere Merton writes:

> There is in us an instinct for newness, for renewal, for a liberation of creative power. We seek to awaken in ourselves a force which really changes our lives from within. And yet the same instinct tells us that this change is a recovery of that which is deepest, most original, most personal in ourselves. To be born again is not to become somebody else, *but to become ourselves.*[16]

This longing or restlessness for "newness, for renewal, for a liberation of creative power" is what compels him and us onward on the quest to "rest in God," as St. Augustine famously put it. Or, as Merton would say, to discover who it is that we really are. This is, as Merton writes in *New Seeds of Contemplation*, often a counterintuitive journey, given that so much energy and effort is placed on our externalizing search for identity, egged on by the manifold distractions of our societies and cultures encouraging us to embrace the appetites of our ego and cultivate our own identities that amount to nothing more than the accumulation of false selves.

In response to this challenge Merton explains:

> Our reality, our true self, is hidden in what appears to us to be nothingness and void. What we are not seems to be real, what we are seems to be unreal. We can rise above this unreality and recover our hidden identity. And that is why the way to reality is the way of humility which brings us to reject the illusory self and accept the 'empty' self that is 'nothing' in our own eyes and in the eyes of

---

[14] Ibid., 61.

[15] Ibid., 280–81.

[16] Thomas Merton, "Rebirth and the New Man in Christianity," in *Love and Living*, 196.

men, but is our true reality in the eyes of God: for this reality is 'in God' and 'with Him' and belongs entirely to Him.[17]

It is in this sense that Merton can say with confidence, "The secret of my identity is hidden in the love and mercy of God," adding, "Therefore I cannot hope to find myself anywhere except in Him."[18] The restlessness that exists in our hearts, that drives our ultimate desires and fuels our insatiable longing for meaning, will only be satisfied by the love of God. Or, as Merton writes: "There is only one problem on which all my existence, my peace and my happiness depend: to discover myself in discovering God. If I find Him I will find myself and if I find my true self I will find Him."[19]

Like the inherent, natural longing for renewal and rebirth that propels us onward toward God and the true self, Merton's spirituality of the restless heart provides a path toward recognizing, embracing, and living true love.

Variations of False Love

Merton writes: "Man cannot live without love, and if the love is not genuine, then he must have some substitute—a corruption of real love. These corruptions are innumerable."[20] While there are certainly other forms that exist within and outside of Merton's accounting, he offers explicitly at least four variations on false love. We shall call these (a) objectified love, (b) romanticized love, (c) legalism masking as love, and (d) the package concept of love. Referring to all of these tendencies, Merton notes that sometimes we are attuned to the falsity of some kinds of "love" and can avoid falling prey to them from the outset. However, there are others that create real difficulty for many people. Merton says: "Those which present a problem do so because they can seem, and claim to be, genuine love. These false forms of love base their claim on appeal to an ideal and their falsity consists precisely in the fact that they tend to sacrifice

---

[17] Merton, *New Seeds of Contemplation*, 282.
[18] Ibid., 35.
[19] Ibid., 36.
[20] Merton, *Disputed Questions*, 105.

persons to concepts."[21] When this sort of pseudo-intellectualization takes over our understanding and practice of love, what results is inevitably a conditional and false sense of love, which is not what Christ calls us to live. Merton elaborates on this contrast, noting:

> Corrupt forms of love wait for the neighbor to 'become a worthy object of love' before actually loving him. This is not the way of Christ. Since Christ Himself loved us when we were by no means worthy of love and still loves us with all our unworthiness, our job is to love others without stopping to inquire whether or not they are worthy. That is not our business and, in fact, it is nobody's business. What we are asked to do is to love; and this love itself will render both ourselves and our neighbor worthy if anything can.[22]

Let us briefly examine each of the four kinds of false love about which Merton speaks in these two essays.

Objectified Love

Drawing on the philosophical and theological insights of the continental thinkers of the early twentieth century without explicitly naming them, Merton highlights the importance of loving another as a wholly free subject.[23] Merton explains:

> The trouble is that love is something quite other than the mere disposition of a subject confronted with an object. In fact, when love is a mere subject-object relationship, it is not real love at all. And therefore it matters little to inquire whether the object of one's love is real or not, since if our love is only our impulsion towards an "object" or a "thing," it is not yet fully love.[24]

---

[21] Ibid., 105.

[22] Ibid., 125.

[23] For example, see Martin Buber, *I and Thou*, trans. Ronald Gregor Smith (New York: Scribner, 2000).

[24] Merton, *Disputed Questions*, 102.

And here we have a summation of the first kind of false love in Merton's unsystematic typology: objectified love.

There is a way in which this kind of love comes to pass unwittingly, not necessarily because an individual is consciously objectifying or dehumanizing another, but because fear of vulnerability, disclosure, openness, and transparency take hold and create a "protective" distance between oneself and the other. Merton writes:

> When we love another "as an object," we refuse, or fail, to pass over into the realm of his own spiritual reality, his personal identity. Our contact with him is inhibited by remoteness and by a kind of censorship which *excludes* his personality and uniqueness from our consideration. We are not interested in him as "himself" but only as another specimen of the human race.[25]

This kind of love is not only destructive because of how it frames and limits the other, but also because of how it serves as a gatekeeping mechanism for the one seeking to love. This kind of love is false because it never seeks to risk what is necessary to know and be known by the other, and it fails to recognize the agential quality and inherent subjectivity of the other. "To love another as an object is to love him as 'a thing,'" Merton writes, "as a commodity which can be used, exploited, enjoyed and then cast off."[26] One never invests in the other or dares to stake a vulnerable claim on behalf of a relationship of mutuality. While there is certainly a degree of selfishness that undergirds such a false love, there is also a tremendous amount of fear and withdrawal.

Merton addresses this dynamic of insecurity when he writes:

> But to love another as a person we must begin by granting him his own autonomy and identity as a person. We have to love him for his own good, not for the good we get out of him. And this is impossible unless we are capable of a love which "transforms" us, so to speak, into the other person, making us able to see things as

---

[25] Ibid., 103.
[26] Ibid., 103–4.

he sees them, love what he loves, experience the deeper realities of his own life as if they were our own.[27]

In other words, Merton says that love without sacrifice and compassion is no real love at all. The false love of objectification feels comfortable because it is an attempt to love someone at arm's length, without letting the messiness of human relationships affect us, challenge us, and ultimately transform us.

Romanticized Love

Despite how the term sounds, romanticized love is not just about romantic or erotic love. Philosophically, what Merton terms romanticized love might rightly be called a Platonic idealization of the concept of love. Merton believed that there was a strong tendency, especially in our modern contexts, to move away from the personal, embodied, imperfect, and finite love of real life to an abstraction or ideal mental conception of love. He explains:

> What we call the romantic approach to love is that love of the good which sacrifices the persons and the values that are present and actual, to other values which are always out of reach. Here a shiftless individualism dignifies itself as the quest for an elusive ideal, whether in politics or art or religion or merely in one's relations with other men. Such love is apparently obsessed with "perfection." It passes from one object to another, examining it superficially, playing with it, tempting it, being tempted by it, and then letting go of it because it is not "the right object." Such love is therefore always discarding the real and actual in order to go on to something else, because the real and actual are never quite right, never good enough to be worth of love.[28]

Merton summarizes with prophetic clarity the state of affairs that so many of us find ourselves embroiled in on the quest for genuine love. As psychologists, sociologists, and demographers have noted in recent decades,

---

[27] Ibid., 104.
[28] Ibid., 106.

the nearly instantaneous availability of information and the curating of digital selves via social media channels have made what Merton describes here about the quixotic quest for the "ideal" or "perfect" experience of love (or "ideal" or "perfect" object of love) all the more pressing.[29]

The falsity of this kind of love is revealed upon closer examination of both its motivations and consequences. Merton writes: "Such love is really only an escape from love, because it refuses the obligation of entering into a real relationship which would render love at the same time possible and obligatory. Because it hates the idea of obligation, it cannot fully face even the possibility of such a relationship." Merton adds: "Its romanticism is a justification of flight. It claims that it will only begin to love when it has found a worthy object—whether it be a person who can 'really be loved,' or an ideal that can really be believed in, or an experience of God that is definitive and binding."[30] The false love of romanticism captures well the temptation to indefinite deferral of true love. Ironically, the claim to delay true love on account of an idealized or abstracted object of love is, in fact, a reduction of the full humanity of those one actually encounters. Merton points out that "romanticized love" therefore "declares an open season on 'perfect objects,' and proceeds comfortably to neglect *persons* and realities which are present and actual, and which, in all their imperfection, still offer the challenge and the opportunity of genuine love."[31]

This romanticized love ultimately results in another form of avoiding commitment and justifying a solipsistic mode of being-in-the-world. Merton explains that this form of false love "is in fact a way of defending oneself against real involvement in an interpersonal relationship and of keeping other persons subdued and humiliated in the status of objects."[32] Admittedly, this is rarely a conscious activity. Instead, it is often a self-defense mechanism arising from insecurity and fear, which unsurprisingly results in barriers to authentic relationship and true love.

---

[29] See Daniel P. Horan, "Digital Natives and the Digital Self: The Wisdom of Thomas Merton for Millennial Spirituality and Self-Understanding," *The Merton Annual* 24 (2011): 83–111; and idem, "Striving toward Authenticity: Merton's 'True Self' and the Millennial Generation's Search for Identity," *The Merton Annual* 23 (2010): 80–89.

[30] Merton, *Disputed Questions*, 106.

[31] Ibid., 106–7.

[32] Ibid., 107.

Legalism Masked as Love

The third kind of false love Merton explicitly names is what we might call legalism masked as love. Merton notes from the outset that the "legalist corruption of love is also a refusal to love on the ground that the object is not worthy." He adds, "But here, instead of undertaking a vast exploration in quest of the worthy object (which can never be found), the presence of the unworthy object becomes the excuse for a tyrannical campaign for worthiness, a campaign to which there is practically no end."[33] In this false form of love "the objectification of personality and of all spiritual values is carried to the extreme."[34]

This distortion is found in predictable places like totalitarian regimes and those persons and groups who subjugate individuals and their particular circumstances, social locations, and realities to some generic part of a collective. But Merton notes that this legalism is also a dangerous threat within the Christian community. He notes that this legalism "is another weak form of love which in the end produces dissension, destroys communion, and for all its talk about unity, tends by its narrowness and rigidity to create divisions among men."[35] Like the trap of romanticism, legalism masquerades as authentic—often as the *most* authentic—form of love. Whereas romanticism perpetually defers the possibility of true love because of the endless and unrealistic quest for a perfect or ideal object of love, legalism offers another form of rejecting authentic relationship and true love on the grounds that others do not measure up to the assumed rigors of disciplinary observance.

We see this play out frequently today within ecclesial circles when religious leaders publicly condemn individuals, especially politicians, for not conforming to this or that particular religious leader's interpretation of the law (religious or secular) and related expectations. Within the Catholic Christian context this is seen when bishops deny individuals access to the sacraments, especially the Eucharist. In a weak but common defense, such self-identified Christians often say that they are merely "following the rules" and that their preferred punishments are, in fact, a form of "tough love." But, as Merton notes, "Legalism in practice makes

---

[33] Ibid.
[34] Ibid., 108.
[35] Ibid., 115.

law and discipline more important than love itself. For the legalist, law is more worthy of love than the persons for whose benefit the law was instituted. Discipline is more important than the good of souls to whom discipline is given, not as an end in itself but as a means to their growth in Christ."[36] While this is evident within the dynamics of Christian life and ministry, it is also present in our interpersonal dynamics. There is in this context of false love a nonnegotiable quality required for admittance into relationship. It is not acceptance of the two subjects and free persons as they are in mutual love and respect. Instead, it is the prioritization of certain abstract policies and measurements over the particularity of the individual.

This setting of a bar, which the other must reach in order to be loved or even deemed lovable, "is in reality a fatal perversion of the Christian Spirit." Merton explains:

> Such "love" is the enemy of the Cross of Christ because it flatly contradicts the teaching and the mercy of Christ. It treats man as if he were made for the Sabbath. It loves concepts and despises persons. It is the kind of love that says *corban* (Mark 7:9–13) [referring to the practice in which one takes personal financial advantage of something that is said to belong to God] and makes void the commandment of God "in order to keep the traditions of men."[37]

It is, we might add, an acquiescence to the logic or wisdom of the world, as St. Paul puts it (1 Cor 1:1–31), rather than an embrace of the logic or wisdom of God.

The Package Concept of Love

Finally, we turn to the last of the four varieties of false love Merton discusses: the package concept of love. Building on the "logic" or "wisdom" of the world—as well as the consistent theme of objectification that threads these false loves—Merton describes love understood in this packaged way as deeply shaped by consumerism and vague pragmatism. He writes:

---

[36] Ibid.
[37] Ibid., 117.

Love is regarded as a deal. The deal presupposes that we all have needs which have to be fulfilled by means of exchange. . . . We unconsciously think of ourselves as objects for sale on the market. We want to be wanted. We want to attract customers. We want to look like the kind of product that makes money. Hence, we waste a great deal of time modeling ourselves on the images presented to us by an affluent marketing society.[38]

This false understanding of love is likely recognizable to most people today. While Merton is writing this in the 1960s, with the advent of social media and an advertising culture that targets its audience directly, what he is describing might appear all the more familiar to people today. Merton explains that this way of thinking leads us "to consider ourselves and others not as *persons* but as *products*—as 'goods,' or in other words, as packages. We appraise one another commercially. We size each other up and make deals with a view to our own profit. We do not give ourselves in love, we make a deal that will enhance our own product, and therefore no deal is final."[39] Merton understands this dynamic to contribute to the instability of relationships today, especially romantic relationships. He surmises that "for many people what matters is the delightful and fleeting moment in which the deal is closed. They give little thought to what the deal itself represents. That is perhaps why so many marriages do not last, and why so many people have to remarry. They cannot feel real if they just make one contract and leave it at that!"[40] To think in such a consumerist—or "package"—manner is to be driven in part by a need for relevance and desirability. The dissolubility of relationships and the avoidance of commitment follow from this way of thinking about love. "Our eye is already on the next deal—and this next deal need not necessarily be with the same customer. Life is more interesting when you make a lot of deals with a lot of new customers."[41]

Merton notes that "this concept of love assumes that the machinery of buying and selling of needs and fulfillment is what makes everything run. It regards life as a market and love as a variation on free enterprise."[42]

---

[38] Merton, *Love and Living*, 29.
[39] Ibid.
[40] Ibid., 31.
[41] Ibid., 29.
[42] Ibid., 30.

Like the capitalistic vortex that propels the false religion of belief in a "free market," the restless heart led astray propels this false love onward. We all hunger for connection, acceptance, fulfillment, and meaning, but this false concept of love insists that satisfaction is only found in our marketability. Pursuing this trajectory of false love only reinforces problematic outcomes and distraction from true love. Merton writes: "The trouble with this commercialized idea of love is that it diverts your attention more and more from the essentials to the accessories of love. You are no longer able to really love the other person, for you become obsessed with the effectiveness of your own package, your own product, your own market value."[43]

Merton goes on to explain that this "package" sense of false love is built on a lie, albeit a lie that is often compelling and attractive—the whole marketing industrial complex is committed to its replication and advancement. But this way of being in the word is not only narcissistic, it is also essentially hollow. Interestingly, Merton makes the point that even those who are fully invested in this false love, who even benefit from matching the consumeristic ideals of beauty and success, will eventually arrive at a point when the hollowness of this false love cannot be avoided. He writes: "The truth is, however, that this whole concept of life and love is self-defeating. To consider love merely as a matter of need and fulfillment, as something which works itself out in a cool deal, is to miss the whole point of love, and of life itself."[44]

And so, this brief examination of four kinds of false love that Merton writes about gestures toward a key question: what does *true* love look like? Let us switch gears now to consider what Merton means when he talks about true love.

The Meaning and Power of True Love

When Merton writes about the discovery of our true self, he makes the point that we come to know something about our true self in coming to know God. This is because God is the one who knows our truest and most essential identity, given that God is the one who loved us into existence. Likewise, when reflecting on the meaning of true love, Merton identifies

---

[43] Ibid., 30–31.
[44] Ibid., 33.

God as the source and model of such love. In *Disputed Questions* Merton ties together the quest for our true self with our inherent capacity for love or what Augustine might call our "restless hearts."

Merton writes that our "vocation to be sons of God means that we must learn to love as God Himself loves. For God is love, and it is by loving as He loves that we become perfect as our heavenly Father is perfect (Matt. 5:48)."[45] This leads Merton to reflect on the centrality of love not only for the Christian community but also for all of humankind and the rest of creation. "Love then is not only our own salvation and the key to the meaning of our own existence," Merton writes, "but it is also the key to the meaning of the entire creation of God. It is true, after all, that our whole life is a participation in that cosmic liturgy of 'the love which moves the sun and the other stars.'"[46]

Offering a contrast with the false love of selfish interest and comfort, Merton notes that "true love leads man to fulfillment, not by drawing things to himself but by forcing him to transcend himself and to become something greater than himself."[47] He adds: "All true love is therefore closely associated with three fundamentally human strivings: with *creative work*, with *sacrifice*, and with *contemplation*. Where these three are present there is reliable evidence of spiritual life, at least in some inchoate form. There is reliable evidence of love. And the most important of the three is sacrifice."[48]

To some readers this prioritization of sacrifice over contemplation is surprising, especially coming from someone like Merton, who dedicated so much of his work and ministry to inviting all people to a contemplative life. However, Merton understood that true love is first and foremost *agapic* love—that self-sacrificial, challenging, at times laborious love that demands something of the lover, that requires patience and persistence, that may at times be messy and uncomfortable. In short, true love is always somehow tied to the love Christ consistently exhibited and called his followers to live. Merton makes this point plainly when he states that a mature person is a person "in Christ" and therefore someone who is "able to live on the level of Christ's love."[49] For those not yet at that

[45] Merton, *Disputed Questions*, 99.

[46] Ibid.

[47] Ibid., 100.

[48] Ibid.

[49] Ibid., 112.

point, those who are in the realm of the various forms of false love, the *agapic* love of Christ appears as foolishness, yet again invoking the Pauline distinction between the wisdom of the world and the wisdom of God.[50]

Throughout much of Merton's writings this sense of true love anchored in the *agapic* love of Christ is present, and he clearly understands the centrality of this view for Christian discipleship. But there is a notice-able shift in the way he writes about the meaning, power, and effects of this true love in the fall of 1966 that is not found as clearly in his earlier reflections, including that essay collected in *Disputed Questions* published just a few years beforehand. In reflecting on the active quality of love as something more than a passive event that merely chances to take place (as if struck from without by cupid's arrow!), Merton writes that the "question of love is one that cannot be evaded. Whether or not you claim to be interested in it, from the moment you are alive you are bound to be concerned with love, because love is not just something that happens to you: *it is a certain special way of being alive.*"[51] Here we begin to sense the lived reality that undoubtedly informed Merton's own experience of true love in ways previously not seen. "Love is, in fact, an intensification of life, a completeness, a fullness, a wholeness of life." He adds, strikingly, "We do not become fully human until we give ourselves to each other in love."[52]

In *Love and Living* Merton brings together the two distinct but related and often elusive realities of the true self and true love. He explains, "Our conception of ourselves is bound to be profoundly affected by our conception—and our experience—of love. And our love, or our lack of it, our willingness to risk it or our determination to avoid it, will in the end be an expression of ourselves: of who we think we are, of what we want to be, of what we think we are here for."[53] In a moving elaboration of this point, Merton writes:

> Love affects more than our thinking and our behavior toward those we love. It transforms our entire life. Genuine love is a personal revolution. Love takes your ideas, your desires, and your actions and welds them together in one experience and one living reality which

---

[50] Ibid.
[51] Merton, *Love and Living,* 27.
[52] Ibid.
[53] Ibid., 28.

is a new *you*. You may prefer to keep this from happening. You may keep your thoughts, desires, and acts in separate compartments if you want: but then you will be an artificial and divided person, with three little filing cabinets: one of ideas, one of decisions, and one of actions and experiences.[54]

While false love is typically solipsistic and self-centered, true love is other-focused, outwardly oriented, and ultimately transformative.

Elsewhere Merton develops this notion of the revelatory and transformative power of true love. He says that when people are "truly in love" they "become different people: they are more than their everyday selves, more alive, more understanding, more enduring . . . They are transformed by the power of their love."[55] Developing this further, he writes:

> Love is the revelation of our deepest personal meaning, value, and identity. But this revelation remains impossible as long as we are the prisoner of our own egoism. I cannot find myself in myself, but only in another. My true meaning and worth are shown to me not in the estimate of myself, but in the eyes of the one who loves me; and that one must love me as I am, with my faults and limitations, revealing to me the truth that these faults and limitations cannot destroy my worth in *their* eyes; and that I am therefore valuable as a person, in spite of my shortcomings, in spite of the imperfections of my exterior "package." The package is totally unimportant. What matters is this infinitely precious message which I can discover only in my love for another person. And this message, this secret, is not fully revealed to me unless at the same time I am able to see and understand the mysterious and unique worth of the one I love.[56]

The condition of the possibility for this powerful, transformative true love is the recognition of the *agapic* or sacrificial quality that it requires.

Again, echoing the wisdom of St. Paul in the First Letter to the Corinthians, this time with hints of chapter 13, Merton states that "love is not a matter of getting what you want" and that "love is not a deal, it is

---

[54] Ibid.
[55] Ibid., 34.
[56] Ibid., 35.

sacrifice. It is not marketing, it is a form of worship."[57] This acknowledgment of the sacrificial and sacramental quality of true love sets Merton up to offer his clearest and most direct explanation of its meaning.

> In reality, love is a positive force, a transcendent spiritual power. It is, in fact, the deepest creative power in human nature. Rooted in the biological riches of our inheritance, love flowers spiritually as freedom and as a creature response to life in a perfect encounter with another person. It is a living appreciation of life as value and as gift. It responds to the full richness, the variety, the fecundity of living experience itself. It "knows" the inner mystery of life. It enjoys life as an inexhaustible fortune. Love estimates this fortune in a way that knowledge could never do. Love has its own wisdom, its own science, its own way of exploring the inner depths of life in the mystery of the loved person. Love knows, understands, and meets the demands of life insofar as it responds with warmth, abandon, and surrender.[58]

This sense of true love is what Merton suggests: a force that changes us when we experience and express it in its genuine form. For Merton that form is always *agapic* in the spirit of Christ, which is why it is also the love that includes enemies as much as it does friends and neighbors. In *Passion for Peace* Merton makes this connection explicit, stating that this transformative power of love for our enemies is "one of the crucial ways in which we give proof in practice that we are truly disciples of Christ."[59]

Called to True Love

The sacrificial, challenging, and transformative power of true love is our shared vocation, what we are called to live in the world in order to participate in the in-breaking of God's reign. It is counterintuitive when viewed through the lens of the "wisdom" of the world, appearing as foolishness in the face of consumerism and capitalist impulses. Merton's

---

[57] Ibid., 34.

[58] Ibid.

[59] Thomas Merton, *Passion for Peace: The Social Essays,* ed. William H. Shannon (New York: Crossroad, 1995), 241.

own personal and spiritual journey led him to a deeper understanding of precisely the challenge and power of true love, manifesting as both love of God and love of his fellow persons in community. Perhaps the greatest experiential teacher for Merton was his relationship with M., which, while imperfect and still not fully understood by those other than the two of them, nevertheless suggests a marked shift in Merton's own language and expression about true and false love. Whatever accounts for the lifetime of growth and learning, we benefit from the wisdom Merton leaves us to help us think through and live out our call to love as God has first loved us.

IV

The Spirituality of Racial Justice

12

A Spirituality of Resistance

Thomas Merton on the Violence of Structural Racism in America

On August 23, 1961, Thomas Merton wrote a letter to his friend and spiritual companion Dorothy Day, the co-founder of the Catholic Worker movement. In this letter Merton expressed his ongoing discernment about the direction of his thinking, writing, and vocation: "I don't feel that I can in good conscience, at a time like this, go on writing just about things like meditation, though that has its point. I cannot just bury my head in a lot of rather tiny and secondary monastic studies either. I think I have to face the big issues, the life-and-death issues."[1] This sentiment reflected the shift in Merton's attention from the interior life toward a greater interest in the social justice concerns of his time.[2]

Among the "big issues, the life-and-death issues" that preoccupied him was violence. His interest was both global and local. On the international level he was concerned with the state of world affairs in the wake of the

<hr>

[A version of this essay was originally published in *American Catholicism in the Twenty-First Century: Crossroads, Crisis, or Renewal*, ed. Benjamin Peters and Nicholas Rademacher (Maryknoll, NY: Orbis Books, 2018), 189–200. Used with permission.]

[1] Thomas Merton, "Letter to Dorothy Day, August 23, 1961," in *The Hidden Ground of Love: Letters on Religious Experience and Social Concerns*, ed. William H. Shannon (New York: Farrar, Strauss, Giroux, 1985), 140.

[2] For more on this shift, see William H. Shannon, *Thomas Merton: An Introduction* (Cincinnati: Franciscan Media, 2005), 60–73; David W. Givey, *The Social Thought of Thomas Merton: The Way of Nonviolence and Peace for the Future* (Winona, MN: Anselm Academic, 2009); and Mario I. Aguilar, *Thomas Merton: Contemplation and Political Action* (London: SPCK, 2011).

Second World War, the emergence of the Cold War standoff with its subsequent and persistent nuclear threat, and the troubling realities of the Vietnam conflict. But his interest in the relationship between the United States and violence appeared on the domestic horizon as well, and in ways not as intuitively related to physical force or conflicts between nation-states. As James Thomas Baker rightfully observed, "Merton believed that the most obvious and continuing sign of America's violence was the racism which had led to its greatest social crisis of the 1960s."[3]

Racism was for Merton more than a series of discrete actions of prejudice or harm. Although he certainly recognized the reality of particular instances of physical, emotional, psychological, and spiritual violence deployed against individuals and communities of color, one of Merton's most notable (if often overlooked and underappreciated) contributions was his ability to recognize and name structural racism or what Bryan Massingale has called "the culture of racism" that permeates historical, cultural, and institutional realities throughout the United States. As Massingale explains: "Racism, at its core, is a set of meanings and values that inform the American way of life. It is a way of understanding and interpreting skin color differences so that white Americans enjoy a privileged social status with access to advantages and benefits to the detriment, disadvantage, and burden of person of color."[4] And Merton— a white, male, Euro-American, straight, ordained Catholic monk, who died in 1968—recognized and named this pervasive reality for what it is: a form of structural and systemic violence. His contributions anticipate much of the contemporary developments of critical race theory over the last thirty years.

This chapter is an exploration of Merton's prophetic and prescient writing on racism in the American context.[5] Despite his ostensibly isolated social location as a cloistered monk, Merton nevertheless scrutinized the

---

[3] James Thomas Baker, *Thomas Merton: Social Critic* (Lexington: University Press of Kentucky, 1971), 99.

[4] Bryan N. Massingale, *Racial Justice and the Catholic Church* (Maryknoll, NY: Orbis Books, 2010), 42.

[5] Though *American* can rightly be applied to many nations in the Western Hemisphere and the persons residing within these nations, for the sake of simplicity (given the frequency that Merton and other authors use the term in this way) *American* is used in this chapter synonymously with *United States* and its context.

"signs of the times in the light of the Gospel"[6] from a "surplus location" at one of the margins of mainstream American society.[7] The result of his writing from this unique social, geographic, and spiritual location was the production of several essays aimed at awakening fellow Christians to the violence of deep-seated structural racism and white supremacy.

What follows in this chapter is organized in three parts. First, I briefly survey Merton's writing on the reality of structural racism, white privilege, and violence. Second, I show how Merton's writings anticipate by more than a decade the work of legal theorist and early founder of critical race theory Derrick Bell, Jr., on the subject of "interest convergence." Finally, I conclude by noting how Merton's work on violence and racism contributes to articulating a *spirituality of resistance* aimed at disrupting the status quo and awakening white American Christians to their complicity with structural sin and their call to *metanoia* or ongoing conversion.

Thomas Merton, Structural Racism, and White Privilege

I believe that Merton's awareness of the complexity of racism in the United States arose from several factors converging in his unique position. One factor was his voracious reading habits, which put him in contact with writers including W.E.B. Du Bois, James Baldwin, Martin Luther King, Jr., and Malcolm X. A second factor was his work with Christian nonviolence movements, which put him in contact with, in addition to King, the Berrigan brothers, Dorothy Day, James Forest, John Howard Yoder, Ping Ferry, and others.[8] A third factor was the deeply mystical and

---

[6] Vatican II, *Gaudium et Spes* (*Pastoral Constitution on the Church in the Modern World*) (December 7, 1965), no. 4.

[7] Here I am borrowing the notion of "surplus" from Joerg Rieger, whose interpretation of Jacques Lacan led him to pose this term as useful in postcolonial critique. See *Christ and Empire: From Paul to Postcolonial Times* (Minneapolis: Fortress Press, 2007), 9: "Such surplus is subversive because it cannot ultimately be controlled by the system. Surplus, in this context, can be anything that points beyond the status quo."

[8] For an excellent overview of Merton's role as an adviser to several key nonviolent activists in the 1960s, see Gordon Oyer, *Pursuing the Spiritual Roots of Protest: Merton, Berrigan, Yoder, and Muste at the Gethsemani Abbey Peacemakers Retreat* (Eugene, OR: Cascade Books, 2014).

contemplative discipline of prayer and reflection he cultivated, especially as he embraced a more eremitical lifestyle in proportion to his social justice work. In this way we might liken Merton to Howard Thurman, who was also a "mystic as prophet."[9]

Speaking as a white male in the context of American religious life and addressing an audience of similar composition, Merton noted his complicity in structural racism, demarcating it from discrete acts of racially based animus while also naming its inherently violent roots:

> There is, however, such a thing as collective responsibility, and collective guilt. This is not quite the same as personal responsibility and personal guilt, because it does not usually follow from a direct fully conscious act of choice. Few of us have actively and consciously *chosen* to oppress and mistreat the Negro. But nevertheless we have all more or less acquiesced in and consented to a state of affairs in which the Negro is treated unjustly, and in which his unjust treatment is directly or indirectly to the advantage of people like ourselves, people with whom we agree and collaborate, people with whom we are in fact identified. So that even if in theory the white man may believe himself well disposed toward the Negro—and never gets into a bind which he proves himself otherwise—we all collectively contribute to a situation in which the Negro has to live and act as our inferior. I am personally convinced that most white people who think of themselves as very "fair" to the Negro show, by the way they imagine themselves "fair," that they consider the Negro an inferior type of human being, a sort of "minor," and their "fairness" consists in giving him certain benefits provided he "keeps in his place," the place they have allocated to him as an inferior. I would like to say that this state of mind is itself an act of inhumanity and injustice against the Negro and is in fact at the root of the trouble with the Negro, so that anyone who holds such opinions, even in the best of faith, is contributing actively to the violence of the present situation whether he realizes it or not.[10]

---

[9] See William Apel, "Mystic As Prophet: The Deep Freedom of Thomas Merton and Howard Thurman," *The Merton Annual* 16 (2003): 172–87.

[10] Thomas Merton, "The Hot Summer of Sixty-Seven," in *Faith and Violence: Christian Teaching and Christian Practice* (Notre Dame, IN: University of Notre Dame Press, 1968), 180–81.

Merton added: "This kind of treatment is part of a whole subtle system of moral and psychological oppression which is essentially *violent*. Anyone who has such an attitude is then partly responsible for what is going on, and in that sense 'guilty.'"[11] The relationship between the particular and the collective as it concerns the violence of racism anticipates what scholars have said in subsequent decades.

Bryan Massingale affirms Merton's intuition that much of the violent and "subtle system of moral and psychological oppression" functions as "a largely unconscious or preconscious frame of perception, developed through cultural conditioning and instilled by socialization."[12] Massingale explains that "racism's manifestations change, sometimes dramatically. But at its core, racism always involves the use of skin color differences for the purpose of assigning social rank or privilege."[13] The shifting iterations or manifestations of racism can lead people to dismiss its enduring and persistent reality, claiming that "improvement" is actually the eradication of racism in society. However, as Merton, Massingale, and many others note, racism is only one side of the coin of this structural injustice. The other side is the privilege that is preserved and protected by racial injustice.

While many white women and men readily admit the reality of racial injustice as it disadvantages some, far fewer are able or willing to recognize their own advantages resulting from the very same system. For many whites the notion of white privilege appears theoretical, especially when the matrix of class, gender, and race come together in the lived realities of individuals. However, as Massingale notes, in the American context "white privilege is not an abstraction; it is real. White privilege is the range of unearned (and at times, unwanted) advantages that come simply from possession of an attribute our society prizes, namely, the status of being considered 'white.'"[14] Merton recognized the reality of white privilege, which arises from a society structured such that supremacy is bestowed on whites by virtue of law, custom, culture, and social systems. He takes particular aim at white Christians and their willful ignorance about white supremacy. "The actions and attitudes of

[11] Ibid., 181.
[12] Massingale, *Racial Justice and the Catholic Church*, 26.
[13] Ibid., 36.
[14] Ibid., 41.

white Christians all, without exception, contain a basic and axiomatic assumption of white superiority, even when the pleas of the Negro for equal rights are hailed with the greatest benevolence. It is simply taken for granted that, since the white man is superior, the Negro wants to become a white man."[15] In other words, in the structurally racist thinking of even those white women and men who, in principle, support civil rights, there is an insidious undercurrent of supremacy that governs what white society will accommodate, when it will accommodate, and for whom it will accommodate those rightfully demanding racial justice. I will say more about this in the next section, but suffice it to say here that Merton's awareness of the violence of structural racism and white privilege allowed him to recognize the failures of ostensible white allies during the 1960s (and beyond).

Recognizing the deep-seated and complex reality of structural racism in America, Merton was distinctive among white Catholic clergy in his time acknowledging what black women and men knew for centuries: racism is essentially a *white problem*. Merton wrote that the work of Martin Luther King, Jr., and his fellow nonviolent activists was, in part, to help bring the social reality of the American context into white consciousness:

> The purpose of nonviolent protest, in its deepest and most spiritual dimensions then is to awaken the conscience of the white man to the awful reality of his injustice and of his sin, so that he will be able to see that the Negro problem is really a *White* problem: the cancer of injustice and hate which is eating white society and is only partly manifested in racial segregation with all its consequences, *is rooted in the heart of the white man himself*. Only if the white man sees this will he be able to gradually understand the real nature of the problem and take steps to save himself and his society from complete ruin.[16]

Although, for Merton, King's nonviolent protest was aimed at ushering in this awakening to racism and privilege, it did not succeed, even in the civil rights legislation that ostensibly advanced racial justice in America.

---

[15] Thomas Merton, "Letters to a White Liberal," in *Seeds of Destruction* (New York: Farrar, Straus, and Giroux, 1964), 58.
[16] Ibid., 45–46.

Merton and Interest Convergence Theory

The entire premise of Merton's essay "Letters to a White Liberal" was that those civil rights milestones lauded by white Christians in the North were insufficient, even perhaps meaningless, in addressing the reality of structural racism in the United States. One of the primary reasons is that white women and men have failed to acknowledge and therefore address the reality of white privilege and supremacy, which they, in fact, are uninterested in surrendering. As Merton puts it strikingly: "We have been willing to grant the Negro rights on paper, even in the south. But the laws have been framed in such a way that in every case their execution has depended on the good will of white society, and the white man has not failed, when left to himself, to block, obstruct, or simply forget the necessary action without which the rights of the Negro cannot be enjoyed in fact."[17] From Merton's perspective, any liberties or rights extended to persons of color are done on the condition that the white supremacist American society maintains its status quo, affording no undue hardships for those who are currently privileged and remain in power.

Merton insisted that "as long as white society persists in clinging to its present condition and to its own image of itself as the only acceptable reality, then the problem will remain without reasonable solution, and there will inevitably be violence."[18] In summary form, Merton lays out the issue:

> The problem is this: if the Negro, as he actually is (not the "ideal" and theoretical Negro, or even the educated and cultured Negro of the small minority), enters wholly into white society, then *that society is going to be radically changed.* This of course is what the white South very well knows, and it is what the white Liberal has failed to understand. Not only will there be radical change which, whatever form it may take, will amount to at least a peaceful revolution, but also there will be enormous difficulties and sacrifices demanded of everyone, especially the whites. Obviously property values will be affected. The tempo of life and its tone will be altered. The face of

---

[17] Ibid., 19.
[18] Ibid., 8.

business and profession life may change. . . . We must dare to pay the dolorous price of change, *to grow into a new society*. Nothing else will suffice![19]

But the problem remains that white society does not want anything to *actually* change, because the result would be another kind of society, a "new society" as Merton puts it, and that society would not hold one race superior to another.

Because of this dynamic Merton sees the white Northerners who are quick to join in the civil rights movement as not only often inadvertently disingenuous, but actually counterproductive in advancing racial justice. He calls these "white liberals," many of whom are Christian leaders, to task for inserting themselves in a controlling position, seeking to set a tone and establish goals that at least do not demand they surrender their material, psychological, or social comforts and status. This is why Merton is incredulous when it comes to passing legislation like the Civil Rights Act of 1964. Merton explains: "The Negro is integrated by law into a society in which there really is no place for him—not that a place could not be made for him, if the white majority were capable of wanting him as a brother and a fellow-citizen."[20] Merton takes fellow white Christians to task for ostensibly supporting persons of color but in fact seeking to control and undermine their righteous effort for true equality and justice. In a scathing rebuke Merton names what he sees as the primacy of the white Northern interests in controlling the civil rights efforts of persons of color:

Now, my liberal friend, here is your situation. You, the well-meaning liberal, are right in the middle of all this confusion. You are, in fact, a political catalyst. On the one hand, with your good will and your ideals, your fine hopes and your generous, but vague, love of mankind in the abstract and of rights enthroned on a juridical Olympus, you offer a certain encouragement to the Negro (and you do right, my only complaint being that you are not yet right enough) so that, abetted by you, he is emboldened to demand concessions. Though he knows you will not support all his

<hr/>

[19] Ibid., 8–9.
[20] Thomas Merton, "Religion and Race in the United States," in *Faith and Violence*, 134.

demands, he is aware that you will be forced to support some of them in order to maintain your image of yourself as a liberal. He also knows, however, that your material comforts, your security, and your congenial relations with the establishment are much more important to you than your rather volatile idealism, and that when the game gets rough you will be quick to see your own interests menaced by his demands. And you will sell him down the river for the five hundredth time in order to protect yourself. For this reason, as well as to support your own self-esteem, you are very anxious to have a position of leadership and control in the Negro's fight for rights, in order to be able to apply the brakes when you feel it is necessary.[21]

White liberals are happy to support persons of color, provided it is on their own terms and in a manner consonant with their own interests.

What Merton identifies in writing anticipates what more than a decade later Derrick Bell will propose in a theory titled "interest convergence."[22] Bell argues that "civil rights advances for blacks always seemed to coincide with changing economic conditions and the self-interest of white elites. Sympathy, mercy, and evolving standards of social decency and conscience amounted to little, if anything."[23] In other words, the ostensibly commonsense reading of advances in civil rights arising from a recognition that injustices needed to be corrected—what Bell and other legal scholars call a "neutral principle" in this case—does not sufficiently account for why the changes actually took place at a given time and manner.

To illustrate his thesis, Bell chose the Supreme Court decision *Brown v. Board of Education* (1954). He believed that, following nearly a century of black protest for equal rights, the *Brown* decision was decided in 1954 because of a "convergence of interests" according to which the interests of elite whites (politicians, business owners, and others) converged with the

---

[21] Merton, "Letters to a White Liberal," 33–34.

[22] See Derrick A. Bell, Jr., "Serving Two Masters: Integration Ideals and Client Interests in School Desegregation Litigation," *Yale Law Journal* 85.470 (1976): 470–516.

[23] Derrick A. Bell, Jr., quoted in Richard Delgado and Jean Stefancic, *Critical Race Theory: An Introduction*, 2nd ed. (New York: New York University Press, 2012), 22.

longstanding interests of the oppressed. Bell identifies three reasons for the decision according to this convergence: First, American politicians feared that legal segregation was weakening the credibility of American democracy internationally in the context of the Cold War; second, the decision would offer "much needed reassurance to American blacks that the precepts of equality and freedom so heralded during World War II might yet be given meaning at home"[24]; and third, capitalists were concerned that the American South could never develop industry beyond its rural plantation society as long as state-sponsored segregation remained intact.[25]

At the heart of Bell's theory lies a view that aligns well with Merton's intuition about why *real* change regarding the violence of racism in America remained so elusive. Given that white elites maintained control of the positions of governmental, social, and economic power, only concessions that did not threaten white privilege would ever be permitted. The alleviation of systemic oppression and structural racism in America would always be circumscribed and determined by unspoken rules that maintain white privilege and social supremacy. Bell describes the mechanism of this phenomenon well:

> Whites may agree in the abstract that blacks are citizens and are entitled to constitutional protection against racial discrimination, but few are willing to recognize that racial segregation is much more than a series of quaint customs that can be remedied effectively without altering the status of whites. The extent of this unwillingness is illustrated by the controversy over affirmative action programs, particularly those where identifiable whites must step aside for blacks they deem less qualified or less deserving. Whites simply cannot envision the personal responsibility and the potential sacrifice inherent in Professor [Charles] Black's conclusion that true equality for blacks will require the surrender of racism-granted privileges for whites.[26]

---

[24] Derrick A. Bell Jr., "*Brown v. Board of Education* and the Interest-Convergence Dilemma," *Harvard Law Review* 93.518 (1980): 524.

[25] Bell, "*Brown v. Board of Education* and the Interest-Convergence Dilemma," 525.

[26] Bell, "*Brown v. Board of Education* and the Interest-Convergence Dilemma," 522–23. The text Bell refers to here is Charles Black, "The Lawfulness of the Seg-

Merton was able to identify and name what critical race and legal theorists would later develop into a substantiated field of study that traces
the relationship of the two-sided coin of structural racism and white
privilege within the American context.[27] Whereas developments in
critical race theory in the decades after Merton's death lend clarifying
language and structure to Merton's observations, analysis, and reflections, Merton's writing offers insight into the spiritual significance of
this work for Christians.

Toward A Spirituality of Resistance

In a sense, Merton's entire written corpus can rightly be described as
a reflection on lifelong conversion. Both his autobiographical texts as
well as the more didactic efforts identify numerous opportunities for
metanoia—a turning—from sin, individualism, or the false self and toward reconciliation, communion, and the true self. And this is the case
in his writings on the violence of American racism, wherein he almost
always draws a connection between what *Guadium et Spes* would call
the "signs of the times" and the Christian response these signs elicit.
I am suggesting we can read Merton's Christian response as a nascent
spirituality of resistance rooted in what he describes as a "theology of
love" that is both a theology of revolution and resistance.[28]

Merton laments the "Christian failure in American racial justice" in
his own time, noting that an increased awareness of what is happening
in society brings out "the stark reality that our society itself is radically
violent and that violence is built into its very structure."[29] What is the
response of the Christian, especially the white Christian, supposed to
be? I suggest Merton offers (at least) three points to be considered in
forming a spirituality of resistance for white Christians in the American
context that arises from his critical reflection on experience.

---

regation Decisions," *Yale Law Journal* 69.421 (1960): 421–30.

[27] What Merton intuited and Bell later argued was confirmed beyond empiricism
and theory in the work of, among others, the legal historian Mary L. Dudziak,
Cold War Civil Rights: Race and the Image of American Democracy (Princeton, NJ:
Princeton University Press, 2000).

[28] Thomas Merton, "Toward a Theology of Resistance," in *Faith and Violence*,
9.

[29] Merton, "Religion and Race in the United States," 144.

First, he explains that the "job of the white Christian is then partly a job of diagnosis and criticism, a prophetic task of finding and identifying the injustice which is the cause of *all* violence, both white and black."[30] The exhortation is to *resist* simply resting in unexamined complicity and instead seek to uncover the injustice already at work in the system. Merton explains that this leaves the Christian with a real choice: either "find security and order by falling back on antique and basically feudal conceptions, or go forward into the unknown future, identifying himself with the forces that will inevitably create a new society."[31] This is the revolutionary dimension that challenges Christians to move outside the cocoon of personal piety to embrace a spirituality of praxis and engagement.

Second, Merton encourages his fellow white Christians to *actually listen* to their black sisters and brothers. Again, the central conviction of his "Letters to a White Liberal" is that the seemingly benevolent "liberal" or Northern whites are in fact deploying control and influence that Bell would describe as interest convergence. For Merton, a spirituality of resistance calls white Christians in particular to step aside and recognize the prophetic voice of people of color. Their message, he believes, can be put in simple terms: "I would say that the message is this: white society has sinned in many ways. It has betrayed Christ by its injustices to races it considered 'inferior' and to countries which it colonized."[32] Merton adds, "What is demanded of us is not necessarily that we believe that the Negro has mysterious and magic answers in the realms of politics and social control, *but that his spiritual insight into our common crisis is something we must take seriously*."[33] The spirituality of resistance Merton imagines is not one in which the prophetic voice arises from the "white savior" within American society, but one of humility and honest reflection that invites white Christians to embrace silence and openness. Merton concluded his "Letters to a White Liberal" with an instruction for what this might look like, invoking a familiar motif from the Gospels in the process. "This is the 'message' which the Negro is trying to give white America. I have spelled it out for myself, subject to correction, in order

---

[30] Thomas Merton, "From Non-Violence to Black Power," in *Faith and Violence*, 129.
[31] Merton, "Religion and Race in the United States," 138–39.
[32] Merton, "Letters to a White Liberal," 66.
[33] Ibid., 69.

to see whether a white man is even capable of grasping the words, let alone believing them. For the rest, you have Moses and the Prophets: Martin Luther King, James Baldwin, and others. Read them and see for yourself what they are saying."[34]

The last point is that white Christians should "get out of the way." Articulated in first-person narrative, Merton concludes his essay "From Non-Violence to Black Power" with these lines: "I for one remain *for* the Negro. I trust him, I recognize the overwhelming justice of his complaint, I confess I have no right whatever to get in his way, and that as a Christian I owe him support, not in his ranks but in my own, among the whites who refuse to trust him or hear him, and who want to destroy him."[35] To move beyond uncritical interest convergence toward actual racial justice, white Christians need to follow rather than lead, listen rather than instruct, and support people of color on their own terms.

For Thomas Merton, racial justice can only be imagined when those who benefit from maintaining the status quo of inequality recognize structural racism and its complement of white privilege. Otherwise, progress is only ever advanced in circumscribed ways governed by the happenstance of interest convergence. As Christians, we are called by virtue of our baptism to work for peace and justice, which according to Merton means that white Americans have to move toward surrendering the unearned privilege and power granted by structural racism. Merton highlights that for white Christians this begins with incorporating into their spiritual practices a commitment to identifying injustice, listening to the people of color, and "getting out of the way" so that the agenda and mission of social change can be set by the hitherto oppressed and not by the oppressor.

[34] Ibid., 70.
[35] Merton, "From Non-Violence to Black Power," 129.

13

Racism Is a White Problem

Thomas Merton, Whiteness, and Racial Justice

In what has become a classic reflection on the pervasiveness of systemic racism, deeply imbedded as it is in so many unwitting presumptions, outlooks, statements, and questions of white women and men, the scholar and civil rights activist W.E.B. Du Bois opened his 1903 collection of essays, *The Souls of Black Folk,* with the following lines:

> Between me and the other world there is ever an unasked question: unasked by some through feelings of delicacy; by others through the difficulty of rightly framing it. All, nevertheless, flutter round it. They approach me in a half-hesitant sort of way, eye me curiously or compassionately, and then, instead of saying directly, *How does it feel to be a problem?* They say, I know an excellent colored man in my town; or, I fought at Mechanicsville; or, Do not these Southern outrages make your blood boil? At these I smile, or am interested, or reduce the boiling to a simmer, as the occasion may require. To the real question, *How does it feel to be a problem?* I answer seldom a word.[1]

The power of Du Bois's unmasking of the tacit anti-black racism in the seemingly innocent queries of well-meaning whites leads to his

---

[A version of this essay was first presented as the Annual Thomas Merton Black History Month Lecture, Bellarmine University, Louisville, Kentucky, February 20, 2019; it was later published in *The Merton Annual* 33 (2020): 63–82.]

[1] W.E.B. Du Bois, *The Souls of Black Folk* (New York: Dover Publications, 1994), 1, emphasis added.

consideration of the "double-consciousness" that the structural, institutional, and historical realities of American racism force upon persons of color in general and women and men of African descent in particular. He adds: "It is a peculiar sensation, this double-consciousness, this sense of always looking at one's self through the eyes of others, of measuring one's soul by the tape of a world that looks on in amused contempt and pity. One ever feels his twoness—an American, a Negro; two souls, two thoughts, two unreconciled strivings; two warring ideals in one dark body, whose dogged strength alone keeps it from being torn asunder."[2]

Du Bois's reflection on the effects of the white gaze on his black body anticipates the reflections of Frantz Fanon half-a-century later, who likewise calls out the subjugating presence of whiteness and the deleterious effects on identity that come from our often unwitting performance of whiteness.[3] "The white man is all around me; up above the sky is tearing at its navel; the earth crunches under my feet and sings white, white. All this whiteness burns me to a cinder," declares Fanon.[4] The generally unspoken—though sometimes terribly shouted—presumption in a white-supremacist context such as the United States is that racism is a "black problem," wherein those who are systemically disenfranchised, oppressed, silenced, and erased are made to believe they are responsible, which is one of many disturbing results of the performance of whiteness seen as identical to normativity and authentic selfhood.[5] And, as

---

[2] Ibid., 2.

[3] It is widely recognized across subdisciplines of critical theory that identity categories such as gender, sexuality, and race are not merely ideological but also embodied realities. As such, one is not simply "white" or "black" but *performs* that racial identity in a manner analogous to the performance of gender in everyday life. One analysis of the performance of whiteness in scholarly literature is found in John T. Warren, "Doing Whiteness: On the Performative Dimensions of Race in the Classroom," *Communication Education* 50 (April 2001): 91–108. Also, see Richard Delgado, *Critical Race Theory: The Cutting Edge*, 2nd ed. (Philadelphia: Temple University Press, 2000).

[4] Frantz Fanon, *Black Skin, White Masks,* trans. Richard Philcox (New York: Grove Press, 2008), 94.

[5] Andrew Prevot, "Sources of a Black Self? Ethics of Authenticity in an Era of Anti-Blackness," in *Anti-Blackness and Christian Ethics*, ed. Vincent W. Lloyd and Andrew Prevot (Maryknoll, NY: Orbis Books, 2017), 77–95.

theologian Kelly Brown Douglas and others rightfully note, in the United States (and elsewhere) Christianity has been complicit in the normalizing and promotion of anti-black racism in this way.[6]

An honest analysis of our national and ecclesial contexts reveals an often-avoided truth that persons of color have known from the time of European colonization of Indigenous American lands and the establishment of a "slavocracy"[7] on this continent: racism is a *white* problem. This simple truth about a complex and historically entrenched reality appears in the writings of Thomas Merton. In "Letters to a White Liberal," occasioned by Martin Luther King, Jr.'s impassioned "Letter from Birmingham Jail," Merton at one point reflects on the significance of the nonviolent protests for racial justice led by King and others:

> The purpose of non-violent protest, in its deepest and most spiritual dimensions is then to awaken the conscience of the white man to the awful reality of his injustice and of his sin, so that he will be able to see that the Negro problem is really a *White* problem: that the cancer of injustice and hate which is eating white society and is only partly manifested in racial segregation with all its consequences, *is rooted in the heart of the white man himself.*[8]

As numerous Merton scholars, historians, and theologians have noted in the decades since the publication of this essay in 1964, Merton was in many ways ahead of his time. His direct criticism of well-intentioned Northern whites—the so-called liberals—for their lack of adequate self-reflection, humility, and openness to the righteous laments of the black population they so eagerly wished to assist, garnered both scathing

---

[6] Kelly Brown Douglas, *What's Faith Got to Do with It? Black Bodies/Christian Souls* (Maryknoll, NY: Orbis Books, 2005).

[7] Alternatively, some historians of Antebellum United States history have referred to this context as a "Plantocracy," alluding to the socioeconomic structures that established and depended upon chattel slavery in a plantation system. For example, see Michael Craton, "Property and Propriety: Land Tenure and Slave Property in the Creation of a British West Indian Plantocracy, 1612–1740," in *Conceptions of Property*, ed. John Brewer (London: Routledge, 1996), 497–529.

[8] Thomas Merton, "Letters to a White Liberal," in *Seeds of Destruction* (New York: Farrar, Straus, and Giroux, 1964), 45–46.

blowback in his time and near-unanimous praise in subsequent decades.[9] Merton is correct. Racism *is* a white problem, and he deserves appropriate credit for recognizing and naming what so many other white women and men could not or would not do in his time (or in ours). But what has received far less attention—to my knowledge, actually no substantive attention—is the role of Merton's own *whiteness* in his outlook and writings on racism and racial justice. In other words, is it enough simply to name the reality that racism is a white problem? What responsibility do those who identify or are perceived as white have to unpack the claim that racism is a white problem? Are there limits to Merton's own self-awareness, shifting perspectives on race in America, and both his diagnostic and prescriptive exhortations? Admittedly, a thorough study of these and other questions would require far more time and space than I have in a single chapter, but it is my intention to at least begin an exploration of these themes here.

This chapter is organized into four parts. First, to understand the role of whiteness in the antiracist writings and outlook of Merton, we need briefly to examine what it means in terms of race, social location, and interpersonal orientation. Here I draw on the work of philosophers and theorists, including Sarah Ahmed, George Yancy, and Robin DiAngelo. Second, I argue that there is indeed a prophetic valence to Merton's antiracist writings, which made notable contributions in his time and beyond, particularly within the Catholic Christian context of the mid-twentieth century. Third, in addition to the constructive contributions of Merton's thought there are also limits to his own white self-criticality that

---

[9] On the contemporaneous criticism, see Martin E. Marty, "An Interview about Thomas Merton," *The Merton Annual* 25 (2012): 13–22; and idem, "To: Thomas Merton; Re: Your Prophecy," *National Catholic Reporter* 3.34 (August 30, 1967), 6. For a sampling of the affirming responses, see Daniel P. Horan, "A Spirituality of Resistance: Thomas Merton on the Violence of Structural Racism in America," in *American Catholicism in the Twenty-First Century: Crossroads, Crisis, or Renewal?* ed. Benjamin T. Peters and Nicholas Rademacher (Maryknoll, NY: Orbis Books, 2018), 189–200; M. Shawn Copeland, "The Watchmen and the Witnesses: Thomas Merton, Martin Luther King, Jr., and the Exercise of the Prophetic," *The Merton Annual* 30 (2017): 156–70; Christopher Pramuk, "'The Street Is for Celebration'": Racial Consciousness and the Eclipse of Childhood in America's Cities," *The Merton Annual* 25 (2012): 91–103; Albert J. Raboteau, *A Fire in the Bones: Reflections on African-American Religious History* (Boston: Beacon Press, 1995); and James Thomas Baker, *Thomas Merton: Social Critic* (Lexington: University Press of Kentucky, 1971).

have largely gone unexamined. While not attempting to be exhaustive, I want to identify some of these limitations in his thought and writing. Finally, I conclude with a brief presentation of the insights Merton provides us with today, particularly in light of recent US bishops' pastoral statements on racism.[10]

Whiteness and the Reality of Systemic Racism

To begin, we need to acknowledge that *race* is a social construct. It is the false belief "that superficial adaptations to geography (skin tone, eye shape) are genetic and biological determinants that result in significant differences among groups of human beings."[11] Many of us have been socialized, generally in a tacit or unwitting manner, to believe that there are biological or genetic distinctions between races that correlate to phenotype, which is the way one appears or is perceived according to skin color. But this is not correct. Scholar Robin DiAngelo explains:

> The idea of race as biological makes it easy to believe that many of the divisions we see in society are natural. But race, like gender, is socially constructed. The differences we *do see* with our eyes, such as hair texture and eye color, are superficial and emerged as adaptations to geography; there really is no race under the skin. The differences we *believe* we see (Lakisha is less qualified than Emily, or Jamal is more prone to violence) are a result of our socialization; our racial lenses. While there is no biological race as we understand it, race as a *social construction* has profound significance and impacts every aspect of our lives.[12]

This recognition of what scholars call scientific racism, tenuous linkages between race and biology, is an important starting point for conversations about race and racism in the United States. When we talk about race, we have to recall that there is a deeply complex social and institutional

---

[10] United States Conference of Catholic Bishops (USCCB), "Open Wide Our Hearts, The Enduring Call to Love: A Pastoral Letter against Racism" (November 2018).

[11] Robin DiAngelo, *What Does It Mean to Be White? Developing White Racial Literacy*, rev. ed. (New York: Peter Lang Publishing, 2016), 101.

[12] Ibid., 98.

context that undergirds and reinforces certain power relations, identity formation, and assumptions associated with how one appears physically with regard to certain spoken and unspoken cultural norms.

In discussions about race in the United States it is commonplace for whites to recognize and talk about the burdens suffered by and the oppression of persons of African descent, Indigenous peoples, and other persons of color, but it is less common for whites to recognize and talk about *whiteness* and its relationship to these burdens and oppression. While there are many reasons why this oversight or ignorance may be the case in a given circumstance, there are two predominant factors that undoubtedly shape this phenomenon within the American context: assumptions of normativity and the denial of structural racism.

First, white women and men do not generally talk about whiteness because the dynamics that make possible the burdening and oppression of persons of color also cover over the reality of "whiteness" as a racial marker within this web of relations. As a result, that which is perceived to be white is viewed—by whites socialized in an anti-black racist society and by persons of color who have internalized this same socialization—to be normative, neutral, acceptable, ordinary, the default, or the ideal. Because it is socially constructed, those who are considered "white" vary with time. As theologian Bryan Massingale has explained, "It is important to note that 'white' is a fluid category that has come to include over the years ethnic groups from other parts of the world" beyond those of Western European descent.[13] Historians note that various groups immigrating to the United States, despite ostensibly shared phenotype, had been considered non-white until those in the position of dominance determined it was socially acceptable to include this or that ethnic population. The historical record of shifting admission to the social category of "white" itself should further trouble any assumption of an objective, static, or scientific grounding for race.

Philosopher Sara Ahmed further highlights this first reason that whiteness is not generally recognized by whites. "It has become commonplace for whiteness to be represented as invisible, as the unseen or the unmarked, as non-color, the absent presence or hidden referent,

---

[13] Bryan N. Massingale, *Racial Justice and the Catholic Church* (Maryknoll, NY: Orbis Books, 2010), 2.

against which all other colors are measured as forms of deviance."[14] To be white is to be normative and without need for a qualifier in this society. As the theorist George Lipsitz explains: "Whiteness is everywhere in U.S. culture, but it is very hard to see. . . . As the unmarked category against which difference is constructed, whiteness never has to speak its name, never has to acknowledge its rule as an organizing principle in social and cultural relations."[15] To sum up the occlusion of whiteness for white people, philosopher George Yancy explains:

> The fact of the matter is that, for white people, whiteness is the transcendental norm in terms of which they live their lives as persons, individuals. People of color, however, confront whiteness in their everyday lives, not as an abstract concept but in the form of embodied whites who engage in racist practices that negatively affect their lives. Black people and people of color thus strive to disarticulate the link between whiteness and the assumption of just being human, to create a critical slippage.[16]

Elsewhere, Yancy likens the socialization of whites into whiteness to the way native English speakers learn English growing up: "One learns English in the context of the everyday by hearing it spoken. The 'subject' of the language-learning process does not self-consciously incorporate the grammar of English. Yet parents engage in correcting the linguistic performances of their children; this is part of what it means to inhabit a linguistic community."[17] Likewise, white people inhabit a racialized community in which they "become white" through subtle, uncritical, and tacit socialization. At times there are stronger signals sent to "correct" the "racial grammar" of white performance.

A second key factor that inhibits whites from recognizing the reality of whiteness is the pervasive denial of systemic or cultural racism today, particularly within the context of the United States. The most common

---

[14] Sara Ahmed, "Declarations of Whiteness: The Non-Performativity of Anti-Racism," *borderlands e-journal* 3 (2004).

[15] George Lipsitz, *The Possessive Investment in Whiteness: How White People Profit from Identity Politics,* rev. ed. (Philadelphia: Temple University Press, 2006), 1.

[16] George Yancy, *Look, A White! Philosophical Essays on Whiteness* (Philadelphia: Temple University Press, 2012), 7.

[17] Ibid., 24–25.

iteration of this dismissal takes the form of a conflation of "racism" with discrete acts of racial animus, such as the use of derogatory slurs or particular acts of violence. In this way white people who do not actively seek to harm people of color or consciously hold disparaging prejudices against non-whites move to exonerate themselves from charges of racism or being labeled a racist. The truth is that racism is not limited to discrete or isolated racist actions but is a deeply imbedded social reality from which no one is immune, whether one appears to benefit from this structure or is harmed by it. Massingale explains: "Racism, at its core, is a set of meanings and values that inform the American way of life. It is a way of understanding and interpreting skin color differences so that white Americans enjoy a privileged social status with access to advantages and benefits to the detriment, disadvantage, and burden of persons of color."[18] It is like the water in which fish swim, the air in which we move and live and breathe. Furthermore, this conflation of discrete acts of racist animus that typifies what a "racist *does*" with the structural and cultural reality of racism is made more contentious by the moral valences associated with the term *racist*—racists are *bad*, but I am good; therefore I cannot be a racist! At issue here is the confusion of culpability and complicity. Indeed, those who act in overtly racist ways, who use derogatory language or promote a white supremacist ideology, are personally *culpable* for the sin of racism. And yet, all of us who benefit from or are advantaged by a structurally racist society are *complicit* in the sin of structural or cultural racism.

As DiAngelo reiterates: "Racism is deeply embedded into the fabric of our society. It is not limited to a single act or a single person."[19] Racism in this context is also not to be confused with "race prejudice" as such, which is when any individual or group—even those minoritized by and oppressed in a given society—hold biases against others based on race. This is *not* racism or "reverse racism," as it is sometimes described. "Racism does not move back and forth, one day benefiting whites and another day (or even era) benefiting people of color. The direction of power between whites and people of color is historic, traditional, and normalized in ideology."[20] This is what is so difficult for those in the

---

[18] Massingale, *Racial Justice and the Catholic Church*, 42.
[19] DiAngelo, *What Does It Mean to Be White?* 108.
[20] Ibid.

dominant position in a racist society to accept: that even if you are not personally guilty of racist actions as colloquially defined, if you are white you are nevertheless complicit in the racist structures of our society, institutions, and even the church. DiAngelo offers a substantive definition of what we mean by racism:

> Racism is a form of oppression in which one racial group dominates others. In the United States, whites are the dominant group and people of color are the minoritized group. Thus in this context, racism is white racial and cultural prejudice and discrimination, supported intentionally *or unintentionally* by institutional power and authority, used to the advantage of whites and the disadvantage of people of color. Racism encompasses economic, political, social, and institutional actions and beliefs, which systematize and perpetuate an unequal distribution of privileges, resources, and power between whites and people of color.[21]

When this reality is avoided or denied, white people further challenge their individual and collective ability to see their participation in a racist context and recognize their own performative whiteness. It is worth noting briefly that, while I am highlighting two major factors at work in the occlusion of whiteness, there are many other factors that contribute to making racism in general and whiteness in particular difficult for whites to see. Such factors include the perpetuation of a "racists are bad, nonracists are good" binary; the consequences of seeing whites as individuals not tied to larger social, cultural, institutional, and religious structures; reinscriptions of the false claim of color-blindness; a sense of entitlement to "racial comfort" (that is, avoidance of hard truths about complicity, privilege, injustice); willful or even invincible ignorance about the impact and power of whiteness in a racist society; and the preponderance of racially segregated contexts in which whites and people of color live, the former by choice, the latter not so much.[22]

Despite these challenges to white self-awareness, philosopher Linda Martín Alcoff notes that research compellingly shows how "whiteness impacts perceptual attunements and modes of interaction as well as

---

[21] Ibid., 107–8.
[22] Ibid., 157–213.

the associations and connotations that affect judgment."[23] Put simply, whiteness shapes identity formation, outlook on the world, and behavior, regardless of whether white people choose to acknowledge it or not. In her analytic of whiteness Alcoff highlights three aspects of social identity in this regard. The first is "empirical whiteness," which is approaching the reality of whiteness from an object of empirical study. Demography, geography, migratory and political shifts, institutional affiliations, and the like constitute the modes in which empirical whiteness is manifest. The second aspect is what Alcoff calls "imaginary whiteness," by which she *does not mean* "make believe" or a sense of falseness. Rather, this an approach to understanding whiteness refers to the manner in which white people construct their understanding of the world and sense of affiliation with or connection to other white people and to "a white dominant community or nation."[24] This is an approach to understanding whiteness as it functions to shade and form perception, both individually and collectively. Finally, the third aspect is "subjective whiteness," which is Alcoff's shorthand to describe the way of white being-in-the-world. Alcoff brings together both the racialized construction of identity of whiteness with the manifold ways white people actively and unwittingly dismiss or ignore its veracity according to the way whites are subjects in the world. She explains:

> To say, then, that whiteness is involved in the constitution of the self means that our core set of routine perceptual and epistemic practices and our everyday habits of social interaction, interpretation, and judgment need to be analyzed in relation to a specific racialization process involving whiteness. Such phenomena are not universal: other groups may have less of an investment in epistemologies of ignorance and their very survival may require better epistemic habits, such as the need to listen carefully to what others have to say. We need to recognize that whiteness is not simply about our conscious awareness, nor is it simply about structural patterns of social inequality or cultural representations that we can simply re-pudiate. We also need to avoid assuming that everyone undergoes

---

[23] Linda Martín Alcoff, *The Future of Whiteness* (Malden, MA: Polity Press, 2015), 89.

[24] Alcoff, *The Future of Whiteness*, 81.

an essentially generic and universal process of personality formation that is only afterward connected to racialized differences.[25]

It is this last aspect that is of greatest interest to me in thinking about Merton's understanding of racism as a white problem. The question remains: What role did Merton's *whiteness*, in all the ways acknowledged so far, including the ways it is overlooked or ignored, play in his understanding of racism and racial justice? Before proposing a response to this question, we must turn to his writings to examine the ways in which his antiracist writings were indeed notably prophetic.

The Prophetic Nature of Merton's Antiracist Writings

There is a lot in Merton's writings on racism that is laudable and reflects a truly prophetic quality, particularly when we view his social location and historical context: he was a white, Euro-American male, renowned author, ordained Catholic priest, and cloistered monk, set somewhat apart from the world in the bluegrass hillside of rural Kentucky during the 1940s, '50s, and '60s. Amid a setting that would appear to be among the least conducive to an experience of ongoing conversion to the "signs of the times," to a growing awareness of the racial injustice that plagued the United States, Merton "turned to the world" (as Merton scholars often say) with conviction and moral clarity not found in many of his fellow white Roman Catholic clergy, let alone members of cloistered religious orders. His attunement to the *sensus plenior* (fuller sense), to borrow a technical scriptural term, of the conditions of racial injustice in the United States is striking. While he does not get everything exactly correct—we will look at some of that in the next section—Merton does arrive at an awareness of and response to several key realities that many if not most whites in his time (and since) have overlooked or willfully ignored. While there are surely other areas that could be discussed, I wish to highlight three notable dimensions of Merton's antiracist writings that reveal a distinctly prophetic character.[26] First, he recognized and called

---

[25] Ibid., 85.

[26] On Merton and the prophetic, see Copeland, "The Watchmen and the Witnesses," 156–70; Daniel P. Horan, "Seeing the World As It Really Is: The Prophetic Legacy of Thomas Merton," in *We Are Already One: Thomas Merton's Message of Hope*,

out the reality of systemic or structural racism beyond the particularity of individual and overt racist acts. Second, he identified the anti-black racist culture imbedded in American Christian communities. And, third, he acknowledged white complicity in the establishment and perpetuation of systemic and institutional racism, which led him to proclaim that racism is a white problem.

The Reality of Systemic Racism

The most widely read of Merton's antiracist writings is his essay "Letters to a White Liberal." Written in 1963 in response to Martin Luther King, Jr.'s, "Letter from Birmingham Jail," this lengthy reflection on the nature of anti-black racism in the United States is presented as Merton's attempt to listen, process, and integrate what he is hearing and reading about the quest for racial justice, especially from the perspective of black authors and civil rights leaders. In the conclusion of the essay Merton explains that his aim was as introspective as it was exhortatory, stating plainly that what is necessary for white people is that they actually listen to their black sisters and brothers. He writes: "This is the 'message' which the Negro is trying to give white America. I have spelled it out for myself, subject to correction, in order to see whether a white man is even capable of grasping the words, let alone believing them."[27] He is modeling a mode of self-education, of awakening to the reality of racial injustice occluded by the performance of whiteness. White people, like him, have to *will* to know, open themselves to the message and experience and instruction of those disadvantaged by the same unjust system that accrues unearned benefits and privileges to whites. Merton explains: "For the rest [of you], you have Moses and the Prophets: Martin Luther King, James Baldwin and the others. Read them, and see for yourself what they are saying."[28]

So what are the modern antiracist "Moses and the Prophets" saying to white people? From Merton's perspective, part of their admonitions is

---

ed. Gray Henry and Jonathan Montaldo (Louisville, KY: Fons Vitae, 2014), 57–63; and William Apel, "Mystic as Prophet: The Deep Freedom of Thomas Merton and Howard Thurman," *The Merton Annual* 16 (2003): 172–87.

[27] Merton, "Letters to a White Liberal," 70.

[28] Ibid., 70.

focused on the pervasiveness of systemic racism. As Merton explains in his preface to the French translation of part of "Letters to a White Liberal," this reality, all-too-often unacknowledged by whites, is something governed by emotions and the unconscious. He explains: "American racism has something of the character of an ineradicable and axiomatic conviction, which is accepted as the basis for an entire outlook on life and becomes the logical presupposition for inhuman conclusions. The chief of these is the justification of any form of violence, hatred, [and] cruelty."[29]

Merton regularly makes the important distinction between individual acts of racist animus and the reality of systemic racism. He describes the inherently unjust laws and structures that ground American society. For example, in an essay written in the fall of 1967, Merton observes:

> It is pointless to say that the laws guarantee the Negro all the same rights as white people. We know that the laws are not enforced and the Negro is often denied his obvious rights; but also economically speaking the Negro remains in the same position as he was before, perhaps worse. He is convinced that there is no real place for him in our established society except the very secondary place which we will give him. It is a psychological impossibility for most white Americans really to accept a Negro as an equal, in every respect, and the violent struggle against open housing has proved it.[30]

Anticipating those whites who would protest the reality of structural and institutional racism by claiming that progress has been made and that there are now clear laws protecting people of color from unfair treatment, Merton responds: "You will point to the Supreme Court decisions that have upheld Negro rights, to education in integrated colleges and schools. It seems to me that our motives are judged by the real fruit of our decisions. What have we done?" To his own question, he responds: "We have been willing to grant the Negro rights on paper, even in the South. But the laws have been framed in such a way that in every case

---

[29] Thomas Merton, "Preface to the French Edition of *The Black Revolution* (December 1963)," in *Introductions East and West: The Foreign Prefaces of Thomas Merton*, ed. Robert Daggy (Ontario: Mosaic Press, 1981), 55.

[30] Thomas Merton, "The Hot Summer of Sixty-Seven," in *Faith and Violence* (Notre Dame, IN: University of Notre Dame Press, 1968), 173.

their execution has depended on the good will of white society, and the white man has not failed, when left to himself, to block, obstruct, or simply forget the necessary action without which the rights of the Negro cannot be enjoyed in fact."[31]

Merton recognized that a structurally racist society such as the United States operates in an inherently unjust and violent manner, though to those in positions of power or dominance—white people in general and white men in particular—the system appears orderly, sensible, and just. In an article titled "Toward a Theology of Resistance," Merton points to how this dynamic plays out within the American context in which the white majority views crime or violence in communities of color, communities segregated by the unjust laws and practices of the racist society, and explains:

> But it must be remembered that the crime that breaks out of the ghetto is only the fruit of a greater and more pervasive violence: the injustice which forces people to live in the ghetto in the first place. The problem of violence, then, is not the problem of a few rioters and rebels, but the problem of a whole social structure which is outwardly ordered and respectable, and inwardly ridden by psychopathic obsessions and delusions.[32]

For Merton, this phenomenon of systemic racism as part and parcel of American culture is not limited to the sphere of civil politics or social norms but also implicates the Catholic Church and Christianity writ large in the United States.

Racism in American Christianity

Debunking the myth that racism exists only in the American South, Merton notes in a 1965 article, "Religion and Race in the United States," that African Americans in the North are quite aware of the deeply imbedded institutional racism of Christianity in this country: "The Northern Negro is, generally speaking, disillusioned with the Churches

---

[31] Merton, "Letters to a White Liberal," 19.

[32] Thomas Merton, "Toward a Theology of Resistance," in *Faith and Violence*, 3.

and with the Christian preaching of moderation and nonviolence. His feeling is that the Churches are part of the establishment (which in fact they are!). They support the power-structure and therefore (he believes) keep the Negro deluded and passive, preventing him from fighting for his rights."[33] In recognizing as he does that the "problem of American racism turned out to be far deeper, far more stubborn, infinitely more complex" than most whites would care to admit, this raises urgent and perennial concerns for the church.[34]

Merton recognized the choice placed before Christians in general and Christian leaders in particular. He writes: "The American racial crisis which grows more serious every day offers the American Christian a chance to face reality about himself and recover his fidelity to Christian truth, not merely in institutional loyalties and doctrinal orthodoxies . . . but in recanting a more basic heresy: the loss of that Christian sense which sees every other man as Christ and treats him as Christ."[35] In a way anticipating Pope Francis's call to address the more radical, that is fundamental and grounded, principles of our Christian faith, Merton speaks across the decades to our modern self-appointed and self-righteous "orthodoxy police," what I have taken to calling the "trolling pontiffs" of social media or others call "alt-Catholics," and says that all the hand-wringing about liturgical preferences or doctrinal debates are worthless unless Christians—particularly white Christians—address this essential social sin. I believe the way Jesus of Nazareth talked about this point was in terms of splinters and wooden beams in one's eyes.

Building on his writing about systemic racism more broadly, Merton makes clear that the consequences of racial injustice within the church is also a white problem and one that requires choosing to acknowledge this reality and accept the conversion necessary to make some radical changes from the status quo. Addressing his fellow white Christians, he says:

In the American crisis the Christian faces a typical choice. The choice is not interior and secret, but public, political and social. He is perhaps not used to regarding his crucial choices in the light of

---

[33] Thomas Merton, "Religion and Race in the United States," in *Faith and Violence*, 131.

[34] Ibid., 133.

[35] Ibid., 143.

politics. He can now either find security and order by falling back on antique and basically feudal (or perhaps fascist) conceptions, or go forward into the unknown future, identifying himself with the forces that will inevitably create a new society. The choice is between "safety," based on negation of the new and reaffirmation of the familiar, or the creative risk of love and grace in new and untried solutions, which justice nevertheless demands.[36]

This focus on the choice at hand impugns the collective innocence of white Christians and the church writ large. Racism is a white problem within American Christianity because, as with the broader American context, the structures, institutions, norms, and loci of power are created and held by whites. And nothing will change until whites take responsibility and dare to risk the cultural and society change that is necessary, which brings us to the third prophetic point of Merton's writings.

White Complicity and Racism As a White Problem

The most notably prophetic dimension of Merton's writings on race is his recognition of white complicity beyond discrete acts of racial animus and the need for whites to acknowledge that the same situation that oppresses others works to their advantage and benefit. For anything to change, white people need to recognize that racism is a white problem. In his "Letters to a White Liberal," Merton explains why the truth of systemic racism is so threatening for most whites to acknowledge:

> Here is why it is a source of uneasiness and fear to all white men who are attached to their security. If they are forced to listen to what the Negro is trying to say, the whites may have to admit that *their prosperity is rooted to some extent in injustice and in sin.* And, in consequence, this might lead to a complete re-examination of the political motives behind all our current policies, domestic and foreign, with the possible admission that we are wrong.[37]

Earlier in the same essay he acknowledges that the laws and social norms of our American society are deeply racist, which simultaneously oppresses

---

[36] Ibid., 138–39.
[37] Merton, "Letters to a White Liberal," 48.

some and advantages others: "If we have got to the point where the laws are frequently, if not commonly, framed in such a way that they can be easily evaded by a privileged group, then the very structure of our society comes into question."[38]

Merton was to some extent aware of how whiteness is performed in a structurally racist society such that, generally unbeknownst to the individual, white people actively participate in, reinscribe, and therefore perpetuate the racist system that is sinful and oppressive:

> There is, however, such a thing as collective responsibility, and collective guilt. This is not quite the same as personal responsibility and personal guilt, because it does not usually follow from a direct fully conscious act of choice. Few of us have actively and consciously *chosen* to oppress and mistreat the Negro. But nevertheless we have all more or less acquiesced in and consented to a state of affairs in which the Negro is treated unjustly, and in which his unjust treatment is directly or indirectly to the advantage of people like ourselves, people with whom we agree and collaborate, people with whom we are in fact identified. So that even if in theory the white man may believe himself well disposed toward the Negro—and never gets into a bind which he proves himself otherwise—we all collectively contribute to a situation in which the Negro has to live and act as our inferior. I am personally convinced that most white people who think of themselves as very "fair" to the Negro show, by the way they imagine themselves "fair," that they consider the Negro an inferior type of human being, a sort of "minor," and their "fairness" consists in giving him certain benefits provided he "keeps in his place," the place they have allocated to him as an inferior. I would like to say that this state of mind is itself an act of inhumanity and injustice against the Negro and is in fact at the root of the trouble with the Negro, so that anyone who holds such opinions, even in the best of faith, is contributing actively to the violence of the present situation whether he realizes it or not.[39]

---

[38] Ibid., 20.
[39] Thomas Merton, "The Hot Summer of Sixty-Seven," in *Faith and Violence,* 180–181.

He is addressing the subtle and destructive ways that racism operates in the daily lives of white people. Part of that complicity manifests itself in the presumption, as we saw in discussing whiteness in the first section of this article, that the white experience is normative and superior. Merton writes, "In simple terms, I would say that the message [black people want whites to hear] is this: white society has sinned in many ways. It has betrayed Christ by its injustices to races it considers 'inferior' and to countries which it colonized. In particular it has sinned against Christ in its lamentable injustices and cruelties to the Negro."[40] Elsewhere Merton reflects on the consequences of a white supremacist society such as ours, noting that its overt violence or legislation is not always as explicit as found in the Jim Crow South, but there are unexamined ways whites benefit financially and politically by the exploitation of persons of color.[41]

This sense of white superiority that pervades American society and collective historical memory is expressed bluntly as Merton reflects on the dynamic of white supremacy instituted in our society as it affects Native Americans in particular. He writes:

> But let us spell out quite clearly what this means. IT MEANS THAT, AS FAR AS WE ARE CONCERNED, THE INDIAN (LIKE THE NEGRO, THE ASIAN, ETC.) IS PERMITTED TO HAVE A HUMAN IDENTITY ONLY IN SO FAR AS HE CONFORMS TO OURSELVES AND TAKES UPON HIMSELF OUR IDENTITY. But since in fact the Indian, or the Negro, is in the position of having a different colored skin and other traits which make him unlike ourselves, he can never be like us and can therefore never have an identity. The lock snaps shut. The Indian, like the Negro (though perhaps less emphatically), is definitively excluded . . . In theory we recognize his humanity. In practice he is, like the Negro, at best a second-class human who tries to dress and act like ourselves but never quite manages to make the grade.[42]

Merton realized with prophetic clarity that racism in the United States is a white problem, which led him to state a sense of cautious hope that our society *could be different*, but it is up to whites. For, as he explains, "as long as white society persists in clinging to its present condition and to its own

---

[40] Merton, "Letters to a White Liberal," 66.

[41] See Merton, "From Non-Violence to Black Power," 129.

[42] Thomas Merton, *Ishi Means Man* (1976; New York: Paulist Press, 2015), 9.

image of itself as the only acceptable reality, then the problem will remain without reasonable solution, and there will inevitably be violence."[43]

Merton knew that the sickness of systemic racism was so pervasive, such an ideological cancer that had metastasized in all parts of American society, that radical change was necessary. But that change had to begin with whites, for as long as white women and men shirked the obligation to recognize the unjust system, it would continue unimpeded to benefit them and subjugate others. To put it bluntly, nothing would change until white people surrendered their privilege and unspoken sense of supremacy and normativity.

The Limits of Merton's White Self-Criticality

While Merton was far ahead of many white Roman Catholic clergy in his time—and, as scholars like Bryan Massingale have noted, still ahead of many white religious leaders in *our time* too—there are nevertheless limits to his understanding and discussion of race in the American context. I briefly highlight three such limitations.

First, the insights in recent decades from scholars of critical race theory offer us points to consider when looking at the role Merton's own whiteness played in his antiracist writings. A helpful starting point is to recognize plainly what scholars like Barbara Applebaum note, "Even whites who are willing to acknowledge that whites are the problem of racism and who are sensitized to the ways that whiteness works through its invisibility are not exempt from being implicated in racism."[44] This stark reminder rightly implicates me as much as it does Merton, which is something for all of us to keep in mind. It is not merely enough to speak the truth of systemic racism and white complicity, or to stake a position of solidarity as Merton does at one point, stating:

Black Power or no Black Power, I for one remain *for* the Negro. I trust him, I recognize the overwhelming justice of his complaint,

---

[43] Merton, "Letters to a White Liberal," 8.

[44] Barbara Applebaum, "Flipping the Script . . . and Still a Problem: Staying in the Anxiety of Being a Problem," in *White Self-Criticality beyond Anti-Racism: How Does It Feel to Be a White Problem?*, ed. George Yancy (Lanham, MA: Lexington Books, 2015), 1–2.

I confess I have no right whatever to get in his way, and that as a Christian I owe him support, not in his ranks but in my own, among the whites who refuse to trust him or hear him, and who want to destroy him.[45]

Genuine and well-intentioned as that statement surely is, Merton's writings could be interpreted at times as an effort to signal his own innocence, awareness, or as it is said frequently today, that he is "woke." As Applebaum reminds us, given the deeply imbedded and socialized reality of systemic racism: "Whiteness continuously 'ensnares' and 'ambushes' white people so that whiteness finds ways to hide 'even as one attempts honest efforts to resist it.' Being an anti-racist white, therefore, is a project that always requires another step and does not end in a white person's having 'arrived' in the form of an idyllic anti-racist."[46]

We can see this dynamic at work in the variation of perspective that Merton offers over the course of his writing on race during the 1960s. In the wake of the increasing violence and the rise of the Black Power movements, Merton appears to equivocate at times in his later writings about the validity and the problematics of civil rights protests toward the end of the decade as things become more violent. He seems to want to hold on to earlier claims he made during the nonviolent demonstrations of Martin Luther King, Jr., and others, that racism is an inherently white problem in the United States, but it appears in his essay "The Hot Summer of Sixty-Seven" that, while the performance of whiteness and the policies of dominance have led to this violence, he calls for a "both sides" approach to responsibility, sublimating the social, political, and cultural problems into a "spiritual crisis." At times he struggles to accept the analogs he himself makes of the violence in search of racial justice, such as when he offers this recapitulation:

To sum it up: the problem as I see it is this. The Negro has in some sense abandoned the struggle for Civil Rights. He has given up Christian non-violence as futile idealism. He has decided that whitey only understands one kind of language: violence. The Negro has concluded that if whitey wants to terrorize Vietnamese with

---

[45] Merton, "From Non-Violence to Black Power," 129.
[46] Applebaum, "Flipping the Script . . . and Still a Problem," 11.

napalm and other cozy instruments of war, he should have a little taste of what fire and terror feel like at home.[47]

The change in tone reflects the ambivalence Merton feels toward maintaining his otherwise consistent theme of racism as a white problem. Here that thesis begins to slip as he signals the blame ought to be shared by at least those people of color who do not subscribe to King's earlier nonviolent approach.

A second limit is the re-inscription of white normativity present in Merton's writing even as he at times explicitly identifies this as problematic. Take for example a brief passage in *Conjectures of a Guilty Bystander* in which, as an aside, he reveals a perception that only non-whites "have race." Merton writes:

> The core of the race problem as I see it is this: the Negro (also other racial groups of course, but chiefly the Negro) is victimized by the psychological and social conflicts now inherent in a white civilization that fears imminent disruption and has no mature insight into the reality of its crisis. White society is purely and simply incapable of really accepting the Negro and assimilating him, because white people cannot cope with their own drives, cannot defend themselves against their own emotions, which are supremely unstable in a rapidly changing and overstimulated society.[48]

We see this elsewhere, too, when Merton ties the reality of American racism to the experiences of colonization and subjugation of populations around the globe. Such is the case when he associates African Americans in solidarity with "colored races in all parts of the world."[49] It would appear that Merton's own white self-criticality was limited by his own socialization, which despite his best intentions nevertheless prevented him at times from recognizing his own whiteness as a marker of race itself. Given his spiritual outlook and concern about the role of the church in a systemically racist context, Merton is notably sloppy about the way he sometimes refers to Christians or Christianity

---

[47] Merton, "The Hot Summer of Sixty-Seven," 175.

[48] Thomas Merton, *Conjectures of a Guilty Bystander* (New York: Image Books, 2009), 24–25.

[49] Merton, "Religion and Race in the United States," 134–35.

in distinctively white terms. Oftentimes the rhetorical device is that "Christians" need to do something about racism, that their complicity in systemic racism is sinful. As true as that statement is, it too often lacks the necessary qualifier "white" in *white Christians.* This oversight, unintentional as it may have been, nevertheless belies an important limitation.

Finally, at least one more limitation in Merton's writings is the way he views the relationship between whites and blacks, the problem and the oppressed. This has two iterations worth noting: complementarity and pedagogy. In terms of complementarity, there are several passages, particularly in "Letters to a White Liberal," where Merton describes the "necessity" of blacks for white folk. While clearly attempting to identify our social and ecclesial interdependence, the framing of the complementary nature of the races could be read as instrumentalizing the existence of black folk for the sake or benefit of whites. "This means to say that a genuinely Catholic attitude in matters of race is one which concretely accepts and fully recognizes the fact that different races and cultures are *correlative. They mutually complete one another.* The white man needs the Negro, and needs to know that he needs him. White calls for black just as black calls for white."[50] There is here a diminished sense of agency and intrinsic identity, leading toward a problematic utilitarian understanding of racial justice.

The second iteration is seen in the way in which Merton at times invokes black authors and leaders as responsible for the education of whites.[51] Again, it seems benign enough, but there is a form of instrumentalizing people of color for the edification of white antiracist intentions when whites expect blacks to "teach" or "educate" them. The proper response is to come to see one's participation in and performance of whiteness as a social field and racial marker in a systemically racist society and then educate oneself. Realizing one's whiteness ought to be the beginning of an ongoing and lifelong process of conversion and education. As philosopher Bridget Newell notes, "The realization itself positions one to take responsibility to learn more about racism and whiteness—accepting the wisdom and experience of others but not

---

[50] Merton, "Letters to a White Liberal," 61.
[51] See ibid., 66–70.

passively waiting for others to impart wisdom or teach her."[52] At times Merton clearly goes out of his way to educate himself, but his overall writing on the importance of whites hearing the voices of people of color is ambivalent in terms of whose responsibility—or problem—it is to learn and be educated.

Conclusion

There is much more that can and ought to be said about Thomas Merton's writings on race and racial justice, as well as the role that whiteness plays in his own experience and outlook. His writings still contain a strongly prophetic valence and remain timely as systemic racism persists today. Nevertheless, this does not mean that his writings on race and racial justice are without fault or limitation. Indeed, his work can and does serve as an important starting point, but we ought to supplement—and at times critique—his writing with the best of critical race theory and other contemporary scholarship, which offers us a more multidimensional understanding of the reality of racism in the American context.

In closing, it is worth noting that Merton's wisdom and striking ability to read the "signs of the times" still exceeds that of the primary ecclesial leaders in the United States. In November 2018 the United States Conference of Catholic Bishops approved a pastoral statement on racism titled "Open Wide Our Hearts," in which the bishops attempt to highlight and discuss the problem of racism today. It was the first major statement in the forty years after the conference had released the abysmally titled "Brothers and Sisters *to Us*" in 1979. Sadly, in the 2018 document the bishops never use the terms *privilege* or *supremacy,* and when they use the term *white* three times, it is always in the context of generally positive historic reference to ages long ago.[53] This newer document discusses in passive and allusive terms the reality of oppression and violence as a result of the racism but fails to identify the cause of the problem or the perpetrator. In an apparent effort to allay the fears of

---

[52] Bridget M. Newell, "Being a White Problem and Feeling It," in *White Self-Criticality beyond Anti-Racism*, 136.

[53] Daniel P. Horan, "The Bishops' Letter Fails to Recognize Racism Is a White Problem," *National Catholic Reporter* (February 20, 2019).

whites, the document presents a false narrative that has been described by scholar Eduardo Bonila-Silva as "racism without racists."[54] For all his contextual and self-critical limitations, at least Thomas Merton was able to plainly state that, in the United States, racism has been and remains *a white problem.*

---

[54] Eduardo Bonila-Silva, *Racism without Racists: Color-Blind Racism and the Persistence of Racial Inequality in America*, 5th ed. (Lanham, MA: Lexington Books, 2018).

14

Martin, Malcolm, and Merton

*The Work for Racial Justice
and the Responsibility of Catholic Spirituality*

On April 4, 2018, we marked a half-century since the life of the Rev. Dr. Martin Luther King, Jr., was taken by assassination. He was thirty-nine years old. He has now been dead longer than he had lived. And over the course of those five decades, the name, memory, speeches, sermons, writings, and legacy of King have gone through numerous shifts and changes. National holidays have been established, a memorial in Washington has been erected, and classroom textbooks that teach the next generation of Americans about his life and legacy have been written. Like the canonical saints in the Christian community, the civil rights saints of this nation are often dismissed by elevation, celebrated in general but ignored in their particularity, remembered for the tragedy of their martyrdom but forgotten for the reason they were murdered in the first place.

It has been said with good reason that the real legacy of Martin Luther King, Jr., the power of his convictions and the admonitions he was not afraid to level against his brothers and sisters, has been, to use an uncomfortably apt term, *whitewashed* by our collective white American imaginary.[1] For many, he is the safe and comfortable patron saint of the American civil rights period, who espoused nonviolent

---

[A version of this essay was first presented as the Jennifer Koon Peacemaking Lecture, Saint John Fisher College, Rochester, New York, April 29, 2018; it was later published in *The Merton Seasonal* 44 (Spring 2019): 3–12. Used with permission.]

[1] For more, see Martin Luther King, Jr., *The Radical King*, ed. Cornel West (Boston: Beacon Press, 2015), esp. ix–xvi.

189

resistance and preached peace. While celebrated as a minister with a powerful voice and a strong presence, his legacy is generally recalled without risk of personal indictment or embarrassment, challenge or exhortation. He is typically thought of as a kind man who would not rock the *white boat* while forging across the river of injustice in a manner befitting George Washington crossing the Delaware. And while there is truth in these memories, there is nevertheless selectivity at play in this recollection.

Our institutional selective memory has painted the United States civil rights period of the 1960s as a tale of two black leaders: one good, the other bad; one peaceful, the other violent; one celebrated, the other feared; one Martin Luther King, Jr., and the other Malcolm X. Such a binary way of viewing our collective history reduces King to a carica-ture and erases the memory of Malcolm. The purpose of this chapter is not simply to restore the full character and dangerous memory of each man—to do so would take more time and space than I have here. Instead, I offer a more narrow restorative focus: to go back to the 1960s accompanied by Thomas Merton to revisit the insights, wisdom, and challenge of King and Malcolm. For Merton, their admonitions were not caricatured or exaggerated, but received in a manner distinctive among white Catholic clergy of his time (Merton's voice is sadly still distinctive in our time too).

Here is how I have organized what follows in this chapter. First, I want to look at Merton and Martin Luther King, Jr. Next, I want to look at Merton and Malcolm X. Finally, I want to consider the insights that arose for Merton from his engagement with the life, writings, and legacies of King and Malcolm X to highlight the responsibility we have as Catholics to incorporate the work for racial justice into our Christian spirituality and practice, especially for those who occupy social locations of privilege in a society that remains deeply scarred by the realities of structural racism.

Merton and Martin Luther King, Jr.

In his influential book *A Fire in the Bones: Reflections on African-American Religious History*, Princeton historian of American religion Albert Rabo-teau opens his final chapter, "A Hidden Wholeness: Thomas Merton and Martin Luther King, Jr.," with a summary of a powerful event that, tragically, was never able to happen. He writes:

> At the time of his assassination, plans were underway for Martin Luther King, Jr., to make a retreat with Thomas Merton at Our Lady of Gethsemani Abbey. We shall never know what might have resulted from a dialogue between this Roman Catholic monk and this black Baptist preacher whose lives still fascinate and inspire us twenty-five [now fifty] years after their deaths. But the act of recalling their common struggle against the evils of racism, materialism, and militarism may enable us to recover what they would have brought to such an encounter and to imagine the joint "word" they might have left those who strive to live out their legacy.[2]

Raboteau is not the first to wonder what might have transpired from an in-person meeting of these two great religious and social justice leaders. However, his reflections, arising from decades of studying the history of African American religious experience in the United States, offer a distinctive and stark reading of their shared experience, shared vision, and kindred spirits. For Raboteau, Merton and King were able to reach a level of prophetic witness in their writings and lives because of their common, albeit distinctive, locations on the margins of American society. He writes: "Our Lady of Gethsemani Abbey and Dexter Avenue Baptist Church, Catholic monasticism and black Protestantism—two very different locations and two very different traditions that nevertheless held one significant trait in common, their marginality. Monks were marginal by profession; they had rejected the 'world.' Blacks were marginalized by discrimination; they were rejected by the dominant white society."[3] Though admittedly very different experiences, this sense of marginalization—one elected, the other forced—led both Merton and King to recognize the religious and moral valence of the issue of civil rights and social justice.

Thomas Merton had no illusion about the radical call that King proposed in Christian prophetic form. Whereas distance and selective memory have inexorably shaped our collective imagination about who

---

[2] Albert J. Raboteau, *A Fire in the Bones: Reflections on African-American Religious History* (Boston: Beacon Press, 1995), 166.
[3] Ibid., 168–69.

King was and what he stood for, Merton recognized the opportunity and threat King's message and witness posed to the dominant white society in the United States.

The opportunity was once described by Merton in terms of a *kairos* moment—a providential time shaped by the Holy Spirit. Merton writes:

> In the Negro Christian non-violent movement, under Martin Luther King, the *kairos*, the "providential time," met with a courageous and enlightened response. The non-violent-Negro civil rights drive has been one of the most positive and successful expressions of Christian social action that has been seen anywhere in the twentieth century. It is certainly the greatest example of Christian faith in action in the social history of the United States. It has come almost entirely from the Negroes, with a few white Christians and liberals in support.[4]

Merton goes on to praise the nonviolent Christian activism of King and his followers as being heroic. And yet, Merton quickly notes the sad reality of why such powerful witness on the part of African Americans does not immediately effect change, even in the American North. The reason is that whites—including and especially white Christians—are not willing to relinquish the unearned power and privilege that comes from the flip side of institutional racism, and the Christian churches are "part of the establishment" that keeps "the Negro deluded and passive, preventing him from fighting for his rights."[5] And while there is an opportunity and sign of hope present in this *kairos* moment of nonviolence, there is also a perceived threat.

Merton was able to recognize in King's message of justice and peace the radical demand of the gospel that calls for *metanoia*, for conversion; but not on the part of black people. The conversion here is for whites— Christian whites in particular—to acknowledge their unearned privileges, the invisible social advantages, to be willing to relinquish them, and to change so that others might have greater civil equality. Merton's most powerful and sustained reflection on this call comes in the form of his

---

[4] Thomas Merton, "Religion and Race in the United States," in *Faith and Violence: Christian Teaching and Christian Practice* (Notre Dame, IN: University of Notre Dame Press, 1968), 130–31.

[5] Ibid., 131.

lengthy essay, "Letters to a White Liberal," written in response to King's famous "Letter from Birmingham Jail." In this essay Merton develops the concurrent reality of King's message—perceived simultaneously as opportunity and threat—noting that African Americans are "not simply judging the white man and rejecting him. [But] on the contrary, they are seeking by Christian love and sacrifice to redeem him, to enlighten him, so as not only to save his soul from perdition, but also to awaken his mind and his conscience, and stir him to initiate the reform and renewal which may still be capable of saving our society."[6]

Interpreting King's writings and witness for a white Christian audience—the so-called "white liberal" here, which is to say those whites who fancy themselves allies in the civil rights struggle—Merton then diagnoses the real problem and hurdle in the movement for civil rights and racial justice. In a manner resonating with the prophetic writings of James Baldwin and W.E.B. Du Bois before him, Merton declares to his fellow white Christians that *we white Christians* are the problem.[7] And the nonviolent efforts of King and others in this providential time are a way for God's Spirit to speak to the hearts of whites while there is still time. Merton explains:

> The purpose of non-violent protest, in its deepest and most spiritual dimensions is then to awaken the conscience of the white man to the awful reality of his injustice and of his sin, so that he will be able to see that the Negro problem is really a *White* problem: that the cancer of injustice and hate which is eating white society and is only partly manifested in racial segregation with all its consequences, *is rooted in the heart of the white man himself.* Only if the white man sees this will he be able to gradually understand the real nature of the problem and take steps to save himself and his society from complete ruin.[8]

Merton saw the way that white American society would view King as a threat, because beyond the call for legislation or superficial concessions, what was at the heart of the gospel message preached by King and

---

[6] Thomas Merton, "Letters to a White Liberal," in *Seeds of Destruction* (New York: Farrar, Strauss, and Giroux, 1964), 45.

[7] For more on this theme in Merton, see the previous chapter in this volume.

[8] Merton, "Letters to a White Liberal," 46.

recognized by Merton was a deeply personal and profound challenge for white Christians to examine their consciences and, in authentic evangelical style, to change their lives.

Merton recognized the resistance to this call, even among those who had convinced themselves and others that they welcomed broader inclusion of African Americans into predominantly white American society. Merton observed that in response to the "lip service" paid to persons of color by whites, African Americans had "come to realize that the white man is less interested in the rights of the Negro than in the white man's own spiritual and material comfort."⁹ Merton articulated this even more plainly elsewhere in his essay when he noted that the time of efficacy for King's nonviolent message was running out and violence would ensue unless whites recognized that they needed to surrender privilege, power, and the status quo to make space for true equity and racial justice:

> The problem is this: if the Negro, as he actually is (not the "ideal" and theoretical Negro or even the educated and cultured Negro of the small minority), enters wholly into white society, then *that society is going to be radically changed.* This of course is what the white South very well knows, and it is what the white Liberal has failed to understand. Not only will there be a radical change which, whatever form it may take, will amount to at least a peaceful revolution, but also there will be enormous difficulties and sacrifices demanded of everyone, especially the whites. Obviously property values will be affected. The tempo of life and its tone will be altered. The face of business and professional life may change. The approach to the coming crucial labor and economic problems will be even more anguished than we have feared. The psychological adjustment alone will be terribly demanding. . . . We must dare to pay the dolorous price of change, *to grow into a new society.* Nothing else will suffice!¹⁰

Developing this point further, theologian M. Shawn Copeland notes:

> In concert with King's position, Merton reminded whites that blacks were not "simply asking to be 'accepted into' the white man's society and eventually 'absorbed by it.'" Such attitudes, Merton

⁹ Ibid., 21.
¹⁰ Ibid., 8–9.

stated, merely revealed just how tightly whites clung to the notion of white superiority. With commanding irony, Merton argued, "It is simply taken for granted that, since the white man is superior, *the Negro wants to become a white man*. And we, liberals and Christians that we are, advance generously, with open arms, to embrace our little black brother and welcome him into white society." Do not expect blacks to be grateful for such attitudes, Merton warned: not only are blacks not grateful, they are not impressed by such falsity. Indeed, with these attitudes and actions, whites do "the gravest harm to Christian truth."[11]

Like King, Merton recognized the problematic nature of otherwise ostensible benevolence as covert or even unwitting signals of white supremacy. Elsewhere, Merton reiterates this point in reflecting on the way Native Americans have been and continue to be treated by the dominant white society of the United States.[12]

Merton recognized that it was not enough for a white Christian simply to be supportive in some kind of general way toward those oppressed by the structures and effects of the culture of racism imbedded in American society. Without working to surrender the concurrent privileges that are accrued by dominant groups in a structurally racist society, no real change can take place. The way that he came to develop a capacity to recognize this truth and its implications arose from his openness to listening and hearing his African American sisters and brothers on their own terms. Merton concludes his "Letters to a White Liberal" with an instruction for what this might look like, invoking a familiar motif from the Gospels in the process. He writes: "This is the 'message' which the Negro is trying to give white America. I have spelled it out for myself, subject to correction, in order to see whether a white man is even capable of grasping the words, let alone believing them. For the rest, you have Moses and the Prophets: Martin Luther King, James Baldwin, and others. Read them and see for yourself what they are saying."[13]

---

[11] M. Shawn Copeland, "The Watchmen and the Witnesses: Thomas Merton, Martin Luther King, Jr., and the Exercise of the Prophetic," *The Merton Annual* 30 (2017): 168.

[12] See Thomas Merton, *Ishi Means Man* (1976; New York: Paulist Press, 2015).

[13] Merton, "Letters to a White Liberal," 70.

Before taking a look at Malcolm X, another one of the modern proph-ets that Merton read and learned from, I think it is fitting to give the last word on Merton and King to Professor Copeland who, in an article about the prophetic witness of both men who died in 1968, summarizes their kindred spirits and legacies well.

> The lives of Merton and King converge in the exercise of the prophetic during the modern struggle *for* civil rights and *against* racism, *for* the common good *against* poverty, and *for* peace *against* militarism. Merton read our human condition as a body of bro-ken bones; King sought to reset those bones through a praxis of redemptive love. Merton and King refused to adjust themselves to the evils of the time—discrimination, segregation, religious bigotry, militarism and violence. They were messengers, witnesses, and watchmen—this Baptist minister and Catholic monk—mediating God's word, testifying to the purifying power of love, reading the signs of the time and declaring what they saw and denouncing social injustice as sin. This Catholic monk and Baptist minister understood that the deepest *telos* or authentic end of social justice and social transformation was *neither* desegregation *nor* integration, but the achievement of beloved community, as a foretaste of the eschatological realization of the mystical body of Christ. And that foretaste could be reached only through *agape*, through active and intentional Christian love.[14]

Merton and Malcolm X

Whereas it seems that Merton was more open to the complexities and radical call of Martin Luther King, Jr., than many of his contempo-raries—and certainly more than our contemporaries who might know only a "toned-down" version of a "safe" and unthreatening King—Merton nevertheless had a more difficult time approaching the writings and re-ceiving the message of Malcolm X. While Merton was certainly aware of Malcolm, Merton's journals and letters reveal a certain ambiguity about

---

[14] Copeland, "The Watchmen and the Witnesses," 170.

the civil rights activist. For example, on February 24, 1965, Merton has a one-line mention of Malcolm X's assassination at the end of the day's entry: "Malcolm X, the Negro racist, has been murdered (I am sorry because now there is bitter fighting between two Muslim factions)."[15] At first glance, the descriptor "Negro racist" strikes the reader as hostile or, at the very least, without appropriate nuance. And yet, three days later Merton writes a letter to William Robert Miller, a Protestant editor, in which Merton mentions the assassination again but with strikingly more nuance and within the context of broader social concerns.

> I used to think that only Communism was as systematically dedicated to a false construction but I think in some ways we have got them beat because we are so much less systematic and there is a kind of virtuosity that gets in there, the concert of phoniness that arises from Madison Avenue. . . . The Goldwater campaign, the Vietnam thing, the continuation of nothing in the race crisis, and now the heartbreaking madness in the aftermath of Malcolm X's murder. (I thought he was rather a good guy and capable of making some sense.) This is a very blind country, and you are right about what is said about love and what is not done.[16]

These brief allusions to Malcolm X provide us with little to work with but illustrate a general sensibility witnessed in Merton's writings on racism in the United States from 1963 until 1967. Then things changed.

The cautious optimism Merton expressed for Martin Luther King's nonviolent Christian movement shifted in the wake of the passing of the Civil Rights Act of 1964, which did little to alleviate effects of the deeply rooted reality of structural racism in the United States. This shift in Merton's outlook and assessment is characterized in, among other places, his essay "From Non-Violence to Black Power," which opens with the stark line: "The non-violent struggle for integration has won

---

[15] Thomas Merton, "February 24, 1965," in *Dancing in the Water of Life: The Journals of Thomas Merton—Volume 5: 1963–1965*, ed. Robert E. Daggy (San Francisco: HarperCollins, 1997), 211.

[16] Thomas Merton, "Letter to William Robert Miller, February 27, 1965," in *Witness to Freedom: Letters in Times of Crisis*, ed. William H. Shannon (New York: Harcourt Brace, 1994), 250.

on the law books—and was lost in fact."[17] Whereas Merton previously described Malcolm X as "the Negro racist" prior to reading the activist's own writings, now Merton boldly declares that "the Black Power movement is not just racism in reverse."[18] The superficial appearance of racism—namely, an anti-white sentiment—is an effect of genuine needs people of color have in their quest for racial justice.

Merton's turn to Malcolm X coincided with his ongoing conversion to the plight of people of color in the United States and the concurrent advantageous reality of white privilege and supremacy. In a short review essay titled "The Meaning of Malcolm X," Merton engages the *Autobiography of Malcolm X* in a notably nuanced and erudite way. At the outset of the essay, he admits: "The picture most of us had of him was inadequate, though not altogether untrue. We saw him as a militant, rigid, somewhat fanatical agitator, absolutely committed to a naive racist mystique and to a religious organization which was made to sound like a Negro SS."[19] Acknowledging the caricature of Malcolm X portrayed by the white media and earlier accepted by Merton himself, Merton goes on to interpret what he believes to be the partial truth of the stereotype as a consequence of Malcolm's involvement with the Nation of Islam. Merton explains: "Malcolm X was undoubtedly more gifted, more intelligent, more flexible than he appeared to be when he was deliberately effacing himself behind the ideas and programs of 'The Honorable Mr. Elijah Muhammad.'"[20] Having studied *The Autobiography of Malcolm X*—which on April 28, 1967, Merton described in his journal as "an impressive book"—Merton believed that Malcolm's initial involvement with the Nation of Islam actually prevented him from finding and expressing his prophetic voice in the most robust way possible. Merton also attributes Malcolm's role as Elijah Muhammad's close disciple as informing the activist's early caustic and absolutist views about whites. Hearing firsthand from Malcolm's accounting of his life and experiences, Merton came to recognize the complexity of Malcolm's positions and the difficult truths about which he spoke, raising the rhetorical question about whether

---

[17] Thomas Merton, "From Non-Violence to Black Power," in *Faith and Violence*, 121.

[18] Ibid., 124.

[19] Thomas Merton, "The Meaning of Malcolm X," in *Faith and Violence*, 182.

[20] Ibid., 182–83.

there was indeed veracity in even the more absolutist views Malcolm had earlier expressed. Merton summarizes his take on Malcolm's shifting perspectives on race relations and the quest for racial justice in America:

> Malcolm X later recognized that his own earlier refusals were too absolute, that some kind of dialogue between the races had to be possible, some kind of collaboration had to be admitted. Yet he felt that the ordinary white liberal professions of sincerity were not enough, and he insisted on a tactic of refusal which declared, both implicitly and explicitly, that however honest the white man might feel himself to be subjectively, the Negro could not objectively accept his protestations of concern at their face value. They were bound to prove deceptive because the white man could not change his essentially distorted view of the relationship between the races. Even when the white man indulged in a veritable cult of the Negro, he betrayed his basic conviction that the Negro was somehow more of an animal, a distinct and exotic species of human being.[21]

In addition to an increased openness to the critical insights Malcolm X presented to Merton in a general societal and ecclesial way, they seemed also to shape his personal outlook at a time when he was discerning a desire for increased solitude that included consideration of moving to, as he described it, a "Third World" country. On May 11, 1967, Merton notes in his journal that he finished writing his essay on *The Autobiography of Malcolm X* and that there were "implications of the racial and neo-colonial situation—for my own life."[22] Earlier in his journals he mentioned concurrently reading the postcolonial theorist Frantz Fanon's influential book *The Wretched of the Earth* alongside Malcolm X's autobiography. It seems that at this point in 1967 Merton was more and more open to views he earlier viewed as radical or hostile, and that these views were having an impact on his own life and thinking. He credits Malcolm X's and Fanon's works as shaping his outlook on the implications of white, North American, members of religious congregations

---

[21] Merton, "The Meaning of Malcolm X," 184.
[22] Thomas Merton, "May 11, 1967," in *Learning to Love: The Journals of Thomas Merton, Volume Six: 1966–1967*, ed. Christine M. Bochen (San Francisco: Harper Collins, 1997), 233.

potentially moving to a systemically impoverished land that Merton himself has romanticized for his own benefit.

What is striking to me about Merton's reading of Malcolm X is the way that, despite initial hesitance, he was open to a voice too often dismissed by others. In a context in which he is interrogating why Malcolm X is so infrequently engaged by theologians and Christian thinkers, theologian Bryan Massingale explains that "Malcolm X conjures up images that can be disturbing, imprisoned as he is by the dominant culture's narrative as a hate-filled demagogue, whose fiery rhetoric is out of place in the calm and dispassionate venue of academic [or ecclesial] discourse."[23] Massingale argues that despite the stereotypes that have led to widespread dismissal of Malcolm X, he and his work should be considered a "classic" in the sense articulated by theologian David Tracy, which is understood to be "any text that always has the power to transform the horizon of the interpreter and thereby disclose new meanings and experiential possibilities."[24] Massingale explains the power contained in Malcolm's story, noting that "his narrative of conversion and constant openness to truth, whatever its personal cost, is a witness of integrity that speaks across cultural and racial divides. . . . Malcolm's thought is a 'classic' in that it describes 'America.' Not only 'Black' America, but an essential part of the entirety of the American experience without which we possess truncated and inaccurate understandings of who we are and why we are as we are."[25]

I believe that what we see in Merton's engagement with Malcolm X's thought and legacy is a tacit affirmation of what Massingale means in describing the activist as a "classic." In a way anticipating Massingale's own articulation of the reasons for this classical status, Merton concluded his essay on Malcolm X by stating: "His autobiography reveals a person whose struggles are understandable, whose errors we can condone. He was a fighter whose sincerity and courage we cannot help admiring, and who might have become a genuine revolutionary leader—with portentous effect in American society."[26]

---

[23] Brian N. Massingale, "*Vox Victimarum Vox Dei*: Malcolm X as Neglected 'Classic' for Catholic Theological Reflection," *CTSA Proceedings* 65 (2010): 65.

[24] David Tracy, *On Naming the Present* (Maryknoll, NY: Orbis Books, 1994), 15.

[25] Massingale, "*Vox Victimarum Vox Dei*," 66.

[26] Merton, "The Meaning of Malcolm X," 188.

Merton on the Responsibility of Catholic Spirituality

Throughout his writings during the civil rights period of the 1960s, Merton consistently called out what he described as the "Christian failure in American racial justice," noting that an increased awareness of what was happening in society brings out "the stark reality that our society itself is radically violent and that violence is built into its very structure."[27] Such an observation, true as it is, elicits a basic question: Then what is the response of the Christian, especially the white Christian, supposed to be? While Merton can rightly be described as a social critic, and one with keen perception at that, he was not a social activist or political figure. He never outlined a strategy for community organizing or proposed a set of political policies. His interest was primarily rooted in the Christian responsibility to promote justice and peace as constitutive of the universal vocation of the baptized. In this way his critique of racial injustice in the American context is, in part, a "Christian failure" and therefore demands a distinctively Christian response. Inspired by both Martin Luther King, Jr., and Malcolm X—each in his own way—Merton offers contemporary Christians some resources for developing an antiracist spirituality. He tacitly highlights the responsibility Christians—especially *white* Christians—have to think spiritually and theologically about the roots of systemic racism and white supremacy and how white Christians can respond from within their religious tradition.

This emphasis on the "Christian failure," and by extension the need for a distinctively Christian response, reminds me of Bryan Massingale's characterization of racism as, in part, a "soul sickness." Racism and its complement of white privilege are wisely likened to a spiritual illness. As Massingale explained in a 2014 address: "There are many ways to understand racism, namely, as a political issue, as a sociological phenomenon, as a cultural divide. But for me, at its deepest level, racism is a soul sickness. It is a profound warping of the human spirit, one that enables human beings to create communities of cold, callous indifference to their darker sisters and brothers. Stripped to its core, racism is that disturbing interior disease that enables people to not care for those who don't look like them."[28] In a 2021 presentation to the Carmelite

---

[27] Merton, "Religion and Race in the United States," 144.
[28] Bryan Massingale, speech, YMCA Southeast Wisconsin event, 2014.

community in Baltimore, Massingale reflected on how he arrived at the coinage of the term "soul sickness."

> This phrasing, "soul sickness," is one that I coined. The phrase came to me when I was sitting in an airport lounge watching news coverage of the St. Louis district attorney's decision not to indict the police for the killing of Michael Brown in 2015. Brown's uncle was being interviewed. He was distraught and overwhelmed with emotion, his angry sobs overtaking him as he lashed out at the failure of the system to obtain justice for his nephew. But as I watched the faces of the overwhelmingly white crowd who viewed the broadcast (I was the only Black person in the area), I saw stony faces, hardened, impervious at this outpouring of grief. White faces fixed in anger at the indictment that was being leveled against American society. I was stunned. I wondered, "What has so twisted the souls of these people that they are not only unmoved, but hardened, at the grief of someone who lost their young child? Would they be so calloused if this were a white young man whose death was being mourned?" This is what led me to talk about white supremacy as a "soul sickness."[29]

Massingale goes on to note that "this soul sickness is a cultural reality, a culturally induced indifference, leading to an unconscious refusal of empathy and concern."

Building on this theme, Womanist theologian Kelly Brown Douglas recently wrote: "Just as white supremacy has not disappeared, neither has the religion that fosters and legitimates it. As white supremacy has transformed itself throughout the nation's history to reflect the customs and 'constraints of the time,' so too have white supremacist versions of Christianity. In our own time, these racist renderings of Christianity have simply adapted to twenty-first-century cultural mores and political sensibilities, thereby manifesting in ways perhaps more subtle . . . but not less blatant."[30] Echoing and building on the observations of her

---

[29] Bryan Massingale, "Toward a Spirituality for Racial Justice: The Transformation of Consciousness and the 'Souls of White Folks,'" unpublished lecture, Carmelite Community, Baltimore, Maryland, November 13, 2021, 3.

[30] Kelly Brown Douglas, *Resurrection Hope: A Future Where Black Lives Matter* (Maryknoll, NY: Orbis Books, 2021), 108.

foremothers and forefathers who have long noted the role of Christianity as "the conductor of white supremacy" in this country, to borrow an image from sociologist Robert P. Jones,[31] Douglas is reminding us of both white supremacy's insidiousness and hiddenness. Pope Francis has also drawn the church and world's attention to this dimension of soul sickness, writing in his 2020 encyclical letter *Fratelli Tutti* that "racism is a virus that quickly mutates and, instead of disappearing, goes into hiding, and lurks in waiting."[32]

One of Merton's greatest contributions to the work of racial justice was his insistence that, like Massingale and Douglas subsequently, systemic racism and white supremacy ought to be prioritized by the Christian community. Writing as a white Christian and Catholic religious, Merton understood that spirituality that only served to make white Christians feel comfortable and affirmed in the status quo was insufficient. Merton celebrated Martin Luther King's clear-sighted grasp of this imperative, especially when King saw the intersecting injustices of racism, violence, and poverty. While it took some time, Merton was clearly open to a conversion of perspective when it came to Malcolm X and his message. While not speaking from within the Christian tradition, Malcolm's message was nevertheless deeply spiritual, particularly after he returned from his Hajj in Mecca. Drawing on the insights of both of these great advocates for racial justice, Merton sought to communicate to his fellow white Christians that they needed to incorporate into their spiritual practices and worldviews a commitment to seeing reality as it actually was, especially when it came to systemic racism and white supremacy. This is the responsibility of Catholic spirituality, to encourage ongoing conversion while also challenging Christians to work for the in-breaking of God's kingdom as the gospel instructs. Anything short of this is, as Merton wrote, a "Christian failure."

---

[31] See Robert P. Jones, *White Too Long: The Legacy of White Supremacy in American Christianity* (New York: Simon and Schuster, 2020).

[32] Pope Francis, *Fratelli Tutti* (2020), no. 97.

V

Social Justice and Ethics

15

All Life Is on Our Side

Thomas Merton's Model of Ecological Conversion
in the Age of Pope Francis

In the spirit of the theme selected for the 2016 Thomas Merton conference in Oakham, UK—"Life Is on Our Side"—this chapter begins with
the question: Whose life or what's life is on our side? Over the course of
his life Thomas Merton grew in what has been described as his "ecological
consciousness," that is, an increasing awareness of the interconnection
and interdependence of all creation that extends beyond the human
family to include *all* life.[1] The shift in his worldview to include the
nonhuman dimensions of the cosmos in his spiritual and theological
reflection anticipates the call Pope Francis has expressed in his encyclical
Laudato Si' for all people to embrace an "ecological conversion," which
calls all people to move beyond an anthropocentric view of the world
and recognize our place as sisters and brothers to one another and to
all creation.

In this chapter I make the argument that Merton's ecological consciousness, which, like Pope Francis's encyclical, was deeply informed by

[Versions of this essay were originally presented at the Eleventh General Conference
of the Thomas Merton Society of Great Britain and Ireland, Oakham, UK, April
1–3, 2016; at the Annual Aquinas Lecture at the University of Utah St. Catherine
Newman Center, Salt Lake City, Utah, January 29, 2017; and published in *The
Merton Journal* 23 (2016): 20–29. Used with permission.]
    [1] This is my adaptation of Kathleen Deignan's attention to what she calls Mer-
ton's "ecological consciousness" and increasing "love of the paradise mystery." See
Kathleen Deignan, "'Love for the Paradise Mystery': Thomas Merton Contemplative
Ecologist," *CrossCurrents* 58 (2008): 545–69.

the Franciscan spiritual and theological tradition, can help contemporary people to imagine and embrace "ecological conversion." This chapter is organized into three parts. First, I elucidate what Pope Francis means by ecological conversion. Second, I highlight some of the ways in which Merton's ecological consciousness unfolded over the course of his life and in his writings. Finally, I present a few insights about how Merton provides a prophetic model and guide for enacting what *Laudato Si'* calls all people to live. I believe this is but one more way Merton continues to be relevant for a new time and generation.

Pope Francis and Ecological Conversion

Pope Francis is hardly original in his advocacy on behalf of the more-than-human world put forward in his at once poetic and 2015 encyclical letter *Laudato Si' (On Care for Our Common Home).*[2] This is something he acknowledges in the preface of the text, identifying his pontifical and ecumenical predecessors, each of whom has focused attention on matters pertaining to the natural world and humanity's place within and among it.[3] Directing his teaching to as capacious an audience as could be imagined—that is, all who inhabit "our common home," the planet Earth—Pope Francis understands this encyclical teaching to both recapitulate longstanding Catholic social teaching and apply it in timely, relevant ways. We can see this in the way Pope Francis loosely structures the encyclical after the pattern for reading the "signs of the times and interpreting them in the light of the Gospel"[4] set out by John XXIII in his 1961 encyclical letter *Mater et Magistra.* Pope John writes:

> These are three stages which should normally be followed in the reduction of social principles into practice. First, one reviews the concrete situation; secondly, one forms a judgment on it in the light of these same principles; thirdly, one decides what the circumstances can and should be done to implement these principles.

[2] All church documents are available on the vatican.va website.
[3] *Laudato Si'*, nos. 3–6.
[4] Vatican II, *Gaudium et Spes*, no. 4.

These are the three stages that are usually expressed in the three terms: observe, judge, act.[5]

This threefold process of observing, judging, and acting is witnessed in the structure of the text of *Laudato Si'*. Francis opens the document with a frank assessment of "what is happening to our common home," highlighting the most egregious of ecological tragedies of our contemporary anthropocene age.[6] In addition to the predictable "sins against creation," to use an apt expression from Ecumenical Patriarch Bartholomew and borrowed by Pope Francis,[7] which include pollution, species extinction, issues surrounding water, and the decrease in global biodiversity, among others, Pope Francis identifies the "decline in the quality of human life and the breakdown of society" that concurrently casts its shadow on our times.[8] In this way, Francis opens with a sober summation of a contemporary "observation."

He moves on to the second stage marked by judging these observed "signs of the times" always according to "the light of the Gospel." For this, he reviews what he calls the "Gospel of Creation" in chapter 2 and offers an insightful recounting of essential Christian principles on creation arising from scripture and tradition. Among the most notable are his explicit rejection of so-called dominion models of creation, which misrepresent the Genesis narratives such that human beings are perceived to have sovereignty over nonhuman creation, and the affirmation of the inherent value and dignity belonging to each and every creature, human and nonhuman alike, by virtue of its being lovingly created by God.[9]

This second stage of judgment continues into the third chapter of *Laudato Si'*, bluntly titled "The Human Roots of the Ecological Crisis."

---

[5] John XXIII, *Mater et Magistra*, no. 236.

[6] By "anthropocene" I mean that geo-temporal epoch that refers to the period of global history when human activities begin to have noticeable and, at times, irreversible effects on the earth's geology and ecological systems. The coinage of this term dates back to at least the year 2000, when Nobel-prize laureate Paul Crutzen and his co-author Eugene Stoermer published the article "Anthropocene," *Global Change Newsletter* 41 (May 2000): 17–18.

[7] See John Chryssavgis, ed., *Cosmic Grace and Humble Prayer: The Ecological Vision of the Green Patriarch Bartholomew*, rev. ed. (Grand Rapids, MI: Eerdmans, 2009). Pope Francis quotes him in *Laudato Si'*, nos. 8–9.

[8] *Laudato Si'*, no. 20.

[9] See *Laudato Si'*, nos. 62–100.

Here Francis does not temper his critique of the human family's responsibility for the ecological crises the world faces at present and in the future. Unlike the fringe global climate change deniers found in United States and some places elsewhere around the globe, Francis does not pretend that the overwhelming scientific data is up for debate. On the contrary, he echoes the vast consensus of climatologists and other professionals that attest to the detrimental effects humanity has wrought on *both* the other-than-human world *and* within the human family itself. This latter part of the judgment process is particularly important given the pope's insistence that this encyclical is not simply about the environment, but rather stands properly among the rest of the church's social teaching. Rampant anthropocentrism, uncritical reliance on technology, disregard for the common good, and other human-centered concerns have developed alongside and have contributed to environmental degradation. Furthermore, Francis notes that the human poor are also the ones most directly affected by global climate change, which only increases the ethical imperative to respond to these troubling signs of our times.

The second half of *Laudato Si'*, composed of chapters 4–6, is almost exclusively concerned with the third stage of the evaluative process, which is action. Arguing for an "integral ecology" that would recognize the dual foci of human and nonhuman justice and concern, Francis outlines several "lines of approach and action," including dialogue and political engagement.[10] It is within this context that we encounter the pope's call for "ecological conversion." In fact, although Francis alludes to the need for our repentance, conversion, and corrective action throughout the text, it isn't until the middle of the last chapter that he focuses an entire short section (nos. 216–21) on ecological conversion. In a sense this concept is a premise for every other part of the encyclical, without which no authentic observation, judgment, and action could take place. It is this concept that is of greatest interest to the current project, for it is Thomas Merton's own life experience and writing that I believe helps contemporary Christians accept the call and engage the experience of ecological conversion as Pope Francis identifies it in this teaching.

---

[10] *Laudato Si'*, nos. 137–201.

So, what is ecological conversion?

At its core, it is a turning toward the world, a moving outside of one's self, a rejection of solipsism and self-centeredness, and a fundamental "renewal of humanity" rooted in the "rich heritage of Christian spirituality."[11] Francis believes that the ecological crises we witness in the world today, and for which we are all in part responsible, should lead us to have a change of heart and a "profound interior conversion," one that would presumably lead to the sort of action that *Laudato Si'* has outlined in terms of the threefold social justice evaluation. Though some members of the human family are certainly in need of radical conversion away from destructive practices such as overt pollution and damage to nonhuman creation, most people are not expressly engaged in activities or decision-making processes that directly affect the community of creation in such explicit ways. Instead, Francis observes that most people in economically developed parts of the world are "passive" or rely on the "excuse of realism and pragmatism" when it comes to the necessary changes required of humanity's relationship to the rest of creation.[12] In this sense the globally affluent are guilty of sins of omission, that is, failure to act or be concerned about what *Gaudium et Spes* describes as the "griefs and anxieties"[13] of the people and the planet of this age; instead, much of the human family consists of guilty bystanders.[14]

Among the many striking dimensions of ecological conversion that Francis describes is his insistence that its necessity arises from our foundational vocation as followers of Christ. In effect, he states that if we claim to be Christian, then our relationship with Jesus Christ should have a direct, positive, and pragmatic influence on our relationship with the world around us.[15] This aspect of our faith is, as Francis puts it, "not an optional or a secondary aspect of our Christian experience."[16] The

---

[11] *Laudato Si'*, no. 216.

[12] *Laudato Si'*, no. 217.

[13] *Gaudium et Spes*, no. 1.

[14] For some of Merton's reflections on related conditions of "bystanding," see his *Conjectures of a Guilty Bystander* (New York: Harcourt Brace, 1966); and idem, "Letter to an Innocent Bystander," in *Raids on the Unspeakable* (New York: New Directions, 1966), 53–64.

[15] *Laudato Si'*, no. 217.

[16] *Laudato Si'*, no. 217.

pope recalls his namesake in summarizing what this means for Christians everywhere:

> In calling to mind the figure of Saint Francis of Assisi, we come to realize that a healthy relationship with creation is one dimension of overall personal conversion, which entails recognition of our errors, sins, faults and failures, and leads to heartfelt repentance and desire to change. The Australian bishops spoke of the importance of such conversion for achieving reconciliation with creation: "To achieve such reconciliation, we must examine our lives and acknowledge the ways in which we have harmed God's creation through our actions and our failure to act. We need to experience a conversion, or change of heart."[17]

Indeed, an awareness and a change of heart that lead us from complacency, self-centeredness, and anthropocentrism toward openness to the process of observing the world around us, judging what must be done, and acting in constructive and penitential ways, are attitudes we should all embrace.

However, Pope Francis makes it clear that this is not simply a matter of individual decisions to act or personal efforts to correct private ecological sins. While those things are important, we must also confront the structural, systemic, and social problems of our age. For, "the ecological conversion needed to bring about lasting change is also a community conversion."[18] The result of the twofold individual and corporate ecological conversion should include an awareness for and gratitude in response to the world in which we live, aware that it reflects God as Creator and also provides all of us with life and sustenance. Furthermore, this conversion should open our eyes wider to see "that we are not disconnected from the rest of creatures, but joined in a splendid universal communion."[19] We are not merely interlopers from some outside system of higher and greater value, but kin to the rest of the cosmos and members of a community of creation not of our making.

---

[17] *Laudato Si'*, no. 218.
[18] *Laudato Si'*, no. 219.
[19] *Laudato Si'*, no. 220.

Merton's Ecological Consciousness

That Thomas Merton had a series of significant, even epiphanic experiences over his lifetime is not news to anyone even remotely familiar with the contours of his lifelong experience of conversion. The map of Merton's life is dotted with conversions, changes of heart, and openness to the creative novelty of the Spirit's work in his life. Among the most celebrated is his "turn to the world," which began in the late 1950s and continued to grow throughout the 1960s until his unexpected death in 1968. There is perhaps no better summary of the seeming shift in attention from a nearly exclusive focus on the interior life of the contemplative monk always seeking more solitude toward a radical openness to the world in which he lived and remained a member despite the imposition of the cloister than the remarks he wrote to Dorothy Day on August 23, 1961:

> I feel obligated to take very seriously what is going on, and to say whatever my conscience seems to dictate, provided of course it is not contrary to the faith and to the teaching authority of the Church. . . . I don't feel that I can in conscience, at a time like this, go on writing just about things like meditation, though that has its point. I cannot just bury my head in a lot of rather tiny and secondary monastic studies either. I think I have to face the big issues, the life-and-death issues.[20]

This general movement and awakening to the social justice concerns in the world of his time anticipated the clarion call of the Second Vatican Council's *Gaudium et Spes*'s famous opening lines, according to which all Christians are called to celebrate the "joys and hopes" as well as to acknowledge and respond to the "griefs and anxieties" of all.[21] Global climate change and environmental degradation are both the source of contemporary griefs and anxieties as well as the symptoms of human sinfulness.

---

[20] Thomas Merton, "Letter to Dorothy Day on August 23, 1961," in *The Hidden Ground of Love: The Letters of Thomas Merton on Religious Experience and Social Concerns*, ed. William H. Shannon (New York: Farrar, Straus, Giroux, 1985), 139–40.

[21] *Gaudium et Spes,* no. 1.

It was around this same time that Merton's ecological consciousness blossomed into an acute awareness of the environmental crises of the era. As Kathleen Deignan and Monica Weis, among others, have noted, Merton's reading of Rachel Carson's important book *Silent Spring* in the early 1960s and the subsequent correspondence between the environmental activist and the Trappist monk reflect an explicit awakening to the ecological "signs of the times."[22] And yet, while the experience of turning to the world included nonhuman creation in addition to the strife Merton witnessed among the human family at that time, the late 1950s and early 1960s were not the first time he was aware of humanity's relatedness to the rest of creation or God's presence within it. Like Pope Francis, whose own vision of creation is expressly influenced by the Franciscan tradition, Merton's understanding of the natural world and humanity's place within has always borne a certain Franciscan sensibility. Kathleen Deignan put this succinctly when she wrote: "In true Franciscan spirit, Merton could sense the 'angelic transparency of everything, of pure, simple and total light.'"[23] This sensibility or spirit is seen in Merton's life and writings explicitly in two ways.[24]

The first way is in his understanding of all creation as a vestige of God. In theological discussions *vestige* is tied to the original Latin root, *vestigium*, which means "footprint." It is the medieval Franciscan theologian Bonaventure whose theological reflection on creation emphasized that everything that God created is, in a sense, a vestige of the Creator. In other words, everything that exists reflects or points back to the Creator, who lovingly brought all creation into existence and whose very presence is capable of being recognized in that same creation. Merton writes about this in a 1967 letter responding to a young man named Mario Falsina, stating: "My idea of the world: first of all the world as God's good creation. I have the good fortune to

---

[22] See Deignan, "'Love for the Paradise Mystery': Thomas Merton, Contemplative Ecologist," 560–66; and Monica Weis, *The Environmental Vision of Thomas Merton* (Lexington: University Press of Kentucky, 2011), esp. 9–21.

[23] Kathleen Deignan, "Introduction," in Thomas Merton, *When the Trees Say Nothing: Writings on Nature*, ed. Kathleen Deignan (Notre Dame, IN: Sorin Books, 2003), 27.

[24] For a fuller accounting of these two ways, see Daniel P. Horan, *The Franciscan Heart of Thomas Merton: A New Look at the Spiritual Inspiration of His Life, Thought, and Writing* (Notre Dame, IN: Ave Maria Press, 2014), 142–55.

live in close contact with nature, how should I not love this world, and love it with passion? I understand the joy of St. Francis amid the creatures! God manifests himself in his creation, and everything that he has made speaks of him."[25]

The second way is in Merton's understanding of the kinship of all creation. Like Francis of Assisi, and in a way anticipating Pope Francis's admonition for humanity to recall its familial ties to other creatures, Merton had a deeply intuitive sense of his own ingrained relationship with the rest of the created order. This understanding of the world finds its roots in both the Hebrew and Christian scriptures and is expressed most directly in the texts of nature mystics such as Francis of Assisi, in his famous *Canticle of the Creatures*, in which all nonhuman aspects of the created order are recognized and celebrated as the saint's sisters and brothers. We can see this in Merton's journal reflections, such as the one written on November 4, 1964, in which he writes:

> In the afternoon, lots of pretty myrtle warblers were playing and diving for insects in the low pine branches over my head, so close I could almost touch them. I was awed at their loveliness, their quick flight, etc. *Sense of total kinship with them as if they and I were of the same nature, and as if that nature were nothing but love.* And what else but love keeps us all together in being?[26]

This sense of kinship with the rest of creation doesn't just appear at the end of his life but can be traced back to at least his time as a young monk with some illustrative examples seen in *The Sign of Jonas* and elsewhere. Monica Weis has even suggested that Merton's awareness of the kinship of all creation goes all the way back to his early childhood as recorded by his mother, Ruth Jenkins Merton.[27] What this suggests is that Merton's ecological consciousness did not appear out of nowhere but was an intuition located in the heart and mind of a

[25] Thomas Merton, "Letter to Mario Falsina on March 25, 1967," in *The Road to Joy: Letters to New and Old Friends*, ed. Robert Daggy (New York: Harcourt Brace, 1989), 347–48.

[26] Thomas Merton, "November 4, 1964," in *Dancing in the Water of Life: Seeking Peace in the Hermitage*, ed. Robert Daggy, Journals of Thomas Merton vol. 5, 1963–1965 (San Francisco: HarperSanFrancisco, 1997), 162, emphasis added.

[27] Weis, *The Environmental Vision of Thomas Merton*, 29.

young man who grew into greater awareness. The process of becoming increasingly open to all creatures as vestiges of the Creator and the kinship of all creation is what we might rightly name a lifelong series of ecological conversions.

Furthermore, these two aspects of Merton's ecological consciousness informed his ethical outlook as much as his mere appreciation for the world around him. This is something that grew from a seed of his spiritual environment in the early years into a large tree that shaded his social justice concerns near the end of his life. In one journal entry Merton writes: "We do not realize that the fields and the trees have fought and still fight for their respective place on this map—which, by natural right, belongs entirely to the trees."[28] Here Merton seems to recognize in the trees a sense of moral agency and subjectivity. They—the trees—have a *natural right* to exist and to be recognized as inherently valuable. This is something that Pope Francis emphasizes in *Laudato Si'*, that the inherent dignity and value of all God's creation exists independently of human utility or consideration.

Conclusion

In a way presciently anticipating the modern encyclical letter *Laudato Si'*, Merton writes in a not-well-known essay titled, "The Wild Places," of Aldo Leopold's concept of ecological conscience. Merton writes:

> Aldo Leopold brought into clear focus one of the most important moral discoveries of our time. This can be called the *ecological conscience*. The ecological conscience is centered in the awareness of *man's true place as a dependent member of the biotic community*. Man must become fully aware of his *dependence* on a balance which he is not only free to destroy but which he has already begun to destroy. He must recognize his obligations toward the other members of that vital community. And incidentally, since he tends to destroy nature in his frantic efforts to exterminate other members of his own species, it would not hurt if he had a little more respect for

---

[28] Thomas Merton, "July 22, 1956," in *A Search for Solitude: Pursuing the Monk's True Life*, ed. Lawrence S. Cunningham, Journals of Thomas Merton vol. 3, 1952–1960 (San Francisco: HarperSanFrancisco, 1996), 51.

human life too. The respect for life, the affirmation of *all life*, is basic to the ecological conscience.[29]

This notion of the ecological conscience strikes me as the well-formed object of Pope Francis's call to ecological conversion. Like the modern pope, the late monk recognized the connection between justice within the human family and justice for the larger family of creation. What Merton's journey reveals to us in the age of Pope Francis is a model for what ecological conversion looks like in a time of environmental and human crisis. Like Merton, each of us has the capacity to return to that deep creational intuition that affirms our shared kinship with the rest of creation and recognize the presence of God in all creatures. Additionally like Merton, we too can form our ecological consciences to recognize the interdependence and deep intersection between the injustice perpetuated against nonhuman aspects of creation and the injustices that affect human beings. Put in the words of Pope Francis, as well as the Brazilian theologian Leonardo Boff before him, Merton helps us to attend to both "the cry of the earth and the cry of the poor."[30] The question is, however, whether we will respond to that cry or not. I believe that reading the writings of Thomas Merton, particularly those reflections on the natural world—and yet not only those—may help to inspire us along the way of our journey of ecological conversion and to imagine better what such a pilgrimage of cosmic awareness entails.

---

[29] Thomas Merton, "The Wild Places," in *Thomas Merton: Selected Essays*, ed. Patrick O'Connell (Maryknoll, NY: Orbis Books, 2013), 450.

[30] See *Laudato Si'*, no. 49; and Leonardo Boff, *Cry of the Earth, Cry of the Poor*, trans. Phillip Berryman (Maryknoll, NY: Orbis Books, 1997).

16

What It Means to Be a Person of Dialogue

When Pope Francis addressed a historic joint session of the United States Congress during his Apostolic Visit on Thursday September 24, 2015, he drew on the wisdom and example of four figures to frame his remarks to the American people. Noting that the year 2015 marked a number of significant anniversaries of "several great Americans," the bishop of Rome explained: "These men and women offer us a way of seeing and interpreting reality. In honoring their memory, we are inspired, even amid conflicts, and in the here and now of each day, to draw upon our deepest cultural reserves."[1] He selected four key figures: Abraham Lincoln, Martin Luther King, Jr., Dorothy Day, and Thomas Merton.

With regard to Merton, Pope Francis explained his selection of the Trappist monk and Catholic priest, who was both a spiritual writer and social critic, by stating: "Merton was above all a man of prayer, a thinker who challenged the certitudes of his time and opened new horizons for souls and for the Church. He was also a man of dialogue, a promoter of peace between peoples and religions." He added that Merton was an exemplar of "the capacity for dialogue and openness to God."[2]

Pope Francis's enthusiastic recommendation of Merton as a model for dialogue leads us to consider several implications that his brief address to Congress leave unaddressed. For example, what exactly does it mean to

---

[A version of this essay was originally published in *What Am I Living For: Seven Lessons from the Life and Writings of Thomas Merton*, ed. Jon M. Sweeney (Notre Dame, IN: Ave Maria Press, 2018), 71–88. Used with permission.]

[1] Pope Francis, "Visit to the Joint Session of the United States Congress," September 24, 2015.

[2] Ibid.

be a person of dialogue? How does one go about engaging in authentic dialogue? In what contexts does or should dialogue take place? And how may Merton provide us with insights into becoming women and men of dialogue who, like Merton, serve the world and church as promoters of peace between peoples and religions?

In this chapter we explore four areas in which Merton engaged in dialogue and invites us to do likewise: dialogue with God, dialogue with culture, dialogue with society, and dialogue with religions. Though this chapter is hardly an exhaustive treatment of the manifold ways Merton's life, writings, and legacy provide us with insight about developing relationships rooted in justice, peace, and mutuality, it is my hope that it offers a contribution to the discussion that Pope Francis invited us to consider during his first visit to the United States.

Dialogue with God

If people know of Thomas Merton, it's likely that they know about him for his writings on the spiritual life, prayer, or contemplation. In the early decades of Merton's religious life, the 1940s and 1950s, his contribution to Catholic spirituality was distinctive in that he extended an invitation to all women and men to develop a life of prayer and faith. Today such an observation might appear obvious, but prior to the Second Vatican Council (1962–65), Roman Catholics generally understood the life of prayer and contemplation to belong to the "professional religious"— nuns, priests, monks, and such—and not to the members of the laity. Merton upended that presumption, suggesting that the world in which all Christians find themselves was in fact a world in which God seeks connection and relationship with all people. Merton suggested that "the ever-changing reality in the midst of which we live should awaken us to the possibility of an uninterrupted dialogue with God."[3] Rather than imagine that prayer is something that operates according to our terms or requires of us a commitment to consecrated religious life, Merton invited us to consider that God is the one who *seeks us first,* and that we can cultivate practices of attunement to that loving presence of God already always near us. "We must learn," Merton wrote, "to realize that the love

---

[3] Thomas Merton, *New Seeds of Contemplation* (New York: New Directions, 1961), 14.

of God seeks us in every situation, and seeks our good. His inscrutable love seeks our awakening."[4] If we imagine prayer as a two-way street, then we can rest assured that God is doing God's part in that form of relational communication. It is we that remain the inactive dialogue partners in our respective dialogues with God, and Merton challenges us to do our part to carry on the conversation with our Creator.

As if to echo the psalmist, who proclaims, "God is in the city" in Psalm 46, Merton asserts that God's presence is not limited to the traditionally "churchy" locations we typically imagine. Instead, Merton's spiritual vision is shaped by the longstanding Christian tradition that unabashedly announces God's presence everywhere in creation: "It is God's love that speaks to me in the birds and streams; but also behind the clamor of the city God speaks to me in His judgments, and all these things are seeds sent to me from His will."[5] The dialogue, the conversation, the *prayer* can take place anywhere and everywhere, and not just on Sunday mornings at mass in the parish.

For Merton, the intimacy of the dialogue with God is beyond all other forms of closeness and relationship. The influence of St. Augustine's spiritual reflections on Merton's own writing is evident in this way. Augustine famously wrote in his spiritual autobiography, *Confessions,* that "God is the one closer to us than we are to ourselves."[6] Merton expands on this intuition when discussing the nature of the dialogue with God in contemplation.

> Contemplation is also the response to a call: a call from Him Who has no voice, and yet Who speaks everything that is, and Who, most of all, speaks in the depths of our own being: for we ourselves are words of His. But we are words that are meant to respond to him, to answer to Him, to echo Him, and even in some way to contain Him and signify Him. Contemplation is this echo. It is a deep resonance in the inmost center of our spirit in which our very life loses its separate voice and re-sounds with the majesty and the mercy of the Hidden and Loving One. He answers Himself in us and this answer is divine life, divine creativity, making all things

---

[4] Ibid., 15.

[5] Ibid., 17.

[6] Augustine, *Confessions,* III.6.11, trans. Henry Chadwick (New York: Oxford University Press, 1998).

new. We ourselves become His echo and His answer. It is as if in creating us God asked a question, and in awakening us to contemplation He answered the question, so that the contemplative is at the same time, question and answer.[7]

Indeed, so close is God's presence to us that it is like an unspoken, unmediated, and uncomplicated conversation or dialogue. The difficulty of this dialogue with God is what Merton calls the contemplative awakening; that is, we must be open and attuned to the invitation of relationship that God extends to us at all times.

When we awaken to the mystery of God's presence in our lives, this is at once the beginning of dialogue with God and the inauguration of our discovery of our true self. For Merton, dialogue with God is both a discovery of who God really is as well as the discovery of who we really are: "The secret of my identity is hidden in the love and mercy of God."[8] Though our modern societies and popular cultures tell us that we need to construct our identities and shape our personal futures, Merton insists that who we really are is known to God alone, for God loved each of us into existence individually and in our particularity. We cannot, Merton contends, merely happen upon or discover our true self by ourselves. "For although I can know something of God's existence and nature by my own reason, there is no human and rational way in which I can arrive at this contact, that possession of Him, which will be the discovery of Who He really is and Who I am in Him."[9]

Merton's encouraging challenge for all Christians to embrace a life of prayer and contemplation is an invitation to cultivate a dialogue with God that allows each person to come to know the Creator better and, ultimately, to discover his or her own true identity. In a preface he wrote to a collection of prayers in 1961, Merton summarizes what a dialogue with God looks like and leads to: "Prayer is not only the 'lifting up of the mind and heart to God,' but it is also the response to God within us, the discovery of God within us; it leads ultimately to the discovery and fulfillment of our own true being in God."[10] This dialogue with God is

---

[7] Merton, *New Seeds of Contemplation*, 3.

[8] Ibid., 35.

[9] Ibid., 36.

[10] Quoted in *Thomas Merton: Essential Writings*, ed. Christine M. Bochen (Maryknoll, NY: Orbis Books, 2000), 82.

not only for a few and the religious elite, but also for every member of the human family.

Dialogue with Culture

On the relationship between an individual and culture, theologian Orlando Espín writes: "We are in culture as in a womb from which there is no birth, because we are already born into it."[11] Culture is at once both a difficult concept to articulate and an inescapable reality and condition of human existence. We are born into it, it shapes our imaginations and dreams, and it informs our fears and prejudices. As theologian Kathryn Tanner notes, culture in our modern sense has several components including a universal dimension (nobody exists outside one or more cultures), variation among social groups (culture can be seen as an attribute of each particular group), and a composition conceived as an entire way of life (it is made of social habits and institutions, rituals, beliefs, values, and so on).[12] For our purposes here, we consider culture to be that "womb" or context in which Merton found himself and that helped shape his particular horizon. Culture is also something that is universally experienced in its particularity, which shapes individual and group identities. In addition to a dialogue with God marked by contemplative prayer, Merton also engaged and encouraged others to engage in a dialogue with culture—both their own and that of others. As Merton scholar Patrick O'Connell explains, "Thomas Merton was both committed to the values of his own culture and open to the contributions of other cultures and an advocate of what he called 'transcultural consciousness.'"[13] *Transcultural consciousness* is the term that best summarizes Merton's commitment to the dialogue between his own culture and familiar traditions and those cultures and traditions of other women and men from around the globe.

---

[11] Orlando O. Espín, "Grace and Humanness: A Hispanic Perspective," in *We Are a People! Initiatives in Hispanic American Theology*, ed. Roberto S. Goizueta (Minneapolis: Fortress Press, 1992), 143.

[12] See Kathryn Tanner, *Theories of Culture: A New Agenda for Theology* (Minneapolis: Fortress Press, 1997), 25–27.

[13] Patrick O'Connell, "Culture," in *The Thomas Merton Encyclopedia*, ed. William H. Shannon, Christine M. Bochen, and Patrick F. O'Connell (Maryknoll, NY: Orbis Books, 2002), 95.

Merton firmly believed that one could not dialogue with another culture or tradition without first being deeply grounded in one's own. Without an adequate rooting in the culture of one's own intellectual and artistic heritage, any attempt to engage another would not be a dialogue but a unidirectional monologue of sorts—it could lead to the pilfering of another culture without anything to provide in return. In order to avoid this intercultural pitfall, Merton believed that, in the words of O'Connell, "to become conversant with our own culture is to recognize its shortcomings and distortions, its past sins, its current problems, its future threats."[14] Merton believed that viewing one's own context with a critical lens is a form of respect, love, and fidelity for that which was inherited from the generations and communities that came before us.

In his 1966 book *Conjectures of a Guilty Bystander*, Merton offers a number of reflections on both his own cultural background—that of a European-born white man who emigrated to the United States and is now a member of a Roman Catholic religious community—and his forays into learning more about other cultures. Regarding his own culture, Merton was able to recognize simultaneously the strengths and weaknesses that arise within the Euro-American context.

> Our ability to see ourselves objectively and to criticize our own actions, our own failings, is the source of a very real strength. But to those who fear truth, who have begun to forget the genuine Western heritage and to become immersed in crude materialism without spirit, this critical tendency presents the greatest danger.[15]

Merton goes on to caution against what he perceives to be a cultural trend toward overreliance on technology and consumerism, which weakens the uniqueness and authenticity of cultural particularity. He insisted that one must intelligently and critically engage with one's own heritage so as to appreciate the distinctive characteristics of what has been handed on from previous generations as well as identify that which is emerging in the present age.

Visual and performing arts, literature and poetry, religion and mythology, history and narrative, language and expression all come together to

---

[14] Ibid.

[15] Thomas Merton, *Conjectures of a Guilty Bystander* (New York: Doubleday, 1966), 62.

form what Merton recognized as the matrix of a given culture. Having sought to secure his own appreciation for and understanding of his own cultural foundation, as best as he could, Merton then turned toward others with a genuine spirit of openness to encounter the cultures of others. He approached this dialogue in a particular way. As O'Connell notes, "It is particularly important, in Merton's view, to comprehend other civilizations on their own terms, not to make any premature attempt at assimilation, to reject the temptation to incorporate congenial elements of another culture into one's own worldview and discard the rest."[16] Merton's concern was to avoid the temptation to succumb to syncretism (the piecemeal selection of what strikes one as subjectively appealing while overlooking or rejecting those views or aspects of a tradition that seem unattractive) or what is often referred to today as cultural appropriation (the uncritical mimicry or adaptation of cultural characteristics or behaviors without sufficient context or understanding).

A touchstone of authentic dialogue between cultures is the profound appreciation for the distinctive integrity of the particular culture or tradition. The goal in this way of dialoguing is "to appreciate the core values of another tradition . . . the sympathetic effort to perceive the world from the standpoint of another, to enter as far as possible into that framework."[17] According to O'Connell, Merton always understood this dialogue with culture to exhibit a spiritual dimension. "On its deepest level, this receptivity [of cultural dialogue] is an openness to the divine present within the other."[18] In this way, mirroring his concurrent commitment to interreligious dialogue, Merton anticipates the wisdom of the Second Vatican Council, in which the Roman Catholic Church proclaimed that the church rejects nothing that is true or good in other religions or cultures.[19]

This sort of dialogue presumes a real relationship that risks vulnerability and humility. The vulnerability emerges in the risk of being misunderstood, while the humility rests in the conviction that one's culture

---

[16] O'Connell, "Culture," 95.

[17] Ibid.

[18] Ibid.

[19] See, for example, Vatican II documents *Nostra Aetate* (*Declaration on the Relations of the Church to Non-Christian Religions*), *Gaudium et Spes* (*Pastoral Constitution on the Church in the Modern World*), and *Unitatis Redintegratio* (*Decree on Ecumenism*).

does not have all of the answers or a monopoly on what is good or true. Dialogue with culture also presupposes the patience necessary to listen, discern, and discuss within a community of difference. One must resist the fear of that which is different or perceived as foreign; or, put more bluntly, one must resist the temptation to espouse xenophobic attitudes and assumptions. The result of such a dialogue is the possibility of mutual enrichment and a return to one's own cultural context with greater appreciation for one's own heritage and social location. In his book *Mystics and Zen Masters*, Merton draws on the possibility of Western European and North American engagement with Eastern cultures and traditions to highlight exactly this point about mutual enrichment. He writes:

> The cultural heritage of Asia has as much right to be studied in our colleges as the cultural heritage of Greece and Rome. . . . If the West can recognize that contact with Eastern thought can renew our appreciation for our own cultural heritage, a product of the fusion of the Judeo-Christian religion with Greco-Roman culture, then it will be easier to defend that heritage, not only in Asia but in the West as well.[20]

Merton's understanding of what it means to become a better Christian is tied to his understanding of what it means to become a better human person more generally. One of the central elements is a simultaneous effort to ground oneself in the depths of one's own cultural context and also express openness to other cultures and traditions.

Dialogue with Society

In his encomium for Merton before the joint session of Congress, Pope Francis emphasized that Merton was admirable for being "a thinker who challenged the certitudes of his time and opened new horizons for souls and for the Church."[21] One of the ways that Merton challenged the certitudes of his time was by being a public intellectual and a social

---

[20] Thomas Merton, *Mystics and Zen Masters* (New York: Farrar, Strauss, and Giroux, 1999), 45–46.

[21] Pope Francis, "Visit to the Joint Session of the United States Congress."

critic. Unlike many newspaper columnists or university professors, Merton's public intellectualism didn't originate in the traditional venues nor typically appear in the usual style of most notable commentators. Obviously, he was a Trappist monk and a Catholic priest whose commitment to a religious life of prayer and work (*ora et labora*) remained rooted in a particular and circumscribed geographic place. For this reason, though he might not have been the most well-traveled observer of social mores and his contemporary *zeitgeist*, he nevertheless had a sense of the collective cultural pulse and recognized the everyday realities of his contemporaries. Merton's commitment to recognizing the "signs of the times" and then interpreting them "in light of the Gospel"[22] governed his dialogue with society, offering something of a view from the margins that was a unique vantage point occasioned by Merton's distinctive location as a kind of resident alien in the American context. A voracious reader and letter writer, Merton was attuned to the ethos of his age, which—particularly in the 1950s and 1960s—was consumed with matters of violence and racism.[23]

Whereas culture is an internalized reality, likened to a womb that always surrounds us and from which we cannot escape, society can be understood as the normative structuring of communities outside of the individual. Though universally found, cultures nevertheless remain understandably intangible and difficult to identify clearly. Societies, on the other hand, are established and systemically organized. As with his commitment to dialogue with culture, Merton's dialogue with society began by grounding himself in his own tradition and social location. In this way Merton anticipated what the Second Vatican Council would teach regarding how to interpret the current events and environment once recognized according to the "light of the Gospel." In a counterintuitive way Merton's writings on war and racism were prescient and insightful while remaining prophetic and deeply Christian.

---

[22] *Gaudium et Spes*, no. 4.

[23] I generally agree with David Givey, who writes: "The two social issues that Thomas Merton considered most urgent to Americans during the 1960s were war and racism" (David Givey, *The Social Thought of Thomas Merton: The Way of Non-violence and Peace for the Future* [Winona: Anselm Academic, 2009], 89). Given the limitations of scope and length for this chapter, I briefly address only these two issues, though Merton was also engaged and concerned about other issues of his time such as technology, the environment, and so on.

Merton wrote at great length about the Vietnam conflict, nuclear weapons, and other instances of corporate and individual acts of violence. In his posthumously published book, *Contemplation in a World of Action*, Merton reflected on the way that his birth at a particular point in history shaped his experience and outlook on war and violence:

> That I should be born in 1915, that I should be the contemporary of Auschwitz, Hiroshima, Vietnam, and the Watts riots, are things about which I was not first consulted. Yet they are also events in which, whether I like it or not, I am deeply and personally involved. The "world" is not just a physical space traversed by jet planes and full of people running in all directions. It is a complex of responsibilities and options made out of the loves, the hates, the fears, the joys, the hopes, the greed, the cruelty, the kindness, the faith, the trust, the suspicion of all. In the last analysis, if there is war because nobody trusts anybody, this is in part because I myself am defensive, suspicious, untrusting, and intent on making other people conform themselves to my particular brand of death wish.[24]

Here Merton lays out his motivation for engagement with broader society, particularly regarding the theme of war and violence. In stark contrast to the commonsense logic of religious life at the time, one governed by a *fuga mundi* ("fleeing the world") mentality, Merton deliberately occupied a place at the margins of society as someone who nevertheless remained in touch with and connected to the world, if not exactly "of the world" (to use an oft-quoted religious phrase).

Rooted in his Christian conviction that authentic gospel life demands a radical nonviolent attitude toward conflict, Merton's dialogue with social actors and about the circumstances of his time often took on a notably critical hue. As James Baker explains, "When Thomas Merton emerged from his monastic hideaway in the early 1950s and looked again upon the America which he had adopted, he saw a land filled with violence, a society whose personality and nature were molded by its violent past and whose ability to change its violent present might cause it to be

---

[24] Thomas Merton, *Contemplation in a World of Action* (New York: Doubleday, 1971), 161.

destroyed."[25] Still, Merton, though he was largely an essayist, never let his dialogue with society on the topic of war and violence devolve into mere monologue. He made great strides to understand the contexts, histories, and internal logics of decision makers and situations. The openness he demonstrated in his dialogical approach to prayer and culture likewise was reflected in his engagement with society.

In the end, Merton occupied a position that advocated Christian non-violence as the normative disposition in the face of conflict. He refrained from appropriating the moniker "pacifist," largely for fear that it was too often mistaken for "passivity" in the face of conflict. As a Christian in the modern world, Merton was convinced that a nonviolent stance was anything but passive; it was a radical response that required imagination and creativity, true dialogue and compromise. Unfortunately, Merton recognized that in the age of the overpowering "military industrial complex," the United States' default solution to domestic and international problems was nearly always military in nature.

Merton's dialogue with society concerning war and violence also included a critical conversation within his own Christian theological tradition. Merton was, in principle, an adherent to the ancient just-war theory, which states that, given a number of specific criteria, it is conceivable that a violent response to a military aggressor can be justified. I say Merton was "in principle" in support of just war because he stated himself that, *in practice*, such a justifiable war could not be conducted in the nuclear age.[26] The conversation in which Merton engaged was one that maintained a fierce loyalty to the Christian intellectual and moral tradition but was also one that did not shy away from challenging questions and propositions. Indeed, as Pope Francis mentioned, Merton was not at all afraid to challenge preconceptions or "certitudes" of his time—both within the church and outside it.

---

[25] James T. Baker, *Thomas Merton: Social Critic* (Lexington: University Press of Kentucky, 1971), 98.

[26] See, for example, Thomas Merton, *The Nonviolent Alternative*, ed. Gordon Zahn (New York: Farrar, Strauss, Giroux, 1971); Gordon Zahn, "Thomas Merton: Reluctant Pacifist," in *Thomas Merton: Prophet in the Belly of a Paradox*, ed. Gerald Twomey (New York: Paulist Press, 1978), 55–79; and Daniel P. Horan, "Becoming Instruments of Peace: How Francis and Merton Challenge Us to Live Today," in *The Franciscan Heart of Thomas Merton* (Notre Dame, IN: Ave Maria Press, 2014), 199–218.

Merton was also deeply concerned with the reality of racism and the struggle for civil rights under way in the 1960s, which he recognized as tied to the larger and overarching ill of American society—violence. James Baker explains this connection well when he writes, "Merton believed that the most obvious and continuing sign of America's violence was the racism which had led to her greatest social crisis of the 1960s."[27] Merton was deeply attuned to the social dynamics of institutional and structural evils that perpetuate racial injustice, prejudice, and discrimination. Long before the twenty-first-century technological revolution of smart phones and social media that have brought wider attention to the systemic injustices of racism in the United States, Merton understood that what was widely characterized by politicians and white-controlled media as isolated instances of violence in communities of predominantly persons of color was in fact symptomatic of a far-more-insidious reality of institutional racism masked as "law and order." In an essay that begins with the line, "Theology today needs to focus carefully upon the crucial problem of violence," Merton writes:

> Hence murder, mugging, rape, crime, corruption. But it must be remembered that the crime that breaks out of the ghetto is only the fruit of a greater and more pervasive violence: the injustice which forces people to live in the ghetto in the first place. The problem of violence, then, is not the problem of a few rioters and rebels, but the problem of a whole structure which is outwardly ordered and respectable, and inwardly ridden by psychopathic obsessions and delusions.[28]

Merton's dialogue with society on the topic of racism and civil rights began in the 1960s with an optimistic look to Martin Luther King, Jr., and the hope that Christian nonviolence would prevail. However, by the mid-1960s, and then with King's assassination in 1968, Merton became disillusioned with the prospect that nonviolent action would work. He never goes so far as to endorse violent action, but he does express a sort of solidarity and empathy with those people of color who

---

[27] Baker, *Thomas Merton*, 99.
[28] Thomas Merton, "Toward a Theology of Resistance," in *Faith and Violence* (Notre Dame, IN: University of Notre Dame Press, 1968), 3.

might consider violent force as a means to overcoming racial injustice in the United States.[29]

Merton's writings on race are simply astounding. What is most striking about his perspective in the national conversation about civil rights is his consistent and clear conviction that the problem of racism is not a black problem but *a white* problem. In his classic, if at the time of its publication controversial, essay "Letters to a White Liberal," Merton offers a lengthy engagement with the "signs of the times" in the context of the struggle for American civil rights. His general thesis is that, while Congress passed the Civil Rights Act of 1964, there remains little beyond the written legislation to enact the desired intention of the law. Racism in the United States is so deeply imbedded in the culture and collective imaginary that it will take much more than some words on a paper to change the status quo. In fact, Merton argues that the white Christian communities in the North (that is, "white liberals"), which seem ostensibly supportive of civil rights for black women and men, are in fact complicit in the subjugation of persons of color and the perpetuation of structural racism because they do not wish to surrender the society with which they are familiar nor do they want to acknowledge and then give up the unearned privileges afforded them because of the color of their skin.

Merton's dialogue with his society on the subject of racism challenges his interlocutors, especially those who identify as Christian and white, to acknowledge their complicity in the continuation of racial injustice. In a powerful essay titled "The Hot Summer of Sixty-Seven," Merton explains:

> There is, however, such a thing as collective responsibility, and collective guilt. This is not quite the same as personal responsibility and personal guilt, because it does not usually follow from a direct fully conscious act of choice. Few of us have actively and consciously *chosen* to oppress or mistreat the Negro. But nevertheless we have all more or less acquiesced in and consented to a state of affairs in which the Negro is treated unjustly, and in which his unjust treatment is directly or indirectly to the advantage of people like ourselves, people with whom we agree and collaborate, people

---

[29] See, for example, Thomas Merton, "From Non-Violence to Black Power," in *Faith and Violence*, 121–29.

with whom we are in fact identified. So that even if in theory the white man may believe himself to be well disposed toward the Negro—and never gets into a bind in which he proves himself to be otherwise—we all collectively contribute to a situation in which the Negro has to live and act as our inferior.[30]

The dialogue with society in this case starts with a humility on Merton's part, acknowledging his own social location and his own identification— "we," "us," and "ourselves"—with those with whom he is engaging. Unless serious, conscious, deliberate efforts to recognize and then surrender white privilege, listen to those oppressed by racism, and then do something to change the status quo are deployed, then nothing will change. And the fault rests with the predominantly white, racist society, which does not exist apart from all those willfully ignorant individuals that compose it.

Merton's dialogue with society always began with his owning his own place within it. Although many were openly hostile and dismissive of Merton's social criticism in the moment, the passage of time has only further clarified his prophetic insight and prescience.

Dialogue with Religions

Pope Francis lauded Merton as a "promoter of peace between peoples and religions."[31] And it is precisely for ecumenical and interreligious dialogue that Merton is best known of the four forms of dialogue we have explored in this chapter. As we have already seen, dialogue with God, with cultures, and with society, Merton's starting point for engaging with other religious traditions—both Christian and non-Christian alike—was to situate himself securely in his own faith tradition: Roman Catholicism. In order for there to be a dialogue, both conversation partners must bring something to the table, must be able to offer a grounded sense of integrity and humility. In a 1965 letter to a man named Marco Pallis, who had studied Tibetan Buddhism for many decades before Merton first

---

[30] Thomas Merton, "The Hot Summer of Sixty-Seven," in *Faith and Violence*, 180.

[31] Pope Francis, "Visit to the Joint Session of the United States Congress."

became interested in Eastern thought, Merton affirms the importance of knowing and embracing one's own religious tradition before one is able to engage in interreligious dialogue in any meaningful sense:

> I agree entirely that one must cling to one tradition and to its orthodoxy, at the risk of not understanding any tradition. One cannot supplement his own tradition with little borrowings here and there from other traditions. On the other hand, if one is genuinely living his own tradition, he is capable of seeing where other traditions say and attain the same thing, and where they are different. The differences must be respected, not brushed aside, even and especially where they are irreconcilable with one's own view.[32]

What we see here is something of Merton's own *modus operandi*, a guiding principle of sorts that establishes the context for how to go about engaging in dialogue between religions. In a sense, Merton is speaking here from his own experience as one who was admittedly naive and hostile to non-Christian (and non-*Catholic*) religious traditions prior to the latter part of the 1950s, when Merton began dialoguing with ministers and students of other Christian denominations, including those from Baptist, Methodist, and Presbyterian churches.[33] As a result of his secure standing within the Catholic Christian context, Merton was genuinely open to the experiences and insights of others. He was able to write in his book *Conjectures of a Guilty Bystander* in 1966 that "I will be a better Catholic, not if I can *refute* every shade of Protestantism, but if I can affirm the truth in it and still go further."[34]

What began as openness to other Christian traditions in the West expanded to include Eastern Orthodoxy communities, writings, spiritualties, and theologies about which Merton read extensively and allowed to shape his own theological outlook, thereby strengthening his own

---

[32] Thomas Merton, "Letter to Marco Pallis, Easter 1965," in *The Hidden Ground of Love: Letters on Religious Experience and Social Concerns*, ed. William H. Shannon (New York: Farrar, Straus, Giroux, 1985), 469.

[33] For more on this, see the recent collection of essays in William Oliver Paulsell, ed., *Merton and the Protestant Tradition* (Louisville, KY: Fons Vitae, 2017).

[34] Merton, *Conjectures of a Guilty Bystander*, 129.

faith and worldview.³⁵ Turning toward the East was not simply limited to the Christian churches for Merton but led then to other faith and philosophical traditions including Buddhism, Hinduism, Islam, and Judaism. The groundedness in his own Roman Catholicism that afforded him the freedom, humility, and openness to engage earnestly in dialogue with other religions was observed by the Chinese scholar John Wu, who once wrote to Merton: "You are so deeply Christian that you cannot help touching the vital springs of other religions."³⁶

Contrary to some misguided views of Merton's ecumenical and interreligious dialoguing, Merton was never interested in—let alone considered—leaving the Roman Catholic Church or his religious community of Trappist monks. Instead, his efforts to dialogue among Christian communities and other faith traditions anticipated and then fulfilled what the Second Vatican Council taught regarding religious freedom, ecumenism, and interfaith dialogue and friendship. Indeed, Merton was a man ahead of his time and ahead of his church when it comes to dialogue with religions just as he was with the universality of holiness and contemplation for all women and men, the importance of Christians engaging with culture, and the need for critical dialogue with society. If there was any doubt lingering among the naysayers as to Merton's fittingness to serve as an exemplar of dialogue or Christian living in the modern world, the Holy Father Pope Francis put an end to that uncertainty on September 24, 2015.

But we might ask what resulted from Merton's engagement and dialogue with other religions. The answer is given to us by Merton himself in the posthumously published volume *The Asian Journal*, which chronicles the last months of Merton's life while traveling to the subcontinent and Southeast Asia. In a lecture given in Calcutta in October 1968, Merton hinted at what he had come to recognize as the deep interrelatedness women and men share despite both real and perceived differences. He remarked that there are always people who dare to live on the margins

³⁵ See Gray Henry and Jonathan Montaldo, eds., *Merton and Hesychasm: The Prayer of the Heart and the Eastern Church* (Louisville, KY: Fons Vitae, 2003).

³⁶ John Wu, "Letter to Merton, November 28, 1961," unpublished letter (Louisville, KY: Thomas Merton Center Archives), as cited in William Apel, *Signs of Peace: The Interfaith Letters of Thomas Merton* (Maryknoll, NY: Orbis Books, 2006), xv, see also 47–63.

of society and therefore see the world in a different way than those in the mainstream. Such people, Merton contends, help point the way to possibility of "communication on the deepest level":

> And the deepest level of communication is not communication, but communion. It is wordless. It is beyond words, and it is beyond speech, and it is beyond concept. Not that we discover a new unity. We discover an older unity. My dear brothers, we are already one. But we imagine that we are not. And what we have to recover is our original unity. What we have to be is what we are.[37]

Merton was motivated to engage in dialogue with other religions because he recognized—guided by prayer and the Holy Spirit—that there is something profoundly unifying about our human condition. If we remain isolated monads of religions, separate and defensive, then we will never come close to encountering a kind of unity that is not novel or faddish or fleeting, but a unity that is original and divinely established. Or, as Merton said simply in his book *No Man Is an Island,* "This truth never becomes clear as long as we assume that each one of us, individually, is the center of the universe."[38] True dialogue is only possible when humility and the recognition of interdependence flow into interreligious friendship and conversation.

Conclusion

In a simple statement found in a 1966 letter to the British scholar Etta Gullick, Merton provides in his own words what we might take away as a summary of his approach to becoming a person of dialogue:

> To me it is enough to be united with people in love and in the Holy Spirit, as I am sure I am, and they are, in spite of the sometimes momentous institutional and doctrinal differences. But where there is a sincere desire for truth and real good will and genuine love, there God Himself will take care of the differences far better

---

[37] Thomas Merton, *The Asian Journal of Thomas Merton*, ed. Naomi Burton, Patrick Hart, and James Laughlin (New York: New Directions, 1973), 308.

[38] Thomas Merton, *No Man Is an Island* (New York: Harcourt Brace, 1955), xx.

than any human or political ingenuity can. Prayer is the thing, and union with the suffering Lord upon His Cross.[39]

Unity among people and between humanity and God was the primary motivation for each kind of dialogue in which Merton engaged. It is this quest for truth, good will, and genuine love that enabled him to dialogue fearlessly and courageously and to encourage others to do likewise.

For Thomas Merton dialogue is an extraordinarily human endeavor that involves the risk of vulnerability and openness and requires humility and listening. One must work to understand better one's own cultural, social, and religious contexts in order to engage genuinely with others about their respective experience, perspective, belief, and history. Analogously, there is a risk in dialoguing with God that can be unsettling or even scary for many. But the messiness of human interaction and relationship is at the heart of all dialogue, which is why Merton explains that one cannot simply retreat to an intellectual or scholarly study, for such a detached approach forestalls the peacemaking and bridge-building that can only come through friendship. This is why Merton writes, "The fact remains that as long as the dialogue proceeds merely between research scholars and concerns only the objective study of documents, it will lack its most essential dimension."[40] That essential dimension is relationship, which is something Pope Francis also understands and models for us by his words and deeds in our own time. No wonder he held Merton up as a preeminent example of what it means to be a person of dialogue.

---

[39] Thomas Merton, "Letter to Etta Gullick, November 29, 1966," in Shannon, *The Hidden Ground of Love*, 378.

[40] Merton, *Mystics and Zen Masters*, 209.

17

Raids on the Impossible

*The Poetics of Nonviolence
in Merton, Caputo, and Hauerwas*

Christianity, when taken seriously, is impossible. It advocates love for the unlovable, forgiveness for the unforgivable, healing for the broken and brokenhearted, and nonviolence in the face of adversity within the context of a very violent and unstable world. It is impossible by the standards of so-called common sense and the logic of the world. It is impossible according to the strictures of popular wisdom that rely on systems of retribution masked as authentic justice; economic inequality couched in the often unacknowledged cycles of racism and discrimination; and selfishness that is encouraged under the guise of capitalistic virtues. To live in the footprints of Jesus Christ, to embrace the *vita evangelica* ("gospel life"), which is the primary vocation of all Christians, is indeed impossible. That is, unless it isn't. Unless the metrics we use to evaluate the possibility of our religious convictions are the wrong ones and the correct measurements can only be made in accordance with the gospel.

Rooted in the proclamation of the kingdom of God, Thomas Merton wrote that nonviolence "is the one political philosophy today which appeals directly to the Gospel."[1] This conviction, the ongoing commitment

---

[A version of this essay was originally presented at the Ninth General Conference of the Thomas Merton Society of Great Britain and Ireland, Oakham, UK, April 13–15, 2012, and later published in *The Merton Seasonal* 37, no. 3 (2012): 3–10. Used with permission.]

[1] Thomas Merton, "Non-Violence and the Christian Conscience," in *Faith and Violence: Christian Teaching and Christian Practice* (Notre Dame, IN: University of Notre Dame Press, 1968), 30.

to the inseparability of nonviolence from the Christian life is found throughout Merton's writings. Such is the case in his collection of essays, *Raids on the Unspeakable*, particularly in the essays "The Time of the End Is the Time of No Room," "Letter to an Innocent Bystander," and "A Devout Meditation in Memory of Adolf Eichmann." The ways in which Merton poetically crafts his reflections on the place of nonviolence in Christian life in relationship to the violence of the world anticipates the work of two well-known contemporary thinkers decades later: philosopher John D. Caputo and the ethicist Stanley Hauerwas.

Caputo's postmodern engagement of the gospel with deconstructionist continental philosophy breaks open a renewed sense of the event that is the *kerygmatic* kingdom of God. The gospel proclamation of the kingdom defies the logical discourse of violence and binary distinction, expressing the event of God's reign in a theopoetics, the realization of the possibility of the impossible in the forms of love and forgiveness. Hauerwas's presentation of a Christian ethics of character, which is foundationally narrative, also draws on the *kerygma* of the kingdom to identify the centrality of nonviolence in the Christian vocation. Hauerwas's work, combined with the grammar of kingdom poetics in Caputo's writing, offers us a path toward a theological praxis of nonviolence. These two contemporary thinkers allow us to read Merton with a renewed sense of his relevance for today. Perennially prophetic, Merton's own proclamation of the kingdom as constitutive of gospel living, expressed in the creative poetics of his *Raids on the Unspeakable* and other later texts, provides us with yet another comprehensive elucidation of what it means to bear the name Christian in a world of violence. Indeed, what these three thinkers read together offer us are raids on the impossible, a re-centering of nonviolence in the discourse of Christian discipleship.

The structure of this chapter is fourfold. I begin with a brief introduction to John D. Caputo's understanding of the kingdom of God as an "event of the (im)possible" expressed in terms we might call *theopoetics,* which inherently deconstructs the binary logic of the world and offers us a glimpse at the Christian alternative to violence. Second, I draw on the work of Stanley Hauerwas to identify the centrality of nonviolence in the Christian narrative, the story to which all Christians belong. Third, I show how Merton's later writing, particularly some of his essays in *Raids on the Unspeakable*, presents us with contemporary resources for engaging with and proclaiming forth the poetic nonviolence of Christian discipleship. This chapter ends with a short conclusion.

On the (Im)possibility of the Kingdom of God[2]

In his acclaimed book *The Weakness of God: A Theology of the Event,* John Caputo is entirely forthcoming about his approach to Christian theology. He writes, "I will make clear that the discourse of the Kingdom rightly understood is governed, not by a 'logic of omnipotence,' which has to do with entities, but by what I will call a *poetics of the impossible,* which has to do with events."[3] Caputo's starting point is the correlation of what the Christian scriptures present as that which "nothing is impossible for God" (Lk 1:37) with Derrida's concept of "the *impossible.*" It is a linkage, as Caputo puts it, between the gospel and deconstruction. And, as Caputo makes clear in his popular book *What Would Jesus Deconstruct?* the prophetic spirit of Jesus is made intelligible in the proclamation of the kingdom of God. He suggests that we are able to experience that event, to recognize what is already always there through deconstruction, and that "deconstruction is good news, because it delivers the shock of the other to the form of the same, the shock of the good (the 'ought') to the forces of being ('what is')."[4]

Caputo explains further what he means by deconstruction and its relevance to Christian theology when he writes:

Deconstruction is organized around the idea that things contain a kind of uncontainable truth, that they contain what they cannot contain. Nobody has to come along and "deconstruct" things. Things are auto-deconstructed by the tendencies of their own inner truth. In a deconstruction, the "other" is the one who tells the

[2] Portions of this section come from Daniel Horan, "The Grammar of the Kingdom in a World of Violence: The (Im)possible Poetics of John D. Caputo," in *Violence, Transformation, and the Sacred: 'They Will Be Called Children of God,'* ed. Tobias Winwright and Margaret Pfeil (Maryknoll, NY: Orbis Books, 2012).

[3] John D. Caputo, *The Weakness of God: A Theology of the Event* (Bloomington: Indiana University Press, 2006), 102.

[4] John D. Caputo, *What Would Jesus Deconstruct: The Good News of Post-Modernism for the Church* (Grand Rapids, MI: Baker Academic, 2007), 26–27.

truth on the "same"; the other is the truth of the same, the truth that has been repressed and suppressed, omitted and marginalized, or sometimes just plain murdered, like Jesus himself, which is why Johannes Baptist Metz speaks of the "dangerous" memory of the suffering of Jesus and why I describe deconstruction as hermeneutics of the kingdom of God.[5]

Accessing the event of truth, inasmuch as one is able to "access" and not only experience an event, calls for a different hermeneutic, one that is tuned to the key of the kingdom and not of the world; a way of seeing through the eyes of Jesus and not simply repeating the status quo. For repetition is indeed a function of the kingdom, a repetition of the impossible made possible in the total gift of forgiveness. As Keith Putt explains, "The kingdom of God is a new creation and, therefore, demands new minds and new hearts; it actually established a new type of economy, a mad economy of excess and extravagance, an economy that does not covet balanced books or safe returns on existential investments."[6]

What Caputo recognizes, what he takes as deadly serious, is what the gospel proclaims about the newness of what is happening in the incarnation of the Word. The good news is more than a repeated trope of some platitude of kindness and the Golden Rule. It is instead precisely what the Angel Gabriel is remembered to have conveyed to Mary—*nothing* is *impossible* for God (Lk 1:37). Even more than Mary, we today find ourselves in a constant state of disbelief. We are, as St. Paul points out to the Corinthians, like the Jews and Gentiles (that is, *everybody*), who actually find the content of the faith foolish and a stumbling block. It doesn't make sense—at least not by the standards with which we ordinarily judge our everyday lives. Hence, we have the ostensible impossibility of Christianity.

Caputo and others readily admit that there is a certain logic to violence in our world. This discursive fact invites further consideration, namely, that the logical grammar that sustains myriad forms of violence in our world is antithetical to the *kerygmatic* proclamation of the kingdom of

---

[5] Ibid., 29.

[6] B. Keith Putt, "Violent Imitation or Compassionate Repetition? Girard and Caputo on Exemplary Atonement," in *Religion and Violence in a Secular World: Toward a New Political Theology*, ed. Clayton Crockett (Charlottesville: University of Virginia Press, 2006), 32.

God. Caputo asserts that the wisdom of deconstruction heuristically identifies the contradiction inherent in so-called worldly wisdom as it seeks to maintain power amid claims of authentic Christian discipleship. Such a nexus—the "wisdom" of the world and a distorted reading of Christian discipleship—enables the context out of which secular liturgies of nationalism and violence (from Constantine's Rome to George W. Bush's America) can be formed, simultaneously (re)scripting the Christian narrative while rendering this novel form of discipleship unrecognizable to the gospel proclamation of the kingdom. So tainted have certain articulations of the Christian tradition become that the language of its expression no longer offers a resource for accessing the "good news," as it were. One way to describe this phenomenon, this worldly wisdom of which St. Paul speaks that is at once and the same time wedded to an obsession with maintaining power, is to talk about the logical grammar of the possible. This worldly discourse is concerned with and bent on the sensible, the logical, the economic exchange of just value and reciprocity. It is a language focused on fairness as conceived in finite, human terms and therefore creates a space where it is not only permissible but logical to seek and endorse systems of retribution and vengeance, economies of debt and control, and liturgies and politics of violence.

To the contrary, Caputo holds that this method of language, this worldly grammar of logic, is not what rightly expresses the kingdom of God proclaimed by Jesus of Nazareth. St. Paul says as much when he confesses the ostensible foolishness and stumbling block the Christian *kerygma* presents to the world. Caputo rejects the logical grammar of the possible as capable of expressing the kingdom of the gospel. Jesus does not speak in logical terms, in language of the possible, but instead proclaims a poetic and eschatological theology that denotes the in-breaking of God's reign. Nevertheless, Jesus is quick to point out that his kingdom is "not of the world" (Jn 18:36), offering Caputo and us yet another deconstructive clue. The *kingdom*, as it were, does not conform to the logic of the world but is structured (or unstructured or *deconstructed*) according to a "divine logic," which is described least-badly as a *poetics*.[7] Caputo explains that by *poetics* he means "a constellation of strategies,

---

[7] John D. Caputo, "The Poetics of the Impossible and the Kingdom of God," in *The Blackwell Companion to Postmodern Theology*, ed. Graham Ward (London: Blackwell, 2001), 470.

arguments, tropes, paradigms, and metaphors, a style and a tone, as well as a grammar and a vocabulary, all of which, collectively . . . is aimed at making a point."[8] This point is, as Caputo creatively describes it, a "rule of the unruly, the possibility of the impossible."[9]

The kingdom is marked by several things that appear illogical and counterintuitive in a world marred by the logic of violence, and because of this, we can understand the kingdom to be an announcement of God's preference for reversals, for preferring sinners over the righteous, for identifying the stranger as the neighbor, for showing that the insiders are actually out and the like. The language of the kingdom must be poetic, cannot be logical, because "the horizon of the world is set by the calculable, the sensible, the *possible*, the reasonable, the sound investment." Caputo goes on, "In the world, we are made to pay for everything. The world is nobody's fool."[10] Yet, it is precisely foolishness that Jesus proclaims and St. Paul affirms. The logical language of the world, the grammar that justifies the perpetuation of violence and vengeance, which inaugurates secular liturgies of nationalism, has no room, no patience, and no time for such poetic discourse and such absurd visions of reality.

Nonviolence Is the Christian Way: There Can Be No Other

As with the previous section on the contribution of John Caputo, an extensive presentation of all the relevant work of Stanley Hauerwas on this theme far exceeds the limitations and scope of this chapter. What I wish to do here is present a brief overview of some of the ways Hauerwas's work helps us to read Merton on the theme of Christian nonviolence in our contemporary setting.

Whereas Caputo's approach is philosophically and methodologically oriented, concerned as he is with language and hermeneutics, Hauerwas's approach is more centered on ethical praxis.[11] His method is one of

---

[8] Ibid.

[9] Ibid., 471.

[10] Ibid., 472.

[11] This is not to suggest that Hauerwas is not committed to linguistic concerns and the role of theological grammar in the Christian life. See, for example, his collection of essays, *Working with Words: On Learning to Speak Christian* (Eugene, OR: Cascade Books, 2011).

character or virtue ethics as the operative lens through which a Christian believer is to interpret life circumstances and judge just actions.[12] The emphasis is an important, if subtle, move from the traditional Christian approach of asking questions similar to "What *ought* I do?" to asking the question "What sort of person do I *strive* to be?" This latter question presupposes a set of virtues or character that is cultivated by appropriating a narrative that guides, defines, and relates to the whole person and his or her particular journey. It is not a matter of compartmentalization, the sequestering of *this* or *that* action or decision, but rather situates morality within the broader context of Christian living. One of Hauerwas's assertions is that among the constitutive dimensions of Christian life stands nonviolence. So antithetical is violence to the Christian narrative, Hauerwas asserts, that a Christian cannot be anything else but a practitioner and advocate for nonviolence.

In his book *War and the American Difference: Theological Reflections on Violence and National Identity,*[13] Hauerwas succinctly expresses his position on the nonnegotiability or the inherently integral dimension of nonviolence in Christian life. He writes: "My claim [is] that Christians are called to live nonviolently, not because we think nonviolence is a strategy to rid the world of war, but rather because as faithful followers of Christ in a world of war we cannot imagine not living nonviolently."[14] At the heart of this conviction stands the tension expressed in the work of Caputo, namely, that the world in which we live does not adhere to the nonviolent priority that Christians must ultimately appropriate. The story at the core of what it means to be a Christian is one, not of passivity (Hauerwas makes it abundantly clear that nonviolence is not passive in the colloquial sense, but instead a way of living in the world nonviolently),[15] but of rejecting the lure of violence and the appropriation of secular liturgies and narratives that reinforce such dispositions.

---

[12] Hauerwas lays this method out in a foundational way in his classic book *A Community of Character: Toward a Constructive Christian Social Ethic* (Notre Dame, IN: University of Notre Dame Press, 1981).

[13] Stanley Hauerwas, *War and the American Difference: Theological Reflection on Violence and National Identity* (Grand Rapids, MI: Baker Academic, 2011).

[14] Ibid., xii.

[15] See Stanley Hauerwas, "C. S. Lewis and Violence," in *War and the American Difference: Theological Reflection on Violence and National Identity* (Grand Rapids, MI: Baker Academic, 2011), 71–82.

One of Hauerwas's more radical claims, one that falls on the side of worldly "illogic," is that

> Christians do not renounce war because it is often so horrible, but because war, in spite of its horror, or perhaps because it is so horrible, can be so morally compelling. That is why the church does not have an alternative to war. The church *is* the alternative to war. When Christians no longer see the reality of the church as an alternative to the world's reality, we abandon the world to war.[16]

Which narratives tell the stories of our lives? Hauerwas makes the point, strongly for sure, that the gospel narrative is the story that should describe the lives of anyone who bears the name Christian. What sort of person do you strive to be? If a disciple of Christ is the answer, then nonviolence is the only way to live in this world of war. The problem, it would seem, is something like "narrative amnesia"—we have forgotten our own story, our own identity. Hauerwas's point is simply to reiterate the truth that so many in our world—particular those in the United States and Europe—have forgotten: we are living a lie. The lie is the outward claim that we are disciples of Christ, when in fact the inward disposition is formed by the narratives of worldly logic of retribution and violence.

Thomas Merton's *Raids on the Unspeakable*

In a way that has come to be identified as classically "later Merton," the collection of essays *Raids on the Unspeakable* provides a creative and entertaining engagement with serious concerns of both a spiritual and social nature. The titular concept, that is *the Unspeakable,* itself denotes a certain impossibility as that which cannot be named precisely because it is privative. It is the absence, or as Merton puts it in the introduction to his collection of essays, "the void that contradicts everything that is spoken even before the words are said," that creates the condition for the possibility of Christian eschatological hope, for the unspeakable marks the location (although not a geo-physical one) of the end of worldly

---

[16] Hauerwas, *War and the American Difference*, 34.

hope.[17] Merton summarizes this as "the void we encounter, you and I, underlying the announced programs, the good intentions, the unexampled and universal aspirations for the best of all possible worlds."[18] I suggest that another way to consider the meaning of the unspeakable is as the foundation and the summation of the logic of the world. Conversely, an alternative way to title Merton's collection of essays might be *Raids on the Impossible.*

The concept of the impossible and the role it plays in the Christian theological tradition as elucidated by Caputo above helps to orient our reading of Merton's writing on nonviolence in an age especially plagued by the unspeakable, particularly as it is made manifest in our contemporary bellicose world. Furthermore, the absolute centrality of the commitment to nonviolent living in the Christian narrative as identified and propagated by Hauerwas helps us to see how Merton recognized a similar ethical prioritization in his own Christian outlook.

Concerning the impossibility of Christian nonviolence in the thought of Merton, we can look to his essay "The Time of the End Is the Time of No Room," in which his introductory note situates the "logic of the world," as introduced above, over and against the "logic of God." This is expressed in terms of two competing eschatologies: that of the world and that of Divine Revelation. Merton writes:

> Biblical eschatology must not be confused with the vague and anxious eschatology of human foreboding. We live in an age of two superimposed eschatologies: that of secular anxieties and hopes, and that of revealed fulfillment. Sometimes the first is merely mistaken for the second, sometimes it results from complete denial and despair of the second. In point of fact the pathological *fear of a violent end* which, when sufficiently aroused, actually becomes a thinly disguised *hope for the violent end.*[19]

The essay's starting point is the "beginning" of the end, which is the incarnation of the Word for whom there is "no room in the inn." The birth

---

[17] Thomas Merton, *Raids on the Unspeakable* (New York: New Directions Publishers, 1966), 4.

[18] Ibid., 4.

[19] Ibid., 65.

narrative of the Gospel of Luke becomes an allegory for the eschatological times in which we live—the times of "no room." The world is in fact "the inn" in which there is no room to be found for the Word-made-flesh. This is not a matter of space but instead a conflict of commitments and a confusion of hopes.

Acknowledging the seeming impossibility of God's entrance into creation as one among us, Merton explains that "all ordinary things are transfigured."[20] Yet, this world is "a world of suspicion, hatred and dis-trust" that cannot recognize the Prince of Peace or hear the tidings of *great joy* proclaimed.[21] Merton continues, "The time of the end is the time of the Crowd: and the eschatological message is spoken in a world where, precisely because of the vast indefinite roar of armies on the move and the restlessness of turbulent mobs, the message can be heard only with difficulty."[22] The good news of the *kerygma* finds no room in the time of crowdedness and chaos, in a world that is marked by the lust for power over against the desire or innate longing for peace. It is, in some sense, sin that clouds those most primordial aspirations for community and peace, but there is some hope if we are only open to the possibility. And for all these reasons, Christ can be found only "with those for whom there is no room. His place is with those who do not belong, who are rejected by power because there are regarded as weak, those who are discredited, who are denied the status of persons, tortured, exterminated."[23]

Christ is found among the marginalized because from that location (of *no location*) there is a theological surplus for eschatological imagina-tion. Those who are part and parcel of the worldly system of power and violence cannot imagine any other way, and their fear of death is the very condition for its possibility. But those for whom there is no room are able to imagine the hitherto unimaginable and glimpse the light that has dawned upon the world otherwise unable to recognize it.

Merton's poetic articulation of the centrality of nonviolence and peacemaking as a constitutive dimension of the Christian narrative takes yet another impossible turn in his essay "A Devout Meditation in Memory of Adolf Eichmann." This reflection focuses on the so-called

---

[20] Ibid., 66.
[21] Ibid., 66–70.
[22] Ibid., 67.
[23] Ibid., 72–73.

distinction made between "sane" and "insane," starting with the fact that a criminal psychologist determined Adolf Eichmann to be sane. In this piece, anticipating the core tenets of Hauerwas's ethics in a key resembling the grammar of Caputo's philosophical explication, Merton warns against the popular tendency for Christians to acquiesce and appropriate some other narrative (nationalism, consumerism, xenophobia, and so on) under the guise of Christianity. He writes:

> The worst error is to imagine that a Christian must try to be "sane" like everybody else, that we *belong* in our kind of *society*. That we must be "realistic" about it. We must develop a *sane* Christianity: and there have been plenty of sane Christians in the past. Torture is nothing new, is it? We ought to be able to rationalize a little brainwashing, and genocide, and find a place for nuclear war, or at least for napalm bombs, in our moral theology. Certainly some of us are doing our best along those lines already. There are hopes! Even Christians can shake off their sentimental prejudices about charity, and become sane like Eichmann. They can even cling to a certain set of Christian formulas, and fit them into a Totalist Ideology. Let them talk about justice, charity, love, and the rest. These words have not stopped some sane men from acting very sanely and cleverly in the past.[24]

What begins with a very contemporary reflection on the trial and execution of a Nazi war criminal serves as a parallel survey of St. Paul's exhortation in his First Letter to the Corinthians: God's wisdom is not of this world and those who seek it in the ostensible logic of one's social, cultural, political or economic context are missing the point. Merton concludes his reflection with this admonition to "modern man": "If he were a little less sane, a little more doubtful, a little more aware of his absurdities and contradictions, perhaps there might be a possibility of his survival."[25]

As with the other two essays from *Raids on the Unspeakable* considered above, Merton's "Letter to an Innocent Bystander" bears a certain apocalyptically poetic feel. It is the most admonishing of the three essays we have considered, and the challenge presented in the text is one that should lead readers to pause to consider their complicity in the systemic

---

[24] Ibid., 48.
[25] Ibid., 49.

structures of violence and injustice in our world. The main point of the essay is to shed light on the possibility that the seeming innocence that is maintained by those Merton characterizes as bystanders might not, in fact, be so innocent. It is the classic consideration of one's sins of omission. But there is a sense of hopefulness that emerges amid the necessary critique of the abstaining. Merton explains:

> There is a certain innocence in a kind of despair: but only if in despair we find salvation. I mean, despair of this world and what is in it. Despair of men and of their plans, in order to hope for the impossible answer that lies beyond our earthly contradictions, and yet can burst into our world and solve them if only there are some who hope in spite of despair.[26]

In a clever way Merton again highlights the hidden contradiction in the pairing of the plans, answers, and logic of "this world and what is in it" with the "impossible answer that lies beyond our earthly contradictions." The latter, "impossible" answer is the wisdom of God that enters our experience as *Sophia*, the Wisdom of God, revealed most completely in Christ.

Conclusion

Despite the trappings of darkness and the specter of apocalyptic context that is found throughout *Raids on the Unspeakable*, Merton's text offers a constructive sense of hope that is—like its real counterpart in the world—difficult to recognize easily. It is a hope that is rooted, not in the logic of the world, but in the seemingly illogical wisdom of God. It is a challenge that calls believers to question the collective "wisdom" of society and the seemingly "easy" prescripts of Christian living. It is a call that Merton offers his age and ours to reconsider the place of violence in our lives—individually and collectively—and how that reality of systemic sin is made manifest by our actions and inactions. The writing of Thomas Merton continues to speak to us in an age of chaos and world crisis. It is my hope that contemporary thinkers like John Caputo and Stanley Hauerwas, among others, might help us to read Merton's work anew and aid us in our living Christian lives as prophets of hope and nonviolence in our world.

---

[26] Ibid., 61.

Acknowledgments

This book is nothing but a labor of love. As I shared in the Introduction, I did not set out to become a Merton scholar but found myself drawn more and more into the life, thought, writing, and legacy of this Trappist monk who died decades before I was born. The essays published in this volume reflect a range of my thinking about Thomas Merton and the manifold ways his brilliance, insight, and humanity continue to speak to the "signs of the times" in which we find ourselves more than a century after his birth. The writing of this book required me to revisit dozens of my lectures, columns, conference papers, book chapters, and journal articles, as well as some material that had never been shared live or in print before. That process was both challenging (any author will tell you that it is painstaking to read and reread one's own work) and a blessing. The blessing was most evident to me in the memories that would flood back as I read through this trove of material, most of which did not make it into this volume. I thought of the venues where I may have first presented an academic paper or public lecture. I thought of the process of researching and writing various lectures and essays, recalling fondly where I was living at the time and what occasioned this or that particular approach to the study of Merton in that moment. But most of all I thought of the people I have met along the way, many of whom I am honored to call my friends and colleagues still to this day. As I wrote about in Chapter 4, Merton's "apostolate of friendship" persists today, bringing together scholars and enthusiasts alike who share a common fascination with Thomas Merton. This book is dedicated to them.

There are others to thank along the way. First, to Robert Ellsberg, publisher of Orbis Books and a fellow "friend of Merton." I'm grateful for his encouragement, support, and friendship over the years. I am especially thankful for his patience and understanding when work on this book had to be delayed because of another urgent project that needed attention some years back. In addition to Robert, I want to express my

249

gratitude to Paul McMahon, who was the acquiring editor of this project. It was a joy to work with Paul on an earlier book for Orbis Books and I am grateful to continue working with Paul on other projects in his new capacity at Paulist Press.

There are so many universities, conference organizers, and others to thank for invitations to speak about Merton and his work over the years. At the risk of leaving out some by accident, I'll just mention a few of the places that have invited me to share my research on Merton: St. Norbert College, Saint Xavier University, St. Bonaventure University, Chaminade University, Boston College, Fairfield University, Bellarmine University, St. Michael's College in Vermont, Nazareth College, St. John Fisher College, Siena College, Aquinas Institute in St. Louis, Catholic Theological Union in Chicago, Ignatius College Preparatory School in Chicago, The University of Utah Catholic Center, The World Community for Christian Meditation Centre in London, Immaculate Heart Retreat Center in Spokane, Bon Secours Retreat and Conference Center in Baltimore, Corpus Christi Church in New York City, the Chicago Chapter of the International Thomas Merton Society, Christ the King Retreat Center in Syracuse, St. Anselm's Abbey in Washington, DC, Glastonbury Abbey in Hingham, Massachusetts, St. Anthony's Shrine and Ministry Center in Boston, St. Peter's Episcopal Church in Cambridge, All Saint's Episcopal Church in Pasadena, Mount Savior Benedictine Monastery in New York, La Casa de Maria Retreat and Conference Center in Santa Barbara, San Damiano Retreat Center in California, the St. Francis Retreat Center in Minnesota, the Stillpoint Center for Christian Spirituality in Los Angeles, the Wasatch Retreat and Conference Center in Salt Lake City, the San Pedro Retreat Center in Orlando, the Religious Formation Conference, the Los Angeles Religious Education Congress, the Margaret Brennan IHM Institute for Spirituality, and so many others.

A special note of thanks is owed to the staff of the Jesuit Institute of South Africa, which invited me to be the 2022 Winter Living Theology Lecturer and to speak across South Africa, Eswatini, and Botswana about Thomas Merton. Over the course of nearly six weeks I had the privilege to lecture about Merton and his legacy in several contexts, which helped shape my thinking about and the ultimate form of this book. I am grateful for the invitation from, hospitality of, and conversations with the JISA team during my time in South Africa: Russell Pollitt, SJ, Ursula van Nierop, Puleng Matsaneng, Morongoa Selepe, Annemarie

Paulin-Campbell, and Gillian Hugo, among others. I am also grateful for the many questions, comments, and discussions I had with so many people in so many places during that lecture tour.

Finally, a note of gratitude to all the editors and publishers who have granted permission for essays that originally appeared in their respective pages to be included in this volume.

Index